SEMIOTICS IN INFORMATION SYSTEMS ENGINEERING

KECHENG LIU holds a chair of Computing Science at the School of Computing, Staffordshire University. He leads a research group on semiotics for information systems. He has created the research (specialist) award of Information Systems with Semiotics, the first of this type in the United Kingdom.

Dr Liu first worked in the Commission for Integrated Survey, China State Planning Committee and Chinese Academy of Sciences. As a programmer and later systems analyst designer, he was involved in and led a number of projects of developing information systems for regional planning and development purposes. Originally trained as a computer scientist in his university education in China, his postgraduate and doctorate education has been shifted towards management and business systems; both of them were received in the Netherlands. He is one of the main contributors to an information systems methodology, MEASUR (Methods for Eliciting, Analysis and Specifying Users' Requirements).

Dr Liu's work is found in various computing areas, such as information systems methodologies, requirements studies, information systems engineering, human–computer communication and collaborative work.

SEMIOTICS IN INFORMATION SYSTEMS ENGINEERING

KECHENG LIU
Staffordshire University

CAMBRIDGE
UNIVERSITY PRESS

CAMBRIDGE UNIVERSITY PRESS
Cambridge, New York, Melbourne, Madrid, Cape Town, Singapore, São Paulo, Delhi

Cambridge University Press
The Edinburgh Building, Cambridge CB2 8RU, UK

Published in the United States of America by Cambridge University Press, New York

www.cambridge.org
Information on this title: www.cambridge.org/9780521118194

First published 2000
This digitally printed version 2009

A catalogue record for this publication is available from the British Library

ISBN 978-0-521-59335-9 hardback
ISBN 978-0-521-11819-4 paperback

To Lily and Jimmy
Their love is my drive

Contents

Preface

Information systems are a multi-disciplinary subject, whose objects of study are information and its functions, information technology and its use in organisational contexts. For nearly three decades, scholars and practitioners have been pursuing effective paradigms, approaches, methods and techniques for developing and engineering information systems. The book is intended to contribute to this direction.

The research work on which the book is based began in 1989 in Twente University, the Netherlands, where I joined a team led by Professor Ronald Stamper. The team has been preoccupied by a series of philosophical and methodological investigations into information systems for a long time. My work at that time, with a focus on information modelling, was just a part of the large programme entitled MEASUR.

The research programme began in 1973, marked by Stamper's book on information. It was first called LEGOL, which aimed to deliver a set of legally oriented techniques for requirements specification. It soon extended into a research effort into Methods for Eliciting, Analysing and Specifying Users' Requirements (hence MEASUR). In the last ten years, the programme has further expanded into a set of methods to deal with all aspects of information systems. The theory of organisational semiotics is a key foundation for the methods and techniques developed within MEASUR. These methods and techniques enable one to understand and articulate the business problem and its context under the study, to capture semantics and intentions of users in requirement models, and also to implement technical information systems that are flexible and adaptable to the organisational change.

This book focuses on the requirements engineering and development of IT-based systems. After introducing basic principles of semiotics and the relevance to information systems, the book presents the methods for

xi

requirements analysis and modelling, and techniques for implementing technical systems. Finally, the last part of the book demonstrates the application of these methods and techniques through a number of case studies.

I am deeply indebted to Ronald Stamper, my mentor and a true hero, who has introduced me to this fascinating semiotic perspective of information systems. Thanks are also due to Peter Andersen and Rodney Clarke, with whom I have had inspiring discussions in the last few years on a number of occasions.

Since I joined Staffordshire University in 1993, I have been working with a team of colleagues in a number of projects, including knowledge sharing, information infrastructure, collaborative and software agent-based information systems and electronic commerce. One particular project is on requirements recovery in legacy systems re-engineering. I am grateful to my colleagues in this team with whom I have had many opportunities to discuss the ideas and apply these methods to various research problems: Albert Alderson, Alan Dix, Hanifa Shah, Bernadette Sharp, Dave Brunskill, Sue Blakey and Geoff Crum.

A research-based master's course of Information Systems and Semiotics, the first of this kind, was launched two years ago at Stafford. I must acknowledge the students on this course and my other PhD students for their enthusiasm in their exploring the relevance and power of semiotic methods to their research work. Their feedback has been highly valued.

I would like to thank David Tranah of CUP, and Peter Jackson, my copy editor, for making this book possible; particularly for Peter's thorough and rigorous editing, which has made this book a smooth and pleasant read!

KL
Stafford

1

Introduction

1.1 Information and information systems

What is information? Many people have attempted to give a definition but most of them are not complete. A typical explanation is that information is processed data that has meanings to its users. But then questions arise in what meaning is. If *information* is to the study of information as object is to physics, and there are many laws by which we can study objects, then what are the laws by which we can study *information*? What is the study of information anyway?

What can be said here is that *information* is not a simple, primitive notion. Devlin (1991) compares the difficulties for a man in the Iron Age to answer the question 'What is iron?' and for a man in today's Information Age the question 'What is information?' To point to various artefacts of iron in order to answer his question would not be satisfactory; to demonstrate some properties of information as an answer to 'What is information?' is not good enough either. People can feel the possession of information, and can create and can use information. They gather it, store it, process it, transmit it, use it, sell it and buy it. It seems our lives depend on it; yet no one can tell what exactly it is.

In order to understand the nature of information, one may have to find some fundamental and primitive notions with which the question can be investigated and explained. The concept of a *sign* is such a primitive notion that serves the purpose. All information is 'carried' by signs of one kind or another. Information processing and communication in an organisation are realised by creating, passing and utilising signs. Therefore, understanding signs should contribute to our understanding of information and information systems (Stamper 1992).

The investigation of *information systems* is an active area where much attention has been paid by other research and industrial communities.

1

2 *Introduction*

Much discussion has taken place on its pluralistic and interdisciplinary nature and its foundations. An increasing number of researchers and prac titioners define information systems as social interaction systems. Social and organisational infrastructure, human activities and business processes are considered as part of information systems. Information systems in this definition can produce messages, communicate, create information, and define and alter meanings. The UK Academy of Information Systems pro vides the following definition of the domain of information systems (UKAIS 1996). 'The study of information systems and their development is a multi-disciplinary subject and addresses the range of strategic, manage rial and operational activities involved in the gathering, processing, storing distributing and use of information, and its associated technologies, in society and organisations.' Many authors emphasise the importance of information systems study in this postmodern society and its interdiscipli nary nature. For example, Avison and Nandhakumar (1995) suggest that information systems encompass a wide range of disciplinary areas such as information theory, semiotics, organisation theory and sociology, com puter science, engineering, and perhaps more.

1.2 Problems and challenges in information systems

Information processing has become a major industry which plays a significant role in a national economy (Machlup 1980). Porat (1977), based on analysis of various sources, suggests that in developed countries such as the USA and west European countries, about 50 per cent or even more of the labour force is engaged in information work. However, the following occurrences have been reported in numerous studies: large company budgets for IT (information technology) made, huge expenses on system development projects spent, and, yet, low economic return from the high investment. Strassmann (1990) argues that there is no guarantee that large investment on information technology will lead to high business perfor mance or an increase in revenue: 'no relationship between expenses for computers and business profitability' on any usual accounting basis across an industry. Some companies use IT well but others balance this positive effect with poor returns on IT investment. Many surveys in industry exhibit evidence that a considerable number of information systems developed at great cost fail to satisfy users or have to be modified before they become acceptable. According to an analysis done by the US General Accounting Office in the late 1980s, among a group of US federal software projects totalling $6.2 million, less than 2 per cent of software products were used a

Shameful numbers

☐ 31.1% of projects are cancelled before they ever get completed
☐ 52.7% of projects go over time and/or over budget, at an average cost 89% of their original estimates
☐ 16.2% of software projects are completed on time and on budget
⟹ In larger companies only 9% of their projects come in on time and on budget with approximately 42% of the originally proposed features and functions
⟹ In small companies 78.4% of their software projects get deployed, with at least 74.2% of their original features and functions

Figure 1.1. Shameful numbers in software development crisis.

delivered, more than half were not used (including those not delivered). The situation has not been improved. In 1993, the Taurus project (Transfer and Automated Registration of Uncertified Stock) of the London Stock Exchange was aborted after the expenditure of £400 million over the preceding five years (*De Volkskrant*, March 12, 1993; *Computing*, March 15, 1993). In 1997, Advanced Technical Strategy Inc. published their study 'The software development crisis' on the Internet, as quoted in Figure 1.1 (Boustred 1997). In this figure, the 'shameful numbers' show a majority of projects cost nearly twice their original budgets. The customer acceptance figures display that more than two-thirds of the software products were never used or never completed. One of the main reasons for these failures is inappropriate users' requirements studies which lead to incorrect systems analysis and design.

The social, cultural and organisational aspects play more decisive roles than technology itself. 'A computer is worth only what it can fetch in an auction', Franke (1987) writes. 'It has value only if surrounded by appropriate policy, strategy, methods for monitoring results, project control, talented and committed people, sound relationships and well designed information systems.' These information systems are composed of organisational infrastructure, business processes and technological systems. An organisation with an improperly designed bureaucracy and unprepared culture will not guarantee that the possession of more information will improve the quality of management; on the contrary, the quality of management will suffer from being overloaded with irrelevant information (see Ackoff (1967)). As Lee (1988) points out, '. . . certainly, this [information] technology has done much to improve bureaucratic efficiency. On the other hand, we claim, it has not helped at all in the management of bureaucratic complexity. Indeed, it has aggravated the problem by obscuring bureaucratic rules and procedures in the form of computer codes. (For instance, many have experienced the frustrations of trying to rectify a computer-generated billing error)'.

There are two other problems observed in systems developments. One is the long lead-time between the commencement of the projects and the systems becoming available. The commencement stage may be to study business strategy of a given organisation, to conduct information systems planning, followed by business analysis, system design, construction design, etc. (see the stages considered in the information systems methodologies framework discussed in Olle *et al.* 1991). Many systems development projects have taken too long in reaching fruition. Hence the immediate risk arises that, during the development processes, the users may wish to change the requirements they specified when the projects began. If the development methodologies do not allow the incorporation of the modified requirements into the developments, then the products after the long lead-time may hardly satisfy the users' present needs.

Another problem observed in practice is related to systems analysis, particularly to analysis documentation. Applications of most development methodologies produce huge volumes of documentation. These documents are supposed to address the technical people involved in the development projects. Because the primary purpose of the analysis documents is usually to function as a formal basis for the next stage, i.e. systems design, the deliverables from analyses are often directed particularly to systems designers in the development teams. The business users, who may actually be the owners of the systems, are not considered as recipients of the information analysis products. As a result, the analysis products are presented in some artificial languages that are specially invented by and for the systems development communities. Syntactic elements such as jargonised notation (of the method of analysis used) and technical disciplines (e.g. logical consistency and data normalisation) receive more attention in those methodologies than semantic aspects. The large volume of documentation may contain a great deal of design symbols and special notation. Each project has to define the meanings of the terms used in the information system in a *data dictionary*. The products of analysis may then be very 'precise' and convenient for the next step, i.e. systems design; they may even be automatically translated into a database schema by a CASE (Computer Added Software Engineering) tool. These documents are too difficult for the systems' owners to understand.

The users need to check above all the meanings incorporated into the specification in order that results of the analysis can be verified. However, documentation in most of the conventional methodologies creates barriers to, rather than facilities for, requirements analysis. Voluminous documentation builds up psychological difficulties; in addition to that, many complicated technicalities have to be learned through undergoing intensive training. Every time the users want to understand a fragment of the representation, the *data dictionaries* have to be used. Even with the help of data dictionaries, the users are still unlikely to be able to make an adequate check on the meanings of words. The risk arising from such a situation is that the users' requirements may be wrongly understood by the analysts. Wrong requirements may be sought, though represented in a correct syntax, as foundations for systems development. In such cases, it is unwise to expect satisfactory information systems to be produced based on these requirement models. As a solution, it is suggested that a method with an emphasis on semantics is needed. Possibilities of preserving and clarifying meanings in requirements analysis should be considered as more important criteria than any others. Therefore, a guarantee of producing a correct requirement analysis is possible only if the users can validate and verify an information systems model, which can be technically implemented. Ideally, this model should be a by-product of the business analysis.

1.3 Approaches and methods for information systems development

Frameworks and methodologies have always been regarded as fundamentals for information systems. Many authors offer comprehensive reviews and critique of frameworks and methodologies for information systems (see, for example, Olle *et al.* (1991), Hirschheim *et al.* (1995), Avison & Fitzgerald (1995)). A suggestion to characterise the methods is made, with three features: *data-oriented, process-oriented* and *behaviour-oriented*. An elaborate analysis and comparison of some methodologies and models for information systems can be found in Hirschheim *et al.* (1995) where methodologies and models are evaluated against some 50 criteria which are grouped into technical, usage, economic and behavioural aspects. It is suggested that there are four paradigms: functionalism, social relativism, radical structuralism, and neohumanism (Hirschheim & Klein 1989; Hirschheim *et al.* 1995). Each information systems development approach may be based on one of the paradigms. Goguen (1992) discovers two cultures in information systems development and requirement engineering: the 'dry' and the 'wet'. Bickerton and Siddiqi (1993) classify some 30 methods for systems development and requirements engineering in a framework in which two of the important considerations are whether the methods are 'hard' or 'soft' in character. More studies and comparisons of information systems development methodologies can be found in the literature.

There are confusions in concepts and theories of information systems which actually contribute to the difficulties of development and selection of a suitable methodology. The FRISCO task group (FRamework of Information System COncepts) of IFIP WG 8.1[1] has set up as its goal the removal of the confusions in concepts and theories (Falkenberg *et al.* 1998). The following passage (quoted from Lindgreen (1990)) manifests dissatisfaction about information systems development:

> There is a growing concern within IFIP WG 8.1 about the present situation, where too many fuzzy or ill-defined concepts are used in the information systems area. Scientific as well as practice-related communication is severely distorted and hampered, due to this fuzziness and due to the frequent situation that different communication partners associate different meanings with one and the same term. There is no commonly accepted conceptual reference and terminology, to be applied for defining or explaining existing or new concepts for information systems.

A great deal of effort has been put into information systems studies. One of the purposes is that criticism and suggestions regarding the methods can be learned from, and improvements can be made. There are some problems noticed in many of the above mentioned studies. One of the problems is that the majority of the commercially available methods for information systems development are 'dry' or 'hard' in nature; social and organisational aspects tend to be ignored. However, as noted in the preface of Galliers (1987), 'Few would argue that the study of information and the need to treat the development of information systems from the perspectives of *social* as opposed to *technical* systems remains as crucial today as it was when Stamper first published his book in 1973.'[2] Motivated by these same reasons, many people have put effort into bringing about workable theories and methods for information systems development enabling people to handle both the social and technical systems (see, for example Mumford & Weir (1979), Checkland (1981), Lyytinen & Lehtinen (1986), Stowell (1995)).

---

[1] WG 8.1, part of IFIP (the International Federation for Information Processing), is one of the Working Groups on Information Systems, and focuses on methodologies and issues of design and evaluation of information systems.

[2] Stamper (1973) began his book with a significant remark that the explosive growth of information technology has not been accompanied by a commensurate improvement in the understanding of information. He appeals for an understanding of both machine and human information systems.

1.4 MEASUR: a semiotic approach to information systems

MEASUR (Methods for Eliciting, Analysing and Specifying Users' Requirements) is a research programme initiated in the later 1970s by Ronald Stamper. The main objective of the programme is to investigate and deliver a set of methods that can be used by researchers and business users in their understanding, development, management and use of information systems. The research programme has evolved in the last two decades. As he later elaborated (Stamper 1993), 'MEASUR' is now a rich acronym:

Methods, Means, Models . . . for
Exploring, Eliciting, Evaluating . . .
Articulating, Analysing, Assessing . . . and
Structuring, Specifying, Stimulating . . .
Users'
Requirements

The various MEASUR methods enable one to start with a vague and unstructured problem, perhaps in a messy problem situation, and gradually 'dry' it out until it is crisp and precise enough to derive a set of technical solutions. MEASUR is focused upon solving business problems in the broadest sense. It helps in solving a wide range of problems, especially those that require organisational or social intervention to solve them. MEASUR addresses information technology problems, as well as organisational problems. In dealing with information technology problems, it can handle the 'up-stream' end of software engineering. In a conventional situation it would primarily serve the managers and other system users, helping them to identify and solve their problems, and lead them to a precise statement of information requirements. In this role it covers the domain of information strategy and planning but it also provides detailed specifications of any problem domain where detailed requirements specifications are needed before designing a computer based system. Further descriptions of MEASUR methods are found in Chapter 4. Here an examination of the major philosophical assumptions will be given.

Stamper (1992) proposed a new paradigm for MEASUR: *the information field*. As opposed to information flow, which is the basis for most of the conventional information systems approaches, this information field paradigm enables to us understand information from a new perspective and therefore to develop information systems more properly. A physical analogy can be used to illustrate this information field paradigm (Huang 1998). Just imagine how a space vehicle in the sky is under the interacting

influences of many different internal and external fields: fields of gravita-
tion, electro-magnetic forces as well as clouds of gas, and internal, elastic
tensions. There is no point trying to explain the vehicle's behaviour in terms
of energy, momentum and materials exchanged between its components –
we need a macro model. The information field paradigm is the macro
model. It helps us to obtain a macro perspective before one works on details
of flows where that is possible.

MEASUR rejects the position taken by many practitioners in this field in
that they tend to consider information systems as devices for representing
and interacting with some objective reality. It takes a different stance.
MEASUR is based on the assumption that the world is constructed socially
and subjectively. It recognises that in and out of a business system, there are
many actors, or human agents. The owners, managers, staff, suppliers,
clients, professional groups, local communities, and so on, are all governed
by the forces in the information fields and therefore behave accordingly.
These forces are related to their interests, assigned functions, tasks, objectives, personal values and organisational goals. These forces may be present
in the forms of formal and informal rules, beliefs, cultural habits and conventions, which can be called *norms*.

This subjective, organisational view of information systems and the
information field paradigm lead to the MEASUR approach to information
systems work. In the development of an information system, particularly in
requirements analysis and representation, the scope of attention should be
the whole organisation instead of only the part of the business operations
that is going to be automated by the technical systems. The foci of analysis
should be actors (i.e. agents) and their behaviour which are governed by
social, cultural, institutional, economic and other kind of norms.
Therefore, an effective way of representing users' requirement is to describe
the agents and their intended patterns of behaviour in terms of social
norms.

1.5 About this book

One of the motivations of this book is to examine the relevant issues in
information systems development. It will then introduce a semiotic
approach with a set of methods initially developed by the MEASUR
research team. This team has now grown to a community with colleagues in
many countries and the MEASUR methods have been applied in many
research and industrial cases. But little systematic account can be found

This book aims to fill this gap amongst many MEASUR paper publications, technical papers, research reports and project documentation.

The structure of the book is in two parts. Part one (Chapters 2–8) focuses on discussion of semiotics, the semiotic framework for information systems, and the semiotic methods for information systems analysis. Part two of the book (Chapters 9–13) puts emphasis on the application of the methods. It describes how the methods are used in systems analysis, design and implementation of a computer information system.

Chapter 2 is about principles of semiotics and the relevance of semiotics to organisations and computing. Chapter 3 examines different philosophical paradigms and then introduces a semiotic framework for information systems. The semiotic framework represents a radical subjective view of the social world, organisations and information systems. It serves as philosophical and methodological guidance for the development and formulation of semiotic methods to be discussed later. In Chapter 4, an overview of the semiotic methods for information systems, MEASUR, is presented. MEASUR comprises a set of methods covering all stages and aspects of planning, developing and maintaining an information system. Although the rest of the book focuses on the tasks of systems analysis and design, with a detailed account of the methods of *Semantic Analysis* and *Norm Analysis*, the chapter also discusses the use of other MEASUR methods.

From Chapter 5 to Chapter 8, aspects in three layers of the semiotic framework are followed: *semantic, pragmatic* and *social* aspects. The reason for such a careful investigation of these aspects is that they are more relevant than another three (*physical, empirical* and *syntactical*) aspects as far as information systems analysis and design are concerned. For example, physical and empirical issues can be important in designing and implementing a computer network, and syntactical issues can be highly relevant in programming and implementing a database. The tasks of systems analysis and design are primarily concerned with capturing requirements, studying business knowledge and representing knowledge at semantic, pragmatic and social levels. Before the semiotic methods are discussed, Chapter 5 explores the basic notions of knowledge representation and information analysis, and presents basic considerations of those methods. When one is equipped with fundamentals of knowledge representation and systems analysis, Chapter 6 begins to tackle the issues at the semantic level. The method of Semantic Analysis, which serves as a core of other methods discussed later, is described here. Chapter 7 tackles the next layer of the semiotic framework, pragmatics and communication. It also examines other approaches before looking at Norm Analysis. Finally in this part, we come to the social layer in Chapter 8, which any technical system should ultimately serve. It is argued that an effective modelling method should enable one to analyse all these issues and it demonstrates that these semiotic methods are capable of this.

The second part of the book (Chapters 9–13) deals with the use of methods in systems development. Chapter 9 displays the performance of analysis to capture semantic and pragmatic information in information model. Chapter 10 shows how semantic and temporal information can be stored in databases, and processed and used with the help of a semantic temporal database language, LEGOL. Chapter 11 exhibits the application of the semantic approach to the entire development process of information systems. In addition, hybrid approaches with input from the semiotic methods are also discussed. Chapters 12 and 13 contain two case studies to illustrate the methods and their applications in systems development projects.

The book also contains two appendices. Appendix A gives a full account of the semantic temporal databases, which helps one to understand and appreciate better the power of such databases. Appendix B presents the CRIS case and illustrates the use of LEGOL.

Part one
Semiotic framework and methods

2
Understanding semiotics

The word 'semiotics' comes from the Greek for 'symptom'. Charles Sanders Peirce (1839–1914), who was primarily a logician and competent in mathematics and many other branches of science, including astronomy, chemistry, physics, geology and meteorology, founded semiotics as the formal doctrine of signs'. At almost the same time, Ferdinand de Saussure 1857–1913) founded semiology, a European school of semiotics. Semiology aims at discovering 'what constitutes signs and what laws govern them' (a quote of Saussure, cited in Hawkes (1977, p. 123)), with a slight emphasis on social psychology and general psychology. Semiotics covers the whole cycle of a sign from its creation, through its processing, to its use, with more emphasis on the effect of signs. Although, in the literature, sometimes no clear distinction is made between semiotics and semiology, it is the former which will be the theme of study in this book.

There are three distinct fields of semiotics: syntactics (or syntax), semantics and pragmatics, which go back ultimately to Peirce (*cf.* Lyons (1977)). Morris (1938) made semiotics more generally familiar as a science of signs, to which he made many important contributions, largely from a behavioural standpoint. According to Morris, pragmatics deals with the origin, uses and effects of signs within the behaviour in which they occur. Semantics deals with the signification of signs in all modes of signifying; syntax deals with the combination of signs without regard to their specific signification or their relation to the behaviour in which they occur.

2.1 Signs and their functions

The notion of sign is essential in semiotics. A sign is something which stands to someone for something else in some respect or capacity. Every sign involves a 'signifier' – the material form of the sign – and the 'signified'

13

– the object, action, event or concept it represents. Note that there is always someone – an interpretant – involved, to whom the signification makes sense. An example is given below to illustrate this.

Sign The written word 'house' or a drawing of a house.
Signified The category 'house'.
Interpretant Anyone who is involved in reading and interpreting the sign

The relationships between the signifier and signified may not be fixed and may differ depending on the context, culture and language. For example the word 'slim', although the spelling is the same in both languages, means *cleaver* in Dutch while in English it means *thin*.

Peirce named three categories of signs: icon, index and symbol. An icon is a sign which resembles the signified. An iconic sign represents its object mainly by its similarity and signifies by virtue of metaphor. Icons could also be verbal by making words onomatopoeic. Examples for iconic signs are images, diagrams, maps, portraits, photographs and icons of the algebraic kind. An indexical sign is inherently connected in some way to the signified object. An index is normally instructive and signifies by virtue of metonymy. Examples are smoke signifying fire, a thermometer, a knock on a door, footprints, and pain in the stomach. The third type of sign is a symbol whose relationship with its signified object is 'arbitrary' or purely conventional. It signifies by virtue of an arbitrary norm which may be rooted in societal or cultural convention; for example, the three colours of traffic lights. The three categories of signs are not separate and distinct; a complex sign may be a mixture of several kinds.

A primary purpose for human beings to create and to use signs is communication, unless a sign is purely for private use. To be able to use signs properly, one needs to understand the relationships between the signs and the things they refer to (i.e. referents). For the three categories of signs, the degrees of connection between the signifier and the signified are different Indexical signs have existential or causal relationships with the signified Iconic signs such as photographs are physically forced to correspond to the objects they represent. However, as discussed by Fiske (1990), there are varying degrees of arbitrary elements with an iconic sign. A portrait is less iconic or more arbitrary than a photograph; a cartoon is more arbitrary than a portrait. But even with a photograph, the cameraman can take the picture of different parts of an object, from different angles and with different lighting, to incorporate some arbitrary elements. Therefore convention, cultural norms in a society, is necessary to understanding of any sign, however iconic or indexical it is (Fiske 1990, p. 53). Norms play an important variety of roles in communication and signification. They can be as formal as the rules to define the relationship between signs and the signified, and to govern how the signs should be used. Think about English grammar in forming singular and plural nouns. There are probably more informal norms that one can learn from experience, for example, the meaning of zooming into some football action and playing it in slow motion on television (a highlight or a mistake?), and the meaning of a sudden start of music in a romantic film. Convention is the social dimension of signs. It is the agreement amongst the users about the appropriate uses of and responses to a sign. One has to understand and to follow social and cultural norms when a sign is created and used; otherwise it will be only private and thus does not function in terms of communication.

2.2 Semiosis and learning

The subjects of study for semiotics are all kinds of signs: verbal language, pictures, literature, motion pictures, theatre, body language, and more. The central concept of semiotics is semiosis, which was introduced by Morris. Semiosis is a process of understanding involving something as a sign to some organism. In his book, Nauta (1972) describes semiosis as a sign-process exercise of 'mediated-taking-account-of'. The mediators are sign vehicles; the taking-account-of is interpreters; what is taken account of is designata. These four elements function in every sign-process or semiosis. The sign vehicle is the 'something which is a sign to an organism' (i.e. the interpreter). 'Sign vehicle' is defined as a particular event or object, such as a sound or mark, that functions as a sign. Thus a 'sign vehicle' is a special kind of stimulus. In its function as a sign, the sign vehicle refers to something, the denotatum; it also has a special effect on the attitude of the interpreter; this alteration of the inner state of the interpreter is called the interpretant.

Figure 2.1 illustrates the basic concepts involved in a semiosis and the relationships between these concepts. A semiosis is the sign-mediated process in which a knowing subject gives meaning to what is taken to be an event or actuality. Formulated in terms of the three universal categories, it is the universal process in which a *first*, a presentation (which could be any quality, any thing or any idea) functions as a representamen or sign in being applied to a *second*. In that, a *second* is an object or actuality, through the intermediary of a meaning-mediation *third* (Kolkman 1993). The notion of interpretant is richer and broader than interpretation. It also includes action and feeling. An interpretant can in turn be treated as a sign in another process of semiosis.

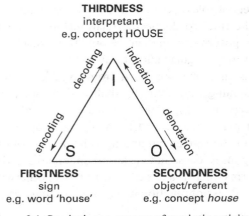

Figure 2.1. Semiosis as a process of semiotic activity.

There are four characteristics for describing semiosis. Firstly, it is univer sal. It is applicable to any type of sign-processing activities. It explains the mechanism for both creating and using a sign. Secondly, semiosis is a process capable of identifying anything present according to a specific crite rion or a norm. The process of representation can be recursive: a sign can be seen as an object in another sign-process, just as an interpretant or an object can be a sign. This will lead to its fourth characteristic which is the possibility of making anything not present identifiable. Finally, semiosis is subject-dependent. It is closely related to the interpretant who can be an individual, a group or a social community with certain knowledge and obeying certain norms. A semiosis process is always partial in representa tion of the object and subjective in interpretation, depending on the view point of the interpretant, and the knowledge and ability the interpretant possesses.

Semiosis can be seen as the building of structures of experience via signs Thinking will involve using signs and inferring an object from its sign. Tha inference, the effect of the sign, is the interpretant (Cunningham 1992). The traditional account of inference usually suggests two processes: deduction and induction. However, Peirce proposed three irreducible, distinct mode of inference in semiosis for understanding and learning. The additional one in the Peircean logic system is abduction. The logic of abduction (the *firstness*) and deduction (the *secondness*) contribute to our qualitative o conceptual understanding of phenomena, while the logic of induction (the *thirdness*) adds quantitative details to the qualitative or conceptual knowl edge (Yu 1994).

The three types of inference are explained below with examples to illustrate the differences between them. In the case of deduction one tries to
make a conclusion or to find a result on the basis of an observed fact by
application of a rule.

Deduction: Rule   : All the apples from the bag are red
　　　　　 Fact   : These apples are from the bag
　　　　　 Result/conclusion: These apples are red.

Induction is related to the generation of a general rule on the basis of a fact
and conclusion.

Induction: Fact   : These apples are from the bag
　　　　　 Result/conclusion: These apples are red
　　　　　 Rule   : All the apples from the bag are red.

Abduction in Peirce's theory is the process of forming a hypothesis that
explains the given observations (see Peirce (1931–58)):

The surprising fact, C, is observed;
But if A were true, C would be a matter of course,
Hence, there is reason to suspect that A is true.

As Yu (1994) summarises, deduction draws logical consequences from
premises. This kind of reasoning does not lead to the discovery of new
knowledge, because the conclusion has already been embedded in the
premise (Peirce [1900] 1931–58). Inductive reasoning is based on generality
and the law of large numbers of cases. Induction generates empirical laws
but not theoretical laws, because the conclusion one reaches from research
with a large number of samples is merely probably (never certainly) true.
Finally, abduction is to look for a pattern in a phenomenon and suggest a
hypothesis. The objective of abduction is to generate hypotheses and,
further, to determine which hypothesis or proposition to test, not which one
to adopt or assert. To achieve a comprehensive inquiry, one should apply
abduction, deduction and induction all together. Abduction and deduction
are the conceptual understanding of a phenomenon, and induction is the
quantitative verification. In short, abduction creates, deduction explicates,
and induction verifies (Yu 1994).

2.3 Semiotics in computing

Semiotics has been an area actively attended to by scientists in linguistics,
media studies, educational science, anthropology, and philosophy of lan-

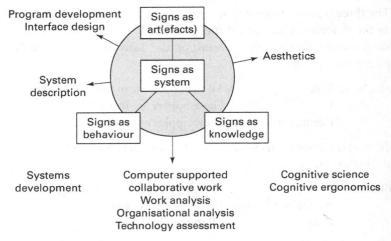

Figure 2.2. Map of a computer semiotics (Andersen 1990, p. 18).

guage. Semiotics as a whole or some of its branches have influenced many of these studies. Computing, including the development and use of computer systems, is another field in which semiotics has shown a great relevance.

Computer semiotics, as defined by Peter Andersen (1991), studies the special nature of computer-based signs and how they function. It is an emerging discipline that will guide people in design and development of computer systems. In Andersen's map of a computer semiotics (Andersen 1990 – Figure 2.2), the perspective of viewing *the signs as systems* occupies the centre. In addition there are three main branches: the psychological view of signs as knowledge, the sociological view of signs as behaviour, and the aesthetic view of signs as artefacts. In the signs-as-systems perspective the individual is considered as a creator, interpreter and referent of signs, or as a user who makes use of a semiotic product from others. In the signs-as-knowledge perspective, the individual is considered as an assemblage of parts: the person's biological ability and psychological mechanism will enable them to learn; so the use of signs is a processing of understanding and learning. Signs, particularly languages, can serve as a means of describing, expressing, designing and constructing both social and computer-based systems. Winograd & Flores (1987) also advocate the same approach and illustrate how information systems development can be started from social reality as the natural foundation.

Applications of semiotics and its methods and techniques can be found in many areas of computing such as computational linguistics, information systems, computer-supported collaborative work, knowledge engineering and artificial intelligence (see, e.g., Benyon (1994), Cunningham (1992), Fiske (1990), Gonzalez (1997), Klein (1996), Liu & Gao (1997), Liu & Dix 1997)).

2.4 Semiotics in organisations and information systems

Organisational semiotics is one of the branches of semiotics particularly related to business and organisations. As manifested in the workshop which was attended by many working in various application areas of semiotics (OSW 1995), *organisational semiotics is the study of organisations using the concepts and methods of semiotics.* This study is based on the fundamental observation that all organised behaviour is effected through the communication and interpretation of signs by people, individually and in groups. The functions of creating, reproducing, transmitting, transforming, preserving and manipulating signs have always been performed with the aid of various technologies. Semiotics, as 'the doctrine of sign', draws from many disciplines to throw light on the ways in which people use signs for all kinds of purposes. The scope of organisational semiotics includes both public and private organisations and concerns their inner workings, their interactions with the environment and with one another. The aims of this study are to find new and insightful ways of analysing, describing and explaining organisational structure and behaviour. The results of this work will in valuable ways relate to and augment current theories about organisations that are based in many disciplines such as economics, social theory, social psychology, anthropology, history, law, information systems, and so on.

Specific problem domains being addressed by people working in organisational semiotics include aspects of such fields as marketing, human resource management, business law and business ethics, the historical development and future evolution of the organs of government, religion, politics, justice, social and health care, as well as private and public businesses. The study is not confined to information expressed in speech, writing or graphics, but takes account of the semiological aspects of the products and productive resources of organisations including the architectural forms which they inhabit. It is relevant to the conservation and the changing of organisational structure and behaviour. Although the subject is wide and touches many other specialist branches of semiotics (e.g. education, law, architecture, media and so on), it only overlaps with them where they are concerned with matters of organisation in their areas.

Semiotics has also been applied to information systems work. During the last decade information systems research has grown dramatically to embrace the insights of several philosophical traditions and semiotics has been one of those contributing to information systems research. It has recognised that within the research community, there are at least two major camps: realists and constructivists. For realists, recognising that the natural language is the ultimate meta-language, their tasks are to devise effective formal languages as means of modelling the structure and behaviour of organisations; and to improve the semantics preserved in the models. Constructivists on the other hand consider that language is not only a medium of expression but also an active force shaping the way the mind functions. By using language, one is engaged in a social process of sense-making and reality construction. Efforts have been made through the study of signs and language to facilitate communication among adherents to alternative philosophical traditions in information systems research (Klein 1996).

3

A semiotic framework for information systems

A semiotics of Stamper (1973), based on the work of Peirce (1931–58), Morris (1938, 1946) and on others, and on 'information theory' (Shannon & Weaver 1949), has evolved into a set of semiotic methods for information systems. A radical, subjectivist stance has been accepted as the basic philosophy for developing the set of methods and tools for information systems development. In this chapter, the discussion will focus on the examination of the subjectivist paradigm and the semiotic framework (Stamper *et al.* 1988).

3.1 Philosophical stance

A paradigm is a set of the most fundamental assumptions adopted by a professional community that allows its members to share similar perceptions and engage in commonly shared practices. Scientific achievements recognised in the particular community and research traditions educate its members to commit themselves to the same rules and standards for scientific practice (Kuhn 1962). Adoption of a certain paradigm will determine the way of exploring the world; it will determine the research theory and method. The usual considerations on scientific paradigms may be complemented by considering a set of presuppositions as paradigmatic, thus relating the discussion to philosophy.

3.1.1 Objectivist paradigm

A predominant philosophical position is the objectivist paradigm which assumes that there is a subject-independent world, some objective reality. Objectivism in its rigorous forms regards the universe as being made up of self-existent entities. The main tenets of objectivism are threefold (Mishra 1982):

The entities (facts, objects) under study in logic, mathematics and the physical sciences are not mental in any usual or proper meaning of the word mental.

The existence and nature of these entities are not in any sense qualified by their capacity for being known.

The degree of unity, consistency or relatedness subsisting among entities is a matter to be empirically ascertained.

In this stance the human mind is treated as a 'blank sheet' on which all the knowledge that it later comes to acquire is 'written' by the external world. Individuals are passively receiving similar ideas. They will arrive at a 'natural' consensus, which is dictated by the external world. Because human perceptions are seen as a kind of mirror image of the world in the mind, it is believed in this paradigm that if one makes the investigation carefully enough one will arrive at the same picture of the world as everyone else. Natural sciences presuppose that there is a body of knowledge which is universally true. The task of scientists is to continuously discover the unknown part of the world and to perfect the knowledge. Sufficient education will enable one to know the right way of learning and to be able to deduce new knowledge, which should reach the same conclusion as that of anyone else based on what is known to him.

These basic assumptions may be justified in some limited circumstances if the area of study is of a mechanical nature, regardless of the human impact. The objectivist position urges one to apply models and methods derived from the natural sciences to the study of human affairs. The social world is treated as if it were some natural world composed of billiard balls (see, for example, Burrell & Morgan (1979), Hirschheim & Klein (1989)). However, a quick observation of day-to-day activities will tell us a different story. In our social affairs, there are always different opinions involved. The notion of true universal knowledge seems not to work as it is supposed to by the objectivist. Differences in political and economic interest, and cultural background, lead to diversified judgements instead of a common conclusion on the basis of the 'objective truth'. To reach a consensus, for example, about a management decision, normally requires a lot of effort in discussion, clarification and negotiation, though members of the management team live in the same physical world. This is because of the subjectivity of knowledge, experience and perception.

This objectivist position leads to a set of basic beliefs in the fields of

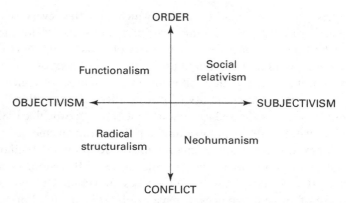

Figure 3.1. Different paradigms for information systems studies (Hirschheim & Klein 1989).

anguage and language use, communication, and information systems. Hirschheim & Klein (1989) illustrated that there are different paradigms of nformation systems development which are named as functionalism, radical structuralism, social relativism, and neohumanism; they can be placed in a coordinate system (Figure 3.1).

In his criticism, Lyytinen (1987) characterises the objectivist position in the systems analysis and development by examining the following four objectivist principles.

1) *Correspondence* There is a fixed, immutable entity-structure in an enterprise. The description of the problem domain is a representation of reality which has a correspondence between the words, and entities and relationships. The problem of this principle arises when dealing with 'soft entities', such as 'legal person', 'loan', 'customer', 'order', etc. A great deal of disputes in legal cases was caused by ambiguous meaning for such 'soft entities'.

2) *Objectivity* This principle suggests that the statements or observations of a problem domain are independent of an observer, because observations by anyone should be the same. According to this principle, a sentence like 'The marketing director believes that the sales have dropped by 10%' is meaningless, because someone's belief suggests that it may not be a fact, which is beyond the scope of discussion. The objectivist position tends to ignore the contextual information associated with the observations. Modalities, purposes and intentions are filtered out from the statements.

3) The *excluded middle* This principle is rooted in one of the fundamental

theories of formal logic, bivalence, which says that every sentence statement or proposition is either true or else false (Note: for more on the definition of *bivalence* see the glossary of Haack (1978)). However social organisations are not built up on the basis of a set of axioms and they do not always function following a finite number of logical rules. Despite a general applicability of norms, there are exceptional situations where one is allowed to violate a rule (Holy & Stuchlik 1983; Lee 1988; Ryu & Lee 1993). For example, a police car in an emergency situation may disobey traffic signals. Norms do provide standards of conduct, but more often than not, deviance of behaviour occurs in society (Gibbs 1981) due to differences in standards and beliefs. Because of these differences, behaviour considered 'right' or 'wrong based on some standard may be judged neutral based on other standards.

(4) *Language neutrality* This assumes a descriptive role of language. A language is seen as a means of representation and not a means of construction of a world.

These objectivist's principles are not suitable for studying problems in social settings, and can lead to some harmful and even dangerous consequences if they are adopted in information analysis and systems development.

3.1.2 Subjectivist paradigm

In daily business practice, and legal and other practical affairs, consensus continually breaks down as individuals see the world differently from each other. This gave rise to the idea of putting the focus on subjectivism in order to investigate whether this doctrine provides a more proper basis for studying the type of problems in social domains. Whereas objectivism assumes a single reality and explains differences of ideas as aberrations, subjectivism treats different ideas of individuals as starting points for a shared reality. In its radical forms it turns away from pretended absolutes and origins, from fixed principles and closed systems. Subjectivism emphasises the abilities of individuals, their freedom to choose courses of action and the moral responsibility for their choice, as well as the uncertainty, novelty and strife they bring about. Importance is also assigned to the affective and cognitive behaviour of people as well as to their cognition. Reality in this stance is experience and it is found within sensible flux. It is not ready-made but in a making process, unfinished and growing in all places where individuals pursue their ends. The subjectivist paradigm rejects the appropriateness of

Table 3.1. *Objectivist and subjectivist views of some key concepts.*

Concept	Objectivist view	Subjectivist view
Reality	objectively given, the same for everyone and composed of entities, their properties and relationships	created subjectively and socially with subtle differences between groups of the knowing agents
Data	a means of representing the truth about reality	a means of indicating intentions and coordinating actions
Truth	the correct correspondence between some real entities	a consensus reached (temporarily) as a basis for coordinated action
Meaning	a relationship between a sign and some real entity	a relationship between a sign and some pattern of action established as a norm within a group
Information system	a kind of 'plumbing' system through which data flow	a semiological system, mainly informal but supplemented by formalised messages
Role of the analyst	to specify the truth data structure and functions of the system needed by the users	to assist the users to articulate their problems, discover their information requirements and evolve a systemic solution

natural science methods for studying the social world and seeks to under-stand the basis of human life by delving into the depth of the subjective experience of individuals. The social world is studied by pursuing an under-standing of the way in which the member of the society creates, modifies, and interprets the world to which he belongs.

Table 3.1 (Stamper 1993) summarises and compares typical objectivist and subjectivist positions in some key concepts related to information systems work. The subjectivist position has increasing influences on com-munication and information systems studies. One of the key influences is that the role of language is seen as not only descriptive, but also construc-tive. The using of language is the performing of actions. A social world can be created, altered, twisted, and moved by the use of language. For example, performative utterances such as 'I do [sc. take this woman to my awful wedded wife],' as uttered in the course of the marriage ceremony, and I name this ship the *Queen Elizabeth*' can create new states of affairs even without any physical actions involved (Austin 1980). All speech acts (Searle 1969) in proper circumstances will have the effect of constructing or alter-ing the world, for example, by creating an obligation or changing a legal relationship in business affairs.

3.1.3 Radical subjectivist paradigm

The research programme MEASUR adopts a radical subjectivist paradigm (Stamper *et al.* 1988). In this paradigm, the reality is seen as a social construct through behaviour of the agents. People in this world share certain patterns of behaviour which are governed by a system of norms. As people argue, communicate, negotiate and interact with each other, the world is constantly changing. The changing world will, in turn, bring about new values, habits and beliefs as norms. When one is trying to understand concepts such as knowledge, truth, language and meaning, then agents and actions should be taken as the starting point. This position can be formulated as the following two axioms on which the major part of the research work is based:

(1) there is no knowledge without a knower; and
(2) there is no knowing without action.

From these axioms, the well-formed formulae for knowledge representation have been built up: there will always be two components in a unit of knowledge representation, the agent (a person or a group) and the behaviour:

or *<knower-term><behaviour-term>*
    <agent-term> <action-term>.

These well-formed formulae require every piece of knowledge to be explicitly tied to the agent who knows it or has constructed it, and is responsible for it. Knowing something or being able to do something becomes an item of knowledge only from the viewpoint of a certain agent. The notion of the universal truth, therefore, becomes irrelevant in this case. Instead, the concept of responsibility becomes as vital as the truth in a classical logic.

3.2 The semiotic framework

Traditionally the divisions of semiotics have been *syntactics, semantics* and *pragmatics*, which deal, respectively with the structures, meanings and usage of signs. Stamper (1973) has added another three. *Physics*, as a separate branch concerned with the physical aspects of signs at the level of signals and marks, has been further added to the taxonomy of semiotics. It gives a handle to deal with the factors governing the economics of signs, which has become important in business contexts. *Empirics* has been

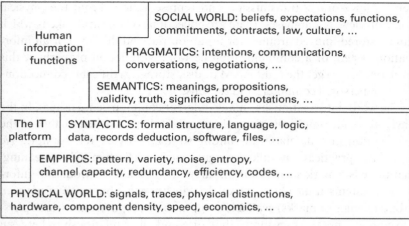

Figure 3.2. The semiotic framework.

introduced as another branch to study the statistical properties of signs when different physical media and devices are used. At the other end of the spectrum, he adds another layer of the *social world* where the effects of the use of signs in human affairs are studied. All these branches of semiotics are organised into a semiotic framework (Figure 3.2).

Issues at the three upper layers in the semiotic framework are concerned with the use of signs, how signs function in communicating meanings and intentions, and what the social consequences are of the use of signs. Studies of issues at the lower three layers will answer questions as to how signs are structured and used in language, how signs are organised and transmitted, what physical properties signs have, and so on.

3.2.1 Physics

A sign in a physical form is a phenomenon. It can be a sign in motion, which is normally termed a 'signal'; and it can be static, then it is a 'mark'. The physical properties of a sign can be its shape, size, contrast, intensity, moving speed, acceleration, loudness, source, destination, etc., depending on the type of the sign. Such physical properties can be studied with methods of physics and engineering. Other related questions can also be investigated, such as material of sign carrier, energy carried or consumed by the signal. The direct relevance to communication and information systems of knowing the physical properties is that people can design physical devices for storage, transmission and representation. From the physical point of view, in databases, there are collections of physical tokens which can be stored, moved around, for input, output and display. For an information system or a communication network to function properly at this level, one has to get the right RAM or disk storage, right cable connections between personal computers and stations.

The word 'information' has many different common-sense usages. In the physical area it simply means a collection of tokens as when we talk of the information in a database amounting to x megabytes, for example. We might, in a practical way, talk of a signal, such as a flash of light, 'meaning' that there is a mark such as a transparent area on a film. Models of information systems at the physical level describe the available range of *physical tokens* (signals or marks) available as input to or output from various physical components and they model the cause-and-effect relationships between them, their energy and material requirements. For example, when developing information systems we model the locations and telecom links between sites, the volumes of information in characters per unit of time which they generate and the volumes they store, in order to discover the capacity of channels and storage devices needed.

3.2.2 Empirics

As a branch of semiotics, empirics studies statistical properties of signs, in which the object of study is a collection of signals or marks. Questions for study at this level are effect of coding, entropy measurement, optimal signal transmission, channel capacity, etc. Information from the angle of empirics can be viewed as a stream of signals which must be transported from one location to another, regardless of what they mean. For example, if binary coding is used for communication between sites, we could have the following coding:

a=00001
b=00011
c=00101
d=00110

In such communications, coding is done at the sending end and decoding at the receiving end. Coding and decoding procedures aim at achieving optimal transmission of information through noisy channels with high accuracy at a rate close to the channel's maximum capacity. There will always be some necessary measures associated with a communication process: imposing a structure on a block of messages before transmission; transmitting some additional messages to describe the structure, and then processing the structure at the receiving end. To get more out of the channel, more elaborate checks, calling for the transmission and storage of larger blocks of signals, subjected to more complex processing, are all necessary. Information should be coded with the minimum number of 'carrier signals' for coding and transmission efficiency. The word 'meaning' in this context means the equivalence of codes.

3.2.3 Syntactics

When there is a satisfactory range of physical tokens that provide a reliable way of encoding diversity of use, physical representation of signs and their statistical properties are covered by *physics* and *empirics*. We can then focus on the complex structures of a language regardless of the actual expression in specific terminal tokens. We can define a syntax using names of syntactic categories and production rules, but we are indifferent about the rules representing the terminal characters.

Syntactics is concerned with rules of composing complex signs from simple ones. Information can be coded following a certain structure; a complex sign, a word, a mathematical expression, or a sentence can be composed of some more basic parts according to the rules. For a formal language, terminal symbols (or vocabulary) are fundamentals of sign construction as far as syntactics is concerned. The rules for generating and parsing formal expressions allow us to measure the complexity of a single formula and a sign system. When a formula can be produced or parsed in two or more ways we have an instance of *syntactical ambiguity*, another semiological phenomenon in the syntactic domain. A formula or an expression carries a piece of information. The meaning of the information at this syntactical level can be studied using the transformation rules. Two sets of formulae have the same meaning (paraphrase each other) if each can be deduced from the other. The meaning of one includes the meaning of the other if it allows the other to be deduced from it.

The rules for combining these parts are called grammar. Grammars of a natural language teach people how to construct grammatically correct sentences, but do not tell how to express semantic meanings. However, if one wants to express oneself precisely, to follow the grammar is one of the conditions.

3.2.4 Semantics

Meaning or semantics of a sign is normally considered as a relationship between a sign and what it refers to: a sign denotes a denotatum. This is its referential meaning. Under this definition of meaning, there has to be a 'reality' assumed, so that signs can be mapped onto objects in the 'reality'. For example, a sign 'table' represents a kind of object with certain properties, such as having legs and a flat surface. This way of treating meaning is reasonable if the problems are simple ones where the boundaries of signs and 'reality' are clear and a shared consensus – for example, properties of objects – is established. Meaning is then a logic function mapping words to reality.

But in most social affairs, this is not the case: there is no agreed unique 'reality'; a consensus does not stay there for ever. People strive for clarifications and consensus. Once a consensus is established, it is soon subject to question, criticism, or modification. Use of signs and languages can clarify ideas, and can also alter or construct the world. Meaning in this respect is more appropriately seen as a relationship between a sign and behaviour. A sign has its behaviour, sign behaviour, behaviour in which signs occur (Morris 1946). The meaning of a sign relates to the response the sign elicits in a given social setting. It signifies any and all phases of sign-process (the status of being a sign, the interpretant, the fact of denoting the significatum), and frequently suggests mental and valuational processes as well (Morris 1946). This is what Stamper calls the behavioural meaning (Stamper 1973). Meaning in this sense is a result of the use of signs, and is constructed, constantly tested and repaired through use of signs.

At the semantic level of use of language, meaning acts as the operational link between signs and practical affairs. People use signs or a language in communication. To enable one person to understand another, there must be some norms governing the use of signs which are established and shared in a language community. These rules regulate people's behaviour in using signs, producing sentences. Norm-confirming uses of signs are acceptable to and understood by the members of the same language community, so that the expected effects can be produced on the audience. To produce effects on the audience, and furthermore to change states of practical affairs, is the ultimate goal of using signs, but the intentional and social effects are embodied in a sentence. In a sense, they are implied in the sentence, and are an extensional aspect of such a sentence. What is firstly reflected in the sentence is the meaning at semantic level which is accommodated by propositions. The sentence can be examined for its validity, signification and correspondence to the business world. However, meaning can only be understood if the context where the sentence is uttered is taken into account. A word, as well as a sentence, can mean anything. The 'literal meaning' of a sentence, as described by Searle (1979, p. 117), is the meaning that is independent of any context whatsoever. One can well imagine how difficult it would be to establish such literal meanings. Winograd and Flores (1987) show with the following example that it is impossible to establish a context-independent basis for circumscribing the literal use of a term even as seemingly simple as 'water':

A: Is there any water in the refrigerator?
B: Yes.
A: Where? I don't see it.
B: In the cells of the eggplant.

Andersen's (1990) example of conversations in a car repair shop illustrates that background information is often necessary to understand the meaning of words, phrases and fragmented sentences. Meaning is highly dependent on the process of using them, dependent on the behaviour of the agents.

A sign's functions at three upper layers of the semiotic framework, *semantics*, *pragmatics* and the *social level*, are concerned with interaction with humans. In a broad sense, they all directly relate to the use and effect of signs. Talking about functions, when people employ a sign or utter a sentence, the first object is to express a meaning. The next goal is to convey a certain intention. The ultimate goal is to produce effects at the social level, such as to set up an obligation, or alter a state of affairs. The fulfilment of the objective at each former level is the basis for the latter. For example, someone tells another person: 'you are stepping on my toes'. The meaning of this sentence is not difficult to understand; the intention is to inform the addressee that he has done something wrong. But the effect of the sentence does not stop there, the speaker is trying to change the situation of being stepped on, and perhaps he is pushing the addressee to feel obliged to apologise to him.

3.2.5 Pragmatics

When a sign has a meaning, it can be used intentionally for certain purposes, such as communication. *Pragmatics*, in such a case of the purposeful use of signs, is a branch of semiotics concerned with the relationships between signs and the behaviour of agents. Within a social community, there exist common knowledge and shared assumptions. These basic assumptions serve as a minimum basis for communication. However, differences in personal experience, values and expectation can create difficulties in understanding. As soon as there is a problem in understanding, people have to come back to the minimum basis, and from there they can expand their common knowledge and reach their new agreement. Dik (1989) calls the personal possession of knowledge and experience 'pragmatic information'.

A process of verbal communication between two people can be modelled like this. The speaker and hearer each have their own pragmatic information base. The speaker's pragmatic information base allows him to form an utterance with an expectation that the hearer will understand both semantic meaning and his intention. For example, by saying 'I'm hungry', the speaker expects the hearer will then interpret the sentence, with his pragmatic information, understanding that the speaker is actually saying 'It's time for lunch, let's go to the cafeteria.' If two participants in a conversation are from the same cultural community, they have a large amount of shared pragmatic information. In this case, they can each assume the pragmatic information of the other. Knowing pragmatic information of the opposite side can shorten the route of conversation and improve the efficiency. On the other hand, incorrect assumption of the pragmatic information of the opposite side can lead the conversation astray. Therefore, it is important for a speaker to know what assumptions he shares with the hearer before communication. Dik (1989) suggests that the speaker should start from shared information, and proceed from there to estimated non-shared information in order to have this added to, or substituted for, pieces of the hearer's information. The shared or non-shared pragmatic information is mainly determined by the cultural differences.

Apart from the shared knowledge, the context where the communication takes place is important to the pragmatic effects. The following elements can be considered in the context: speaker, hearer, intention, purpose, theme, time, location, and psychological states of the speaker and hearer, such as intentions, desires, beliefs, etc. Relative positions of the speaker and hearer, as discussed by Searle & Vanderveken (1985), are also an important aspect of the context. For example, suppose there are two different relative positions of the speaker and hearer: in one, the speaker has an authority over the hearer and, in the other case, the two are peers. An utterance of the sentence 'Leave the room' produces different pragmatic effects. In the former case, it may be an order while in the latter it may be a request. The speaker has an intention when he begins the conversation by uttering his speech act. The following words, for example, either in verb or other forms, can characterise intentions: 'report', 'inform', 'announce', 'declare', 'suggest', propose', 'require', 'order', 'allow', 'permit', 'inquire', 'suppose', 'assume', hypothesise', 'apologise', etc. When the speaker in his utterances uses such words, one can know the speaker's intention as whether he wants either to report his observation or to require something. But in an actual conversation, these words may not need to be used and the speaker is still able to express his intention. In such cases, analysing the intention by means of formal modelling is difficult. However, it is always possible for the hearer to grasp the speaker's intention by applying his pragmatic information with intuition in an informal way. Some techniques for capturing intentions will be found in Chapter 9, where the semiotic method for systems analysis is presented.

The purpose of the conversation is set up by the speaker and is related to the speaker's intention. The speaker can conduct a series of speech acts to pursue the purpose which may be clearly stated by him or hidden. For example, if the speaker 'suggests' something to the hearer, his purpose in carrying on the conversation may not be simply to 'suggest' but to persuade the hearer to join him in some action. Such a purpose is difficult to detect from the beginning of the conversation; it may become clear to the hearer as the conversation develops further. The hearer's perception of the purpose can change in the course of the conversation. In this example, at the beginning of the conversation: the hearer may understand it as merely 'suggest'. But as soon as he changes his perception of the purpose of the speaker, he may interpret 'suggest' as 'persuade'. The purposes of communications are difficult to model by formal means. However, we can understand the underlying mechanism by studying social and cultural norms at the social level. The theory of functional grammar (Dik 1979, 1989) provides an elaborate method of handling pragmatic functions of sentence constituents such as theme, tail, topicality and focality. The analysis of these constituents is useful for one to establish a view on functions of a sentence in relation to the wider communicative setting in which the sentence is uttered. It can help one to obtain a continuous picture of the flow of communication. Time and location are also important aspects in studying communication effects. Effects of the communication acts cannot be studied in isolation, they have to be related to surrounding communication phenomena, for which time and location are aspects of the context indispensable for understanding.

3.2.6 The social level

When a conversation takes place between two or more people, a change at social level will be caused. A conversation can be seen as a proper chain of speech acts. It begins with the speaker expressing some intention in an illo-cutionary act. As soon as the speech act is addressed to the addressee, an obligation is usually already built up for the addressee that he has to respond regardless of the content of the conversation. For example, suppose a person simply says 'Good morning' to a small group of col-leagues. Following social convention, there is an obligation immediately on individuals of the group to acknowledge his greeting. If someone did not do so, he might not feel at ease. In a social setting, norms or social conven-tions govern people's behaviour. Communication must follow a certain pattern. Any deviation from the normative patterns may be unexpected, and may either require an excuse or otherwise be regarded as unacceptable. For example, an 'invitation' can lead to either 'acknowledge but not accept', or 'accept'. The obligations are established on both sides by the speaker and the addressee. As soon as the invitation is issued, the speaker must be pre-pared to be able to entertain the guest. In case of acceptance, the invitee has actually made a promise to the inviting person that he will fulfil his obliga-tion, i.e. going to the party or dinner at the agreed time. Meanwhile, the inviting person has committed himself to receiving the guest. The interpre-tation of the communication acts, under a given circumstance, produces social consequences.

The process of performing communication acts is sometimes a complex process of invoking, violating, and altering social norms. Consciously or not, people interact with each other and make interpretations according to norms, while sometimes they deviate from the normative for their own interest. As Stamper (1973) remarks, for man, a social animal, the norms are a biological necessity. Norms have long been classified into several cate-gories: perceptual, cognitive, evaluative and behavioural. Perceptual norms are implicitly agreed ways of seeing the world. With these norms, words can be assigned meanings that enable people to use them as labels on the hap-penings around them. People can code the message picked up by the eyes and ears in a way that is useful to other people. Cognitive norms are the standardised beliefs and knowledge possessed by a group. These norms ensure that the members of the group acquire the knowledge and expecta-tions about the world which have been accumulated by other members of the cultural group. Evaluative norms direct the group towards common ends. They provide a framework of valuation with which people's behav-iour can be assessed. Behaviour norms govern people so that they behave in an appropriate manner in a given cultural setting.

The nature of a group to which people belong can vary from just a cul-tural group, an informal meeting group, a gang formed in the street, or a

Table 3.2. *Types of norms.*

	Formal	Informal
Explicit	officially documented norms, e.g. laws, legislation, organisational regulations	unofficial but agreed verbally, e.g. each one sharing this big office will buy coffee supply in turn
Implicit	not applicable	habit or convention never verbally mentioned but people follow, e.g. the Club members wear formal dress when attending their monthly meetings

business establishment, to a government organisation. Accordingly, various degrees of formality of norms can be found. For a casual, informal group, very often the norms are informal while in the case of a highly formalised group, such as an administrative department of government or business organisation, most of the norms are formal. Besides, there is a horizon of norms being explicit or implicit. Table 3.2 shows examples of these types of norms.

3.3 An example of semiotic analysis

At a strategic level, semiotics can guide one in understanding how an organisation works as an information system. Operationally, it can also help one in analysing how to make a simple communication process such as a telephone conversation successful. Here a simplistic example of a telephone conversation is used to illustrate how a simple Semantic Analysis can be conducted to diagnose possible problems in the communication.

A successful telephone communication is determined by the factors in six semiotic aspects.

At the physical level, the telephones must be connected by the phone line through telephone service providers.
At the empirical level, the voice signals will be converted into electronic (or optical) signals and transmitted between two telephones.

These two levels are the technical infrastructure which is provided by the telephone companies. They are normally not the concern of the users.

At the syntactical level, the two people involved in the telephone conversation must follow the same grammatical rules, i.e. speak the same language.

At the semantic level, the words, the technical and non-technical terms, and the things referred to in the conversations must be understood by the two people. The sentences and the contents of the conversation must make sense to both of them.

At the pragmatic level, there is a concern with the intention (of the caller), and there may be 'silent' messages beneath the surface. For example, if person A calls person B and says 'I'm interested in your goods but the price is a bit too high', A's intention will be to ask whether B can lower the price a bit.

At the social level, social commitments and obligations can often be created or discharged as the result of a conversation. Following the above example, if B answers 'You'll get ten per cent discount if you buy ten or more of the PCs', there will be an obligation on B to give the discount if A buys ten or more PCs.

A communication, from the caller's point of view, can be said to be successful only if his or her messages are understood by the listener; intentions are learned by the listener; and social purposes are met.

4

A semiotic approach to information systems development

Development of a computerised system normally goes through several stages, and this whole process is termed a system development 'lifecycle'. There are various lifecycle definitions (see Leslie (1986), Macro & Buxton (1987), Olle *et al.* (1991) for example). Many researchers have been engaged in bettering methods for each of the phases in a lifecycle. Some of the methods are aimed at one of the phases while others are claimed to be useful for more than one of them. Recently, a great deal of attention has been paid to user requirement analysis and specification. This is because, on examining the sources of difficulty for large systems projects, we find that the incorrect code is a relatively insignificant factor, dwarfed by incorrect functional specification and (even more significantly) incorrect requirements (Boehm 1981; Goguen 1992).

There are many ways to phase activities in systems development. Macro & Buxton (1987) point out that many models may be excessively simple while others are extremely elaborate. In general, activities of systems development can be grouped under a few headings: conceptualisation of systems scope, requirement analysis, systems design, implementation, validation, acceptance, maintenance, and, finally, obsolescence (which may be followed by activities of developing a new version of the system). The research programme MEASUR (Stamper 1993) has developed a set of methods to deal with all aspects of information systems development.

4.1 MEASUR

MEASUR, a radically new set of norm-oriented methods for business systems modelling and requirements specification for software development, is the result of a research team working in the field of information systems since the later 1970s. The concept underlying MEASUR is that

37

organisations, themselves, are information systems and the social norm is the appropriate unit of specification. MEASUR provides five major methods to cope with the tasks in these phases.

Problem Articulation Methods (PAM) These comprise a set of methods that can be applied at the initial stage of a project when one encounters a vague, complex problem. The methods help the user to identify issues worthy of attention. In the case of solving a problem or a project for an innovation, the central task will be identified as the focal system. The situation in which the problem resides and the envisaged system must operate is seen as the infrastructure, and will be treated as a composition of many collateral systems. In order to characterise the problem situation, the user of the method will be assisted in defining unit systems which have a start, a finish and affordances which are valued by the stakeholders (the user himself may be one of the stakeholders). By using the method, undesirable omissions from analysis and specification can be reduced. The results can provide a basis for socio-economic analysis, and lifecycle and project control. There are four specific methods under the heading of Problem Articulation (Kolkman 1995):

(1) *Unit System Definition*, a method which provides handholds to describe an action course and list interdependent agents who might take an interest in it;

(2) *Valuation Framing*, a method which can be used to reveal the cultural behaviours of the constituents in relation to the benefits and drawbacks of an action course;

(3) *Collateral Analysis*, a method which assists in structuring a problem situation into a kernel course of action and surrounding or collateral activities and subsequently gives names to each part;

(4) *System Morphology*, a method which can be used to clarify three basic functional areas of social systems. Each of these components can in turn be treated as a unit for continued analysis.

Semantic Analysis Method (SAM) This method takes an articulated unit system or focal problem as the input of analysis. Within the agreed boundary of the focal problem, one of the major objectives of Semantic Analysis is to assist the user or problem-owner in eliciting and representing their requirements in a formal and precise form. Possibly with the help of a facilitator, required functions of the envisaged system will be specified in the ontology model which describes an acceptable view of the responsible agents in the focal business domain. The meaning of a word used in the semantic model to represent the business world is treated as a relationship between the word and appropriate actions.

Norm Analysis Method (NAM) This method gives a means to specify the general patterns of behaviour of the agents in the business system. The analysis of the regularities of behaviour is focused on the social, cultural and organisational norms that govern the agents' actions in the business domain. A norm can define responsibility for an agent occupying a certain incumbency (e.g. a person playing a certain role); a norm can specify conditions in which some action *may* (or *must, must not*, etc.) be performed by some agent. The norms can be specified in NORMA, a knowledge representation language, and further be translated into a computable language, LEGOL, for further processing. The systems specification can be directly implemented in the dedicated software development environment, Normbase, or be implemented in any other programming languages. Each specified norm is associated with a pattern of actions described in the computer system. For a computer information system, the norms are effectively used as function definitions or constraints on system functions.

There are two more methods: *Communication and Control Analysis*, and *Meta-Systems Analysis*. The former assists one in analysing the various communications between all the responsible agents and unit systems (identified with the Problem Articulation Method) and within the focal system. The communication messages are classified as informative, coordinative, and control, according to the intentions of the sender. The norms will be added to the governed procedures, message passing, rewards and punishments. The latter of these two methods, *Meta-Systems Analysis*, treats the whole project of innovation or system development as the object of study. It requires one to step outside the object system and helps one to treat the meta-problem in planning and management of the project.

4.2 How MEASUR can help in information systems development

There is no absolutely fixed sequence of the activities engaged in an information systems project; and therefore the application of MEASUR methods need not follow a fixed order. However, the following major phases are often found in a systems development project: infrastructure analysis, systems analysis and systems construction; MEASUR methods can be used in each of the phases. This section will describe how an infrastructure analysis can be conducted, with illustrations of a number of

MEASUR methods. The discussion of systems analysis, design and implementation will be brief in this chapter, because they will be the main focus of discussion in the following chapters.

4.2.1 Infrastructure analysis

The objectives of this phase are to understand the social, organisational, cultural and technical contexts, to understand business objectives and strategies in the organisation, and to identify business and technical problems and the feasibility of solving the problems. To achieve these objectives, one can apply the semiotic framework for a semiotic diagnosis, followed by the Problem Articulation Methods (PAM).

Semiotic diagnosis

A semiotic diagnosis examines the organisation as a social system which is constructed through the use of information. The main steps of diagnosis are the same as the layers described in the semiotic framework (Figure 3.2). The framework links the physical and social worlds through the information mechanisms people use in the organisation, rather than separating the issues into problems for the experts on production engineering and logistics, versus problems for the experts on social psychology, industrial relations and organisations. Let us see how each of the levels in the semiotic framework can be used.

Physical problems concern the media for carrying and storing signals. Word of mouth, paper, electronic devices are examples. The diagnosis at this level will focus, for example, on whether stocks contain the same information as in the inventory, placement of machines matches the plan, and production processes are the same as reported. As far as the informal information system is concerned the physical locations of the participants are crucial to their communication. Thus architecture and travel arrangements are important aspects of the physical aspects of communication. Business issues arise because of the economics of the physical resources. Information technology can often enable us to substitute a cheap medium for an expensive one (email for snail-mail) but it may even allow us to eliminate several lorries and a depot full of stock by using information more skilfully.

Empirics is concerned with the problem of the unexpected, the randomness of the entropy which so-called 'information theory' treats as the root of all information. When you run an organisation you have to cope with many different streams of events that are loaded with randomness. Therefore we organise to turn unpredictable raw materials into uniform products, to give clients a predictable service to cope with their unpredictable problems. You try to keep the plant running smoothly despite randomness in the supply of labour, the functioning of machines, failures of the transport systems and the irregularities of demand. You also want to generate diversity and unpredictability in order to innovate, keep competitors guessing and keep on your toes. Business issues are frequently prompted by considering the management of uncertainty – overcoming it or generating it. These are not necessarily primarily concerned with information systems; but one should not forget that the ultimate goal of having information systems is to help with the management uncertainty.

Syntactics is the aspect of semiotics concerned with structure. At one level it concerns the structure of sentences in a language but it can be treated much more broadly for this diagnostic purpose. The activities we have to manage are often chaotic and the issues of interest here are how to impose order and regularity, and hence operate far more efficiently. That is what production engineering is about in the factory and also systems analysis in its office analogue. One looks for the right kind and degree of formality. Only when one has succeeded in this can one introduce a computer system to support.

These three levels are all concerned with the efficiency issues. This class of problems can normally be solved using technology. They receive nearly all the attention when classical methods of requirements analysis are used. MEASUR is able not only to draw attention to the next three levels but also to provide methods for tackling the problems they raise. They are always information oriented problems, and they are becoming continually more important.

Semantics concerns meanings. When people from different backgrounds have to work together they need to understand one another. On a smaller canvas we can depict semantic problems that organisations constantly encounter – the need to respond to a new technology, a new marketing concept, a social change affecting the consumers, a new organisational concept. Effectiveness is a matter of doing the right thing and that entails a continual search for such new ideas. They all throw up problems of semantics.

Pragmatics concerns intentional behaviour. Signs are used to indicate intentions. Doing business is largely a mater of getting things done through signs that are both meaningful and charged with intention. The characteristic of an organisation with pragmatic problems is muddle. Sometimes this is caused because there is no consensus about goals, the commonly accepted intentions of a team, but sometimes the muddle is caused by misunderstandings about intentions. Issues in this area have to be resolved at the highest level in strategic planning but they also have to be resolved at the micro-level in the design of the organisation and its information systems.

Social problems are essentially those about how people do or should behave, that is problems of norms and expectations. The culture of the organisation is significant, because all information systems are ultimately dependent for any of their capacity to use signs upon the culture in which they are embedded. MEASUR is based on the analysis of the norms of an organisation, so MEASUR takes the social level as the starting point and is ideally suited for elucidating issues in this area.

MEASUR concerns itself with the three upper levels in the semiotic framework, those constituting the human functions. Thus, the use of methods is not constrained by any technical platform on which the human information system stands.

Organisation and context valuation

The next major task in the systems development project may be to conduct a total valuation of the organisation and the context for the proposed project. This analysis can take place later if the impact of the project is not considered a crucial and urgent concern at this stage. This valuation can also be conducted in parallel with other analysis.

All the stakeholders involved will be identified and the valuation will be done taking into account the interest of all stakeholders. The total system will be the object of valuation. Let us imagine that a company is going to initiate a project to develop a computer information system. The stakeholder groups in this case will include the owners of the company, the management, the operational staff, the IT department, the clients, suppliers, competitors, bystanders, the general public and so on. Each group will have a cultural system that governs how it will value this kind of innovation. The different stakeholders may react differently to the proposed project. To enable a comprehensive valuation, valuation framing has been developed which is based on an anthropological classification of cultural norms (Figure 4.1). The management, for example the stakeholder C in the figure,

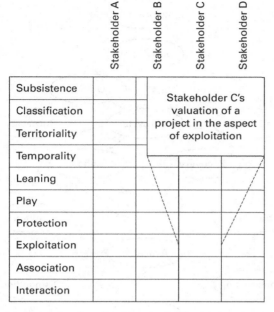

Figure 4.1. Valuation framing for organisation and context analysis.

may see the proposed IT project, in the aspect of exploitation, as an opportunity for improving the productivity, which is viewed differently by the operational staff.

The valuation framing can also be applied at a more refined level such as the unit systems that comprise the total system.

Relationships between unit systems

The method of collateral analysis helps in analysis and articulation of relationships between unit systems that comprise the large, complex system. PAM takes the central task in an innovation, such as an IT project, as the focal system. The scope of the analysis is the focal system and its infrastructure in which the focal system resides and operates. Suppose the proposed IT system has been approved to go ahead, then the focal system will be the new IT system in operation. But it does not spring out of nothing and it can only function successfully in the right infrastructure. Collateral analysis forces one to take the total system apart into a number of unit systems around the focal system. The collateral systems are interrelated and form an infrastructure for the focal system (Figure 4.2).

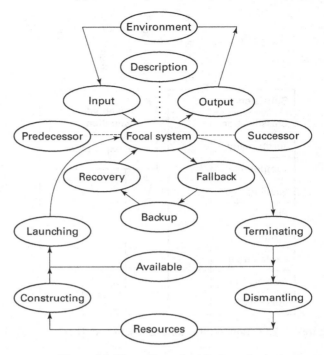

Figure 4.2. The collateral analysis method.

The collateral analysis method takes the fuzzy, total system and locates its effective boundary in a given environment. The method, as a checklist for any innovation, guides people to identify unit systems and organise them into the collateral structure. This method will be most valuable if the social and technological infrastructure is poor. An innovation project may become unexpectedly complex and a larger scale operation than expected. Just consider placing a new plant for electronic products in the 'silicon valley' of any of the economically advanced nations compared with launching it in a developing country. The lack of a piece of electric wire, for example, may make it impossible to connect a personal computer to a power supply, and therefore will make the machine fail to work in a remote undeveloped area. In order to bring the focal system into operation and sustain the situation, the analysis for planning and management of the innovation project must cover all these collateral systems.

System component analysis

For this purpose, the method of systems morphology can be applied as a complement to collateral analysis. Systems morphology looks inward at the

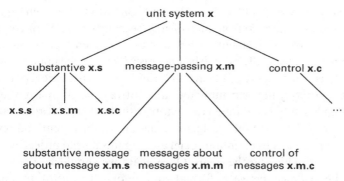

Figure 4.3. Systems morphology for analysing unit systems.

structure of each unit system. The approach taken is similar to the 'top-down', structured methods for requirements analysis, but the focus of attention is radically different. It focuses on the identification of norms that govern people's behaviour in a unit system. Each unit system can be divided into three subsystems: substantive, communication and control subsystems (Figure 4.3). The *substantive* behaviour is governed by the assignments and tasks, rules and norms, that are derived from the organisational objectives within a given institutional structure. Results of the actions in this category are supposed to contribute directly to the attainment of the business goals of the organisation. The actions will normally result in changes physically or socially.

Communication (message passing) is the second type of behaviour, which is concerned with signs, the 'input' and 'output' of the communication process. Communication norms direct the passing of messages from one agent to another for the purpose of supporting successful performance of the first type of actions. Signs are employed and sent between agents with agreed meanings by both parties involved in communication to express intentions. People who have a substantive task to perform will communicate anyway. The norms in this category are those which supplement this informal kind of communication by adding the formal exchange of messages. When people are widely separated by space and time, the informal system is less effective. This is obviously necessary between organisation for most inquiries, orders, invoices, reminders, etc. However, it is quite easy to introduce more formal communication than necessary for running the business effectively. One way of re-engineering is to look at the communications, possibly with a view to making better use of the informal system.

The third type of organisational behaviour, *control*, is governed by some enforcement or inducement norms. Within an organisation, the power of enforcement may be stipulated in rules and regulations. Between organisations, it may be generated from inter-firm agreements, treaties, or contracts. But the power of enforcement both within and between organisations ultimately rests upon socially established norms which may be underpinned by the law. This control part of behaviour within a firm ensures every relevant agent acts properly in performing the substantive tasks. If an agent understood what his duty is but failed to comply with the rule, the organisational control will be imposed on the agent. Sanctions (punishment and reward) are necessary means to maintain social and organisational orders as well as incentives for achieving the goals. Once again we should be prepared to adjust the balance between formal and informal control to increase effectiveness.

4.2.2 Systems analysis, design and implementation

The result of the infrastructure analysis gives us the power to explain the situation and articulate the innovation project into a better defined and structured problem. It also generates sufficient terminology to represent all the relevant actions. The major tasks in the further stages of a systems development project will be as follows.

> *Requirement analysis*, which includes information analysis and functional analysis;
> *Construction*, which includes systems design and implementation;
> *Operationalisation*, which includes the use, monitoring and maintenance of the system.

This section briefly describes how MEASUR can help in coping with these tasks; details will be found in the following chapters.

The *Semantic Analysis Method (SAM)* can be used to elicit and specify users' requirements. The method requires one to start by identifying the agents in the problem domain. The agents are people in different roles, with different responsibilities and authorities in an organisation. A semantic model, as the result of analysis, will capture the possible actions (or patterns of behaviour) of the agents. These patterns of behaviour are called affordances, the actions that are afforded by the agents, and that the agents are potentially capable of doing. The affordances depend on the agents, which is called *ontological dependency*. Because the information about which agent is capable of doing what action is the most important content in the semantic model, it is also called the *ontology model*.

The *Norm Analysis Method (NAM)* can then be used to capture norms

Table 4.1. *MEASUR methods and major systems development activities.*

Major phases	Major activities	MEASUR methods
Infrastructure analysis	business strategy analysis	PAM
	information planning	PAM/SAM
Requirement analysis	information analysis	SAM
	functional analysis	NAM
Construction	design	Normbase
	implementation	Normbase
Audit	audit	PAM, SAM, NAM

(i.e. rules, regulations, etc.). The norms act as conditions and constraints; they govern agents' behaviour, normally in a prescriptive manner to decide when certain actions are performed. Norms, in conjunction with the semantic model, define clearly the roles, functions, responsibilities and authorities of agents

The knowledge representation language used for semantic modelling and norm specification is called *NORMA* (a language for describing NORMs and Affordances). The specification can be translated into a computation language *LEGOL* if a computer system is to be implemented.

A semantic model, as the result of Semantic Analysis, not only is rich in semantics, but also contains information such as temporal and ontological dependencies between agents and affordances. All these information features can be captured in a pre-defined, uniform data structure in the *Semantic Temporal Database (STDB)*. The STDB constitutes the most important foundation for an integrated software environment, *Normbase*, which supports Semantic Analysis and Norm Analysis, and ultimately produces a computer information system that is based on semiotic principles and MEASUR methods.

4.3 Summary

A project of information systems development may pass through a number of major phases, each of which comprises some activities. These activities and phases are not totally sequential. Many of them take place in parallel and may re-occur a few times during the project. Table 4.1 shows major phases and activities, and the MEASUR methods that can be used to assist the activities.

The MEASUR methods can be used in virtually any sequence and may be mixed with other techniques at many points. For example, at the design stage, one may turn to using the entity–attribute–relationship method, or at the implementation stage one may adopt a fourth-generation language or an object-oriented language. But to use the MEASUR methods throughout all the phases may potentially bring in great benefits to the entire project. This is because, first of all, all the methods are consistent with one another and based on the same underlying principles. The result of analysis at an earlier phase always lends itself readily to the MEASUR method at the next phase. Secondly, there are software tools developed to assist activities at all stages. The Problem Articulation Tool (PAT) is a computerised analytical facility. With the help of PAT one will be guided to define all the unit systems, to identify the relationships between the collateral systems and the stakeholders, to assess the business strategy of the organisation, and to establish project plans. One can also use PAT for project management if the plan is constructed with this tool. Normbase is the computerised environment which provides support to cover the whole range of the systems development activities. It supports the whole process of a Semantic Analysis, a Norm Analysis and production of the systems documentation.

5
Knowledge representation and information analysis

Information analysis is also called information requirements analysis, or requirements studies. It shares with *knowledge representation* many fundamental concepts and principles. Similarities are found in techniques and methods for both. They both address how people understand the world and how to represent their understanding. Meaning of symbols and languages used in modelling is a central issue for both.

'All men by nature desire to know' – said Aristotle in his book *Metaphysics*. As an agent experiences in the flux of the world in which he acts, his faculty of sensation enables him to feel and observe affairs around him. His memory helps him to accumulate the observations and from them he learns about the world and knows what he can act upon in given circumstances. Many philosophers and scientists, such as psychologists and linguists, have been preoccupied with the study of knowledge. As computer scientists have joined in the inquiry, new perspectives of the study have been suddenly broadened. Knowledge representation has become one of the most important areas of study, because it is directly related to the exploitation of human knowledge by means of artificial intelligence, (deductive) databases, and other computer-supported methods. Each theory of knowledge (epistemology) presupposes a semantic theory; otherwise knowledge cannot be captured and represented with any language or sign system. Knowledge representation is about meanings, which are relationships between signs and the other things that they stand for. It in many respects shares the same concepts and principles as information analysis.

This chapter will look at some considerations and approaches in knowledge representation, followed by a discussion on information analysis.

5.1 Some basic considerations in knowledge representation

In philosophy or epistemology, it is often thought that *knowledge* is *indefeasible, justified true belief* (Bradley & Swartz 1979), though there is no agreement on what counts as justification, as exhibited by Lacey (1976). In Knowledge Representation (KR), *knowledge* is about 'any kind of belief a rational person might hold'; therefore, the exercise may be more suitably named as *conceptual modelling* (Way 1991). The conceptual modelling deals with questions about the 'knowledge' or beliefs that are held by some agents. The beliefs are concerned with the status of universals, abstract ideas, and concepts which are supposed to be reflected in a model.

5.1.1 Expressive adequacy and notional efficiency

A formal language or method for knowledge representation is devised with the intention of encoding knowledge and describing practical affairs. The notion of expressive adequacy questions whether a method is capable of describing all kinds of information needed in knowledge representation. A few crucial elements have to be taken into consideration when a formal language or method is developed. Knowledge or belief can be subjective. This subjectivity must be capable of being expressed in a knowledge model. General knowledge and belief can evolve or change (for example, human knowledge about the universe); knowledge about particular events is more dynamic. Therefore, it is important that temporality of knowledge be expressed in a knowledge model. In a given circumstance, knowledge can help the agent to make decisions. The decision-making process can be a quite complex one, in which knowledge about the past and predictions and hypotheses about the future will be involved. Modalities (typified by the auxiliary verbs in English such as 'must', 'could', 'may', 'shall', etc.) will be needed in such kind of reasoning processes.

The notational efficiency of a representation language concerns the syntactic usage of the language. An important question regarding efficiency is how easily the language can be understood and worked with. This is often referred to as *conceptual efficiency*. Another consideration is the *computational efficiency*.

5.1.2 Semantic primitives

The primitives of any system are a set of basic units or structures which cannot be analysed further into component parts and of which all other complex structures are composed. Brachman (1979) identifies five levels of primitives in KR: implementational, logical, epistemological, conceptual and linguistic. Apart from the primitives of these categories, Way (1991) suggests another type of primitives that are at the level of the *presentation scheme* itself. At this level, the primitives would be how the general structure of the knowledge is conceived, for example, as predicates organised in the logic approach, as semantic nodes and links in the semantic networks, and as frame structures in the frames. The representation scheme of any method, as a whole, has to consider how the primitives of the first five layers are treated. Another notion of primitives in the representation scheme, which must be distinguished from the syntactic notations, is the *semantic primitives* or basic units of meaning. In her book, Way (1991) quotes Wilks' explanation of semantic primitives (see Wilks (1978)):

Primitives are philosophical atoms, usually corresponding to words in a natural language such as English, and are said to name basic concepts underlying human thought.

A semantic theory, which every KR method must have and be associated with, will enable one to express one's beliefs with the primitives in the formal notations used in the method, and also enable one to understand the model. Meanings specify the correspondence between the signs and the referents. The semantic theory can also be a guide to eliciting knowledge from verbal and non-verbal actions and expressions, and organising them into the formal representation. This means that the knowledge representation would be trying to find meta-models for the models of the world that underlie our everyday reasoning. Such a model is an ontological model: it consists of a catalogue of objects and properties with law-like relations between them (Way 1991). Way calls this approach 'scruffy', which is typically in contrast with some axiomatic approach which has been confined within the consequences based on axioms whose truth depends only on guesswork.[1]

5.1.3 Types of knowledge

Ryle (1949) distinguishes two types of knowledge: *declarative* and *procedural*. The former knowledge is *knowing that* while the latter is *knowing how*.

---

[1] Sowa (1984) comments that the *scruffies* versus the *neats* have different views of AI. The neat view assumes that a few elegant principles underlie all the manifestations of human intelligence. Discovery of those principles would provide the magic key to the working of the mind. The scruffy view is that intelligence is a *kludge*: the ways people solve problems are so much dependent on *ad hoc* approaches and heuristics that no universal principles can be found.

Declarative knowledge is theory-oriented. It consists of an explicit description of relations between concepts. The relations can be definitional dependencies in terms of concepts, and functional dependencies between quantities. This type of knowledge can be conveniently represented in many representation methods, for example, semantic networks and frames. Procedural knowledge is practice-oriented. It often consists of a set of prescriptions for actions in relation to certain types of conditions. They are referred to as *situation-action rules* or *production rules*. Rule-based systems form a typical example of a suitable representation approach for this type of knowledge. Winograd (1975) summarises the arguments in the procedural–declarative controversy as follows:

> *Economy* Procedures specify knowledge by saying how it is used, and every use requires a different procedure. A declarative approach requires only a single copy for all uses.
>
> *Modularity* Procedures bind knowledge and control in a single package. By keeping them separate, a declarative approach makes it easier to update and generalise the knowledge base.
>
> *Exception handling* Procedures can do anything, and problems that are not covered by the formal theory can often be handled by an *ad hoc* piece of code. A declarative approach may find difficulty with exceptions that were not anticipated by the theory.

All the three arguments are important considerations for anyone who develops a method for knowledge representation. Fortunately, advantages and disadvantages of the two representation strategies are recognised by the AI community. Many methods developed so far can also be characterised as being suited to more one type than another. But since the *procedural–declarative controversy* arose over the role of procedural knowledge in intelligence in the late 1970s (*cf.* Winograd 1975), many developers try to cope with both types of knowledge in their methods, because of the necessity for both.

5.2 Representation approaches

5.2.1 Typical examples

There are some well-recognised typical approaches to knowledge representation, such as the logic approach, semantic networks, frames, rule-based methods and conceptual graphs. The book of Ringland and Duce (1988) offers an overview of those typical approaches and some research issues.

The logic approach is mainly based on first order logic, though other non-classical logic, e.g. modal logic, has a role to play there. The system of logic is known as definite Horn clauses, which are essential rules of the form:

A if B_1 and B_2 and . . . B_n

Such a clause has exactly one conclusion A, but zero or more conditions B. Propositions are basic elements and can be translated further into several predicates. Propositions have truth-values that are determined by a certain interpretation function. That is to say, any proposition must be TRUE or FALSE under the interpretation which sets up a correspondence between the symbols of the language and objects or values in some domain. The predicates can be connected with connectives (e.g. $\wedge$ (and), $\vee$ (or), $\neg$ (not), and $\rightarrow$ (implies)) and quantifiers (i.e. $\exists$ (existential quantifier), and $\forall$ (universal quantifier)). Thus, take a piece of 'knowledge' as follows:

John gives a book to Mary

The constituent concepts can be first of all identified as 'John', 'Mary', 'book', and 'give'. A decent representation can be obtained as follows:[2]

$giving(e)$	e is a giving 'event'
$agent(e, John)$	John was the giver
$recip(e, Mary)$	Mary was the recipient
$\exists b, book(b) \wedge object(e, b)$	a book is the object of giving
$time(e, T)$	the giving was at time T
$\forall e,y,t,x\ giving(e) \wedge recip(e, y)$	if y was the recipient of x at time t
$\wedge\ time(e, t) \wedge object(e, x) \rightarrow$	then he becomes the owner for all
$(\forall t1, t1 > t \rightarrow owns(y, x, t1))$	time after this.

Semantic networks are designed as a means to describe the concepts behind word meaning and the ways in which such meanings interact. A network is a net or graph of nodes joined by links. The nodes in a semantic network usually represent concepts (e.g. BOOK, GREEN) and the links (or labelled directed arcs) usually represent relations (e.g. a book IS COLOURED green). Semantic networks may be loosely related to predicate calculus by following the substitution: *terms and relations replace nodes and labelled directed arcs.*

Frames are ways of grouping information in terms of a record of 'slots' and 'fillers'. The record can be thought of as a node in a network, with a

² Based on Pavelin in Ringland & Duce (1988).

Figure 5.1. Concept and relation in conceptual graphs.

special slot filled by the name of the object that the node stands for and the other slots filled with the values of various common attributes associated with such an object. This approach can be conveniently suitable for representing knowledge about structure domains or structured knowledge. The intuition behind the frames is that the human brain is less concerned with defining strictly the properties that entities must have in order to be considered as exemplars of some category, and more concerned with the salient properties associated with objects that are typical of their class.

5.2.2 Conceptual graphs

Charles Peirce had many extensive treatments of graphs. He proposed that a graph can be used as a consistent system of representation, founded upon a simple and easily intelligible basic idea. It can represent facts, concepts and relationships iconically (see Peirce (1931–58)). Graphs have recently been used for developing many methods of knowledge representation, such as semantic networks (see Brachman (1979), Randal (1988)), conceptual dependency graphs (Schank 1972, 1975), knowledge graphs (Hoede 1986, Smit 1991), and conceptual graphs (Sowa 1984). Graph methods generally claim to capture some deeper cognitive properties than syntactic structures. Many studies in this direction try to discover some basic concepts and types of relations so that meanings of words can be described by 'case relations' (i.e. semantic relation primitives linking verbs to some other structures and elements). For example, Schank (1972) identifies a set of primitive actions, states, and 'conceptual cases'. Knowledge expressed in natural language can be represented by employing these primitives.

Conceptual graphs are devised as a language of knowledge representation by Sowa (1984), based on philosophy, psychology and linguistics. Knowledge in conceptual graph form is highly structured by modelling specialised facts that can be subjected to generalised reasoning. In the graphs, concept nodes represent entities, attributes, states, and events, and relation nodes how the concepts are interconnected. A concept is drawn as a box, a conceptual relation as an oval; an arc with an arrow links a box to an oval (see Figure 5.1).

It can also be expressed in a linear form; then the boxes may be abbreviated with square brackets, and the ovals with round parentheses. Therefore the equivalent expression for Figure 5.1 in the linear form is as follows:

[*concept 1*]→(*relation*)→[*concept 2*].

The reading of the expression in both forms can be: the '*relation*' of a '*concept 1*' is a '*concept 2*'. Sometimes the reading of an expression may sound grammatically awkward. Consider the following example:

[Vehicle]→(part)→[Trailer].

The reading of it, 'A part of a vehicle is a trailer', can be simplified as 'a vehicle with a trailer'. These readings are helpful mnemonics, not linguistic rules for mapping the graphs into English sentences. Conceptual graphs are finite, connected, bipartite graphs. Conceptual relations may have any number of arcs; however, most of the common ones are dyadic. Some are monadic, such as the *past tense maker* (PAST) or the *negation* (NEG); others are triadic, like *between* (BETW); and any other number of arcs.

The primitives of the conceptual graphs are *concept types, concepts* and *conceptual relations*. The *concept types* represent classes of entity, attribute, action, state and event. Examples of such concepts are: CAT, ANIMAL, ARRIVE, ATTRIBUTE, BIG, COMMAND, COLOUR, JUSTICE, LOVE, and WARM. Any conceptual graph system may have a set of types as a basis. This set of concept types is organised using a relation _ defined over the set. The concept types can be partially ordered according to the super-type and sub-type relations. For example, consider concept types, PHYSICAL-OBJECT, ANIMAL, MAMMAL and CAT, they can be arranged as in the following order:

CAT _ MAMMAL _ ANIMAL _ PHYSICAL-OBJECT

which means that CAT is a kind of MAMMAL, every MAMMAL is a kind of ANIMAL, etc. CAT is said to be a sub-type of MAMMAL, MAMMAL a super-type of CAT. The type hierarchy is not a tree-like structure, but a lattice structure. This can be seen from the organisation of the following concept types:

ELEPHANT _ MAMMAL
ELEPHANT _ WILD-ANIMAL
RATTLESNAKE _ WILD-ANIMAL
TIGER _ MAMMAL
TIGER _ WILD-ANIMAL

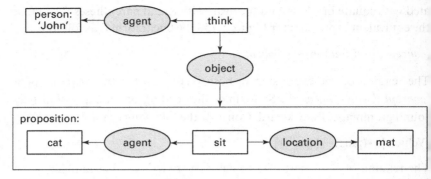

Figure 5.2. An example of a conceptual graph (Jackman & Pavelin 1988).

Concepts are instances of concept types. For example, a concept 'the mammal known as Clyde' can be written in the conceptual graphs of Polovina and Heaton (1992):

[MAMMAL: Clyde].

A concept that appears without an individual referent corresponds to a generic referent. Such generic concepts could be denoted as *[<Type_Label>: *]*. Writing *[<Type_Label>]* is merely a convenient shorthand. Generic concepts may take up an individual referent (Clyde would have a particular trunk). A unique number referent can suffice to make a concept distinct. Thus the generic concept *[TRUNK]* may become *[TRUNK:#1234]* in respect of *[MAMMAL: Clyde]*. The following would be produced:

[MAMMAL: Clyde] → (part) → [TRUNK: #1234].

Conceptual relations are links between concepts, and they indicate the *role* that each concept (or percept, in terms of referent) plays. Typical examples of conceptual relations found in the dictionary in Sowa (1984) are *agent, cause, duration, experiencer, instrument, location, negation, part, past, point-in-time, successor*, etc. Figure 5.2 shows an example of how a propositional attitude *think* is handled in a conceptual graph. Other information on contexts, such as negation, tense, modality, and propositional attitudes can also be incorporated in this way.

5.3 Some fundamental issues of information analysis

Any method of information analysis must adopt fundamental assumptions in these four aspects, which one can always examine: ontological position,

epistemological position, social context and presentation (Hirschheim *et al.*
1995, p. 156).

The ontological position is concerned with the questions of the nature of
reality or of what is being studied. Is there an objective reality that is
independent of anyone? How does the world come to exist? What constitutes the application domain that is being studied and modelled? Is
the object system (or the application domain) that is being studied
defined, created and sustained by physical components, operations,
roles, decisions, social actions, speech acts, or something else? These
are typical questions concerning ontological assumptions.

The epistemological position explains how people are to come to understand the world, how to acquire knowledge about the application
domain. Is there an objective truth? How do we justify the knowledge
acquired about the application domain? How do we define the validity
of knowledge and how do we prove it? The epistemological position a
method adopts is to a large extent determined by its ontological position.

The assumption on *the social context* determines first of all how to see
the relationship between information and action. Information is
created and processed by people and will serve people in their decision
making and actions. The value, relevance and validity of information
are all related to the social context in which information is used.
Secondly, a proper information analysis exercise can only be done if
the people involved use the same language and have a substantial
common understanding of the problem domain.

Finally, *the assumption in respect of presentation* determines the information type to be presented and the form of presentation. For example,
some methods present information in a way that is close to the use of
natural language, while the relational data model recommends nor-
malised data entities (i.e. tables). Efficiency of the presentation is also
part of the concern.

In addition, a sound method of information analysis must meet these criteria.

Adequate A method of information analysis normally includes
identification of information requirements, followed by elicitation and
specification of requirements. Techniques for defining the scope of the
application domain for analysis should be available. In many cases,
prospective users of an information system may not know exactly
what they want. The information requirements are difficult to know

beforehand. The method, therefore, should assist people involved in analysis to elicit the requirements systematically as the requirement specification develops.

Instructive A method should not be like a cooking recipe; it should provide guidelines and allow creativity. But it should provide clear instructions on how to perform analysis step by step.

Capable of capturing rich business semantics An information model should reflect the patterns of behaviour and rules of the business domain, which explicates the meaning of the application domain, or business semantics. The business semantics should be clearly expressed and treated as the focus of the modelling, not the technical design issues (such as data formats for storage).

Rigorous An information model resulting from an analysis should be precise in representing meaning. It should not lend itself to ambiguous interpretation.

Easy to verify/falsify the validity of the information model An information analysis is often a process involving a group of people with multiple roles and perspectives. The prospective users, who are stakeholders, will normally have to approve the result of analysis, based on the outcome of validation of the information model. A sound model should be possible for users to understand – without having to go through a lengthy training process in order to make sense of the model – comment on, critique and finally approve or disapprove the model. Many methods in fact discourage users from checking the analysis with complicated syntactical notation, technical jargon and implementation-related issues, and therefore they have to approve the analysis without really understanding the information model which often leads to a computer system that they are committed to.

These fundamental issues and criteria can be useful when one evaluates and selects methods of information analysis for systems development or other purposes.

5.4 The role of information analysis

Ultimately, an exercise of an information analysis addresses two issues. First of all, it is concerned with understanding of the business itself and business needs. Secondly, it is about how the needs can be met by providing an organisational and technical system. So the information analysis deals with both understanding of a problem and production of a solution. A proper information analysis will enable system developers to ensure that

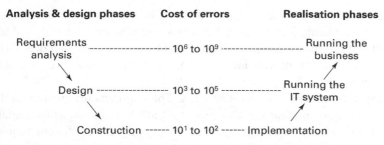

Figure 5.3. Cost of errors at different phases of information systems development (after Liu *et al.* (1994)).

they address the right problem and answer the right questions. It should then deliver the right information requirements on which a system solution can be designed. Therefore an information analysis is extremely important in the development of information systems.

Empirical studies show on many occasions an information system project did not address the right questions because the requirements were understood wrongly. Evidence also shows that an error at the information analysis stage can be incredibly expensive. Figure 5.3 summarises these findings and shows the orders of magnitude of cost of errors at major phases of an information systems lifecycle. From this diagram, one can see that activities in the analysis and design phases have effects on the relevant phases on the side of realisation. For example, the quality of the requirements analysis affects the running of the business. The design of an IT system solution influences the running of the IT system. The construction and delivery of an IT system determine the installation and overall result of the system implementation in the business organisation. An error at the phase of requirements analysis can cost tremendously more than an error of coding at the construction phase. Therefore, an adaptation of proper methods and a careful analysis of information requirements are important because they deal with the activities of the first phase in systems analysis and design.

An information analysis normally involves a group of participants and covers a range of activities. These participants are called stakeholders who all have an interest in the system development. The stakeholders are the concerned parties who are either involved in the system development, the owner of the system, or the user of the system (much literature can be found in stakeholder analysis, e.g. Kolkman (1995)). The process of information analysis carried out by the parties concerned is characterised by these activities (after Kotonya & Sommerville (1998)).

Requirements elicitation The information requirements and system requirements are discovered through consultation with stakeholders, from system documents, domain knowledge and market studies. Other names for this process are requirements acquisition and requirements discovery.

Requirements analysis and negotiation The requirements are analysed in detail and different stakeholders negotiate to decide on which requirements are to be accepted. Stakeholders may have different requirements in terms of information and system functions. Conflicts may exist in these requirements. There are also possible ambiguities in the requirements captured. The negotiation and analysis allow clarification of the meaning of requirements. They also provide opportunities for stakeholders to decide on the set of agreed requirements for the system.

Requirements documentation The agreed requirements are documented at an appropriate level of detail. The requirements document should be understandable by all stakeholders, so that all stakeholders can check and validate the requirements (the objective of the next activity).

Requirements validation The requirements must be checked for consistency and completeness. To achieve this, it would be essentially beneficial that all stakeholders can take part in the validation. The involvement of stakeholders can boost the quality of the requirements, and hence improve the quality of the system. (However, this might be difficult to achieve with many methods because of technical complexity embedded in the presentation of the requirements.)

The information analysis and requirements engineering are not a straightforward process. It normally requires several iterations before a set of requirements with a reasonable accuracy and confidence can be produced. The method of Semantic Analysis enables analysts, with the participation of other stakeholders, to produce correct and accurate requirements in a rigorous manner.

6
Semantic Analysis

A business system is a real information system, which is infinitely rich and complex. One can never exhaustively study a social or business organisation. What is modelled is always a part of it; and what is seen is just a realisation (or an instance) of a pattern of behaviour of some agent. If one wishes to model a business system one has to focus on the level of pattern of behaviour. The method of Semantic Analysis provides a means for these purposes by devising a canonical formalism with focus on the responsible agent and his repertoire of behaviour. This method covers a range of activities in information modelling such as requirements elicitation, analysis, specification and representation.

6.1 Theoretical aspects of Semantic Analysis

The relationship between behaviour and knowledge is in two directions. In one direction, an agent learns about the world through his actions to gain knowledge so that he gets to know exactly the meanings and boundaries of objects, concepts and relations. On the other side, the behaviour manifests knowledge that the agent possesses. The functions of both sides work at the same time, i.e., what he knows tells him what to do; what he does reflects what he knows (partially, because what he does may be a kind of trail to learn some new knowledge). Any rational action of the agent is constrained by the repertoire of behaviour and directed by his knowledge of the world. This repertoire of behaviour can be seen as affordances.

6.1.1 Affordances

'Affordance' is the word that Gibson (1968) and the 'direct perception' school of psychologists (see Michaels & Carello (1981)) use for behaviour

61

of an organism made available by some combined structure of organism and its environment. 'The affordances of the environment are what it offers the animal, what it provides or furnishes, either for good or ill', Gibson (1968) writes. He gives an example to show that, if a terrestrial surface is horizontal, flat, sufficiently extended, and firm, then the surface *affords support*. It is a surface of support. It is stand-on-able, permitting an upright posture for quadrupeds and bipeds. It is therefore walk-on-able and run-over-able. It is not sink-into-able like a surface of water in a swamp. The properties of the surface, when they were measured as an affordance of support for a species of animal, have to be measured relative to the animal, not just treated as physical properties. According to ecology, a species of animal is said to utilise or occupy a certain niche in the environment. The natural environment offers many ways of life, and different animals have different ways of life. The niche implies a kind of animal, and the animal implies a kind of niche. They together constitute the totality of the world that we inhabit.

The theory of affordances can be naturally extended to the social world for studying social behaviour. The society acting as environment makes many patterns of behaviour possible. People are agents living in a world of flux. This world is socially constructed through agents' actions, on the basis of what is offered by the physical world itself. The agent-in-its-environment makes it possible to acquire certain abilities of behaving which may be completely impossible if the agent is separated from the environment. While an agent acts, he experiences the environment and alters it at the same time. His previous actions build up a possibility of some new type of action. For example, a person's ability to recognise a telephone is socially afforded by the fact that there is an artefact called a telephone. Only if he has the ability to recognise a telephone can he be taught how to operate it, and can he then be able to make a telephone call. An agent learns his direct knowledge through detecting *valuable invariants by act-in-relation-to-environment* physically and mentally. By knowing the invariants, the values of certain ranges of behaviour are learned. Having sufficient experience in the social environment and knowing the invariants enough, an agent can know the boundaries of behaviour which are socially acceptable. However, what he learns is only his direct environment, here and now. To be able to know anything beyond here and now, signs must be employed so as to compose propositions and images.

By using signs, another dimension of the world is opened up for the agent, and he can then get access to the part of the world which is beyond the *here-and-now*. Signs afford appropriate action at a distance. In particular, they afford coordinated actions among members of a society. People create signs and assign meanings to them, and use them to refer to the future and past. This ambience, full of man-made signs, is called 'culture', which supports most of the daily social interactions. A natural deduction, which can be socially confirmed, is that different cultures, for example the western or eastern, Christian or Buddhist, provide different affordances, hence different perceptions of reality.

6.1.2 Ontology and some other fundamental notions

Lacey (1976) offers the following explanation about *ontology*:

A central part of metaphysics is *ontology*. This studies BEING, and in particular, nowadays, what there is, e.g. material objects, minds, PERSONS, UNIVERSALS, numbers, FACTS, etc . . . A particular theory about what exists, or a list of existents, can be called an ontology.[1]

Questions that an ontological theory tries to investigate are fundamental and general. It seeks an inventory of kinds of things that exist and asks what can be said about anything that exists, just in so far as it exists. Can we classify all that exists into different fundamental kinds (categories), in one way or more ways? Is there any hierarchy among kinds of things? Do some depend on others for their existence? These are typical questions concerned in any ontological study, and involve the relations between very general notions, such as *thing, entity, object, individual, universal, particular, substance*, and also *event, process, state*.

In a paper, Stamper (1985) examines three very different ontologies which have strong influences on the studies of information and knowledge. The first one only recognises symbol structures; this is the ontology of a relational database language. The second ontology recognises distinct, individual, identifiable objects; this lies behind predicate logic as its formal semantics is based on set theory. The third ontology assumes that the only thing we can know is our own behaviour in our own environment; this is the ontology that Semantic Analysis bases itself on. This ontology assumes that the world known to a particular agent comprises only the actions he can perform in his environment.

The agent can be as simple as an individual person, and complex as a cultural group, language community or society. What exists in the world relies on the repertoire of behaviour of the agent. For example, an ink pen may exist in a sense of an *ink pen* in one cultural community, but of an *unknown object* in some other cultural community; a particular sword may exist as a

---

The capitals used by Lacey indicate his view that some of these categories are more important than others.

weapon in one society but as only an ornament in another. In these examples, the existences of the pen and the sword depend on the agent whose affordances allow him to recognise them, to assign meanings to them, to know their properties. This leads to the notion of dependency in this ontology: the agent learns abilities; these affordances enable him to act, in ways that determine the shape of the world he inhabits. The affordances the agent has gained are universal invariants which constitute the repertoire of his behaviour, and allow him to react recurrently and circumstantially. Every particular action he performs is a realisation of a universal pattern of behaviour. The two main categories of the *construction blocks* of the world are *agent* and *affordance*, but the definition of agent and affordance is context-sensitive. Some simple agent, for example a person, is ontologically dependent on some other complex agent, say society; in this case, the agent, person, is an affordance itself. Nevertheless, a criterion for determining whether an affordance can ever be an agent is that an agent must be able to act responsibly. Properties of the agents and affordances are another fundamental class of the *construction blocks*, labelled as *determiners*, which result from complicated measurements of the agents and affordances.

Actions of agents normally should be modelled at the universal level concerning the universal patterns of behaviour in knowledge representation and requirement analysis, though in the end they will be recorded in a database at both levels. Loux (1978) reports that Aristotle's definition of the universal is 'that which is of such a nature as to be predicated of many objects'. Frege considers that concepts are the referents of predicate-expressions. Russell states that 'substantives, adjectives, prepositions, and verbs', the expressions which serve as predicate-terms, 'stand for universals'. In NORMA, the universals represent invariant patterns of behaviour, or mechanisms. The universals can have realisations which are particular instances. This universal–particular conceptual construct is found in conceptual graphs as well (see Sowa (1984)). Universals are represented as the concept types, while particulars are concepts. However, the representations of both universals and particulars in NORMA are done in the same way, because there is no fundamental difference between the universals and particulars. Both of them represent repertoires of behaviour. Similar treatments of both universals and particulars can be found in Semantic Analysis in later sections.

6.2 NORMA

NORMA is a knowledge representation language developed in the MEASUR research programme (Stamper 1992, Stamper *et al.* 1988). A primary function of this language is for conducting semantic analysis. *NORMA* comes from NORM and *Affordance*, and is devised as a language for specifying norms and affordances as systems analysis and requirement specification. The purpose of this section is to introduce NORMA in terms of some of its most important concepts and syntax.

6.2.1 Well-formed formula

The focus of systems analysis is the agents in action. No matter how complex the agents are in a social environment, they can be studied by observing their actions and detecting the invariants, i.e. general patterns of behaviour. Two axioms stated earlier, in Chapter 2, that dominate basic formulation of the language are

there is no knowledge without a knower, and
there is no knowing without action.

These axiomatic, philosophical assumptions suggest that the only feasible way to depict any fragment of knowledge is to model the agent and his action at the same time. The meaning of representation of action is only determined if the viewpoint is chosen; therefore, the place of the agent in a knowledge representation model is essential. Following this, a well-formed formula (wff) for knowledge representation is derived as always having the following structure:

$$<knower\text{-}term><behaviour\text{-}term>,$$
or
$$<agent\text{-}term>\ <action\text{-}term>.$$

For example,

Ax, where *A* is an agent and *x* stands for a pattern of action, e.g. *person stand.*

This wff requires every piece of knowledge to be tied to the agent who is responsible for it. The knowledge can be about universal patterns of actions or particular instances. In any case, the agent is responsible for possessing the knowledge, performing the action, or designating meanings to actions.

6.2.2 Affordance and ontological dependency

Some affordances can be possible only if certain other affordances are available. This kind of dependency is *ontological*, which is taken as an essential theme in representing knowledge. For example, for a person to be able to stumble, he must first walk; for two persons to be separated, they must have a marriage or other relationship which involves being together. In these two examples, 'walk' and 'marriage' are *ontological antecedents* for 'stumble' and 'separation' respectively which are called *ontological dependants*. These ontological antecedents are more direct extensions of affordances of the agent or agents. An agent with affordances can be seen as a *modified agent*, the affordances being treated as extensions. To represent the above two examples, the following expressions can be obtained:

person walk stumble,	where '*person walk*' is the modified agent which affords '*stumble*'; and
(person₁, person₂) marriage separation,	where (person$_1$, person$_2$) is a complex agent, the modified agent is '*(person₁, person₂) marriage*' on which a further affordance '*separation*' is an ontological dependent.

These two expressions have employed syntactic formulae:

Axy,	e.g. *person walk stumble*; and
(A,B)xy,	e.g. *(person₁, person₂) marriage separation.*

In most of the cases, analysis of agent (either a simple one, such as a person, or a complex one, such as a corporate body or an institution) with his behaviour would be a recursive application of this principle of modified agent to obtain the expressions in the wff.

The affordance can be composite. When an agent is doing one thing, he might also be doing another. Thus,

$A(x,y)$, where ',' reads as 'while', a restriction. E.g. *person(stand, speak)*, meaning: a person stands while he speaks.

The agent may do one or another or both of two things at a time. The syntax for this is:

$A(x:y)$, where ':' reads as 'or-while', a conflation. E.g. *person(speak: sing)* for 'a person either speaks or sings.'

If the agent has an affordance of doing one thing while the other is not experienced, the following syntax is designed for designating that:

$A(x;y)$, where ';' reads as 'while-not', an exclusion. E.g. *person(sit; sing)* for 'a person sits while he is not singing.'

A composite affordance can be partitioned into several parts. The notation in NORMA is defined as follows:

Ax.y, which means *y* is a part of *x*. E.g. '*university student-council. chairperson*', the student-council is ontologically dependent on the university, and the chairperson (the role or incumbency in the office rather than the person) is a part of the student-council.

6.2.3 Semiotic behaviour

Two types of behaviour have to be identified: substantive and semiotic. An agent can perform an action and he can also use signs to describe the action (though the using of signs itself is an action). Without involving signs, the agent is confined within his here-and-now environment, for example, he stands, walks, and moves about. If he wants to make his actions linked with the past and future, he must use signs. The abilities to use signs in various ways are called semiotic affordances, while the behaviour directly bringing in a change of a physical or social world is considered substantive. For example, '*marriage*' can be considered as a substantive behaviour of the two persons concerned. The associated semiotic behaviour with '*marriage*' would be announcing the start or the finish of the marriage where production of semiotic entities (signs), such as speeches and documents, is involved. Such semiotic behaviour can be represented in the following form:

B "Ax", where *B* is the agent performing the semiotic action, and between and including the quotes are signs employed by *B* in his behaviour. *Ax* is the meaning or referent of the semiotic action. E.g. '*Mary "John happy"*'.

6.2.4 Time

Time is one of the most effective measures to determine the meanings of concepts, actions, and events expressed in our language. Affordances have an ontological nature which allows them to be placed into the flux of the world in terms of time. The benefit of using time is exploited in NORMA in many ways. When an agent and an affordance are identified and defined, their existence period must be determined, marked by *start* and *finish*, for both a universal and a particular. The determination of the boundaries in terms of time is the minimum as a guarantee that the meanings of the words and expressions appearing in an analysis are clear. It is also used as a clue for seeking agreed meanings from different viewpoints. Several operators are defined in NORMA to enable one to describe patterns of behaviour that are related to the *start* and the *finish* of the affordances. Two of them are *beginning* and *ending*:

$Ax<$, e.g. '*person stand<*', meaning: a person begins to stand, which may terminate an action of sitting and leads to a start of standing, if the *beginning* process is successful.

$Ax>$, e.g. '*person stand>*', meaning: a person ends standing, which may bring the action of standing to a finish, if the *ending* process is successful.

6.2.5 Determiner and identity

Agents and affordances have properties which are invariants of quality and quantity that differentiate one instance from another. This kind of invariant is called a *determiner*. Typical examples of determiners are names, addresses, weights and hair-colours of a person. To describe the determiners, the following mechanism is devised:

$A\#x$, or $Ax\#y$ where the hash sign indicates what follows is a determiner, e.g. '*person#name*', '*person#weight*', or '*person salary#amount*', etc.

An agent may have many roles to play when he is involved in many actions or relations. For example, a person can be seen as a father, a husband, a manager, and a customer, depending on the circumstances in which the person is looked at. The role name, essentially serving the same purpose as the other properties discussed above, is also a determiner of individuality. See the following expression as an example:

(person#husband, person#wife)marriage

This describes that a marriage is a joint affordance of two persons, of whom one has a role name '*husband*' and the other '*wife*'.

6.2.6 Generic–specific relationship

Agents and affordances can be placed in generic–specific structures according to whether or not they possess shared or different properties. The generic–specific classification is normally determined by norms which may be socially or culturally formed. In some cases, the classification rules can be defined by the parties involved in the particular practical affairs. The formula to represent the generic–specific relationships is as follows:

$A((b:c:d:e) \rightarrow f)$, where b, c, d, and e are specific affordances of the
generic f. E.g. '*society ((natural-person:corporate-body:government) → legal-person)*', which means in a society, there are several specific kinds of legal persons,

such as natural persons, corporate bodies and
governments.

The generic–specific structures are contingent on social decisions and are
not logically necessary. For example, one may classify a whale into the category of fish or mammal, or both.

6.2.7 Defining authority and responsibility

The notion of *responsibility* is as essential in NORMA as the notion of
truth in classical logic, because in NORMA any recognition of affordances,
and their existence periods, are tied to the agents. Realisations of actions
and changes of states are all decided by the responsible agents in accordance with the authorities. For example, the commencement and termination of a studentship are authorised by someone who is in a role of student
registration officer; and the qualification of enjoying a social security
benefit is determined by the special government office. The responsibility
and authority over realising each instance of the affordances are analysed
and traced in the analysis. The following way is defined for denoting
authority in NORMA:

$A(x@ \rightarrow y)$ which means the authority for x is y. E.g. *'nation(law@ $\rightarrow$
parliament)'*.

6.2.8 Graphic representation – ontology chart

An old Chinese saying says 'A picture is worth a thousand words'.
NORMA offers a way of graphic representation. Agents and affordances
are nodes in the graphic representation, and linked with lines. The
antecedents are placed on the left of the dependants. In other words, the
left–right positioning reflects the ontological dependencies. The example in
Figure 6.1 explains how the ontological relationships can be represented in
the graphic form of NORMA.

The '*society*' is the root agent in this model, and it has two affordances:
'*person*' and '*thing*'. Here 'person' is an agent and 'thing' is a normal
affordance. Both are ontologically dependent on the society, which means
both are defined in the context of a certain society. If the society does not
exist, then the concepts of person and thing become undefined. Therefore,
it is the '*society*' which has affordances of recognising the '*person*' and
'*thing*' and the other dependants. If the society is seen as a modified agent
with the extension of affordances of person and thing, it makes it possible

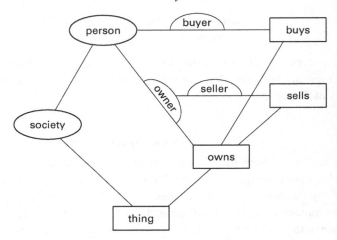

Figure 6.1. An illustration of NORMA in graphics.

to talk about '*owns*'. More straightforwardly, a person can own a thing.
Agents are placed in ovals, such as 'society' and 'person'. Role names are
put in half-curves, e.g., owner, seller and buyer. Actions and other kinds of
affordances are put in rectangular boxes. Notice the action '*sells*' is ontologically dependent on the '*owner*' (the role) and '*owns*', and the action '*buys*' is
built upon *person* and *owns*. This suggests that selling is only possible for
the owner who owns the thing, while buying is for any person. Selling and
buying are referred to the affordance '*owns*.' That means when people are
trading, it is the ownership rather than the physical thing itself that is dealt
with. In this sense, the representation ontologically reflects the social practice which is dominated by the shared norms in the social context.

The example in Figure 6.2 involves the representation of affordances
having generic–specific relationships. The root agent '*nation*' affords '*legal
person*' within the given social and legal context. Under the generic
heading, more specific items can be found: '*natural person*,' and '*corporate
body*.' Within the heading of 'corporate body,' there are more specifics:
items '*company*,' '*government*,' and '*learned society*.' The specific kinds of
affordances under a generic heading share some properties; for example, all
specific kinds of corporate body have a '*management*' as part of the organisation. Any natural person can be employed by a corporate body, in which
he is called '*employee*' and the other party is '*employer*.' The '*management*' is
a part of the 'corporate body.' Therefore a line with a dot associated is
drawn to indicate the whole–part relationship between them. To be a

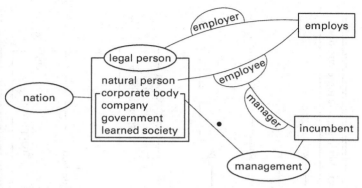

Figure 6.2. Another illustration of NORMA in graphics.

manager, one is first of all considered as an 'employee' of the 'corporate body,' which is represented by putting *'being an employee'* as an ontological antecedent for the *'incumbent.'* This constraint is assumed, when the analysis is conducted, as a norm generally residing in the social organisations.

The ontological relationship is considered as the most fundamental relationship to model in NORMA. All other relationships, such as generic–specific, whole–part, determiners, roles, etc., are treated on the basis of the ontological relationship. Therefore, the process of producing a graphic representation in NORMA is called *ontology charting*, and a complete conceptual model represented in NORMA graphic notation is called an *ontology chart*. Table 6.1 presents some of the syntax notations of NORMA in both textual and graphic forms, and summarises briefly some of the discussions in this section.

6.3 Using LEGOL to specify norms

LEGOL is a knowledge manipulation language that can be used for handling data that have rich semantic and temporal features. In this section, some LEGOL operators will be used even before the language itself is introduced in Chapter 10.

The ontological structure of the agents and the affordance depicts the most fundamental norms of behaviour. The complex behaviour which is built up on the fundamental patterns of behaviour can be described in the form of norms. In addition, although the ontological structure offers an understanding of what patterns of behaviour are ontologically available, the detailed conditions and constraints of the realisations of the behaviour

Table 6.1. *Part of NORMA syntax and examples.*

Textual	Graphic	Meaning	Example in graphic representation
Ax	A ——— x	x is an affordance of A	person ——— walk
			society ——— person
Ax.y	A ——— x •—— y	y is a part of x; they all are afforded by A	nation ——— school •—— department
Ax#y	A ——— x ——— #y	A affords x which has a determiner y	society ——— person ⌐———#weight
A((a:b:c:d)→f)	A ——— ⌐ f ⌐ a b c d	a,b,c,d are specifics of f	nation ——— ⌐ legal person ⌐ person corporate-body
(A#x,B#y)z	A ⌐(x) ⌐z B ⌐(y)	A with role name x, and B with role name y jointly afford z	(employer) corporate-body ⌐ employs (employee) person

patterns are not covered. Norms are needed for specifying conditions and constraints of the actions as well. Norms have the following general structure:

<condition> → *<consequent>*.

Norms exist in a community. Rules are signs for norms. At the analysis stage, the norms can be identified and specified in natural language, but complex or subtle norms may not be capable of representation in formal rules. Specified norms can be used to understand the organisations as well as to be programmed for automatic execution. The following are some examples of norms specified in LEGOL. These examples are based on the IFIP case study on information systems (Olle *et al.* 1982), and a complete semantic model and more detailed illustration of LEGOL are presented in Appendix B.

contributor(paper) → *author(paper)*
contributor(report) → *referee(paper)*
    These two norms define the roles of author and referee.

member(WG **or-while** *TC)* → *eligibility#priority#1*
author(paper#selected) → *eligibility#priority#1*
    These two norms define the conditions for assigning the first priority to the applicants of the conference. A person who is a member of the working group (*WG*) or the technical committee (*TC*) is assigned the first priority, and the author of a selected paper is assigned the first priority (boldface words appearing in the expressions are LEGOL operators).

6 month **before** *start-of meeting#CRIS-2*
    while (*selected(paper)* **while-not** *invited(author(paper))*)
    → **print** *author*
    This is a trigger norm for actions, a reminder for the IFIP 'CRIS-2' conference secretary: a check to be done half a year before the conference. If there is any author of a selected paper who has not been invited, his name will be printed (then, the secretary can send him an invitation to the meeting).

6.4 Conducting a Semantic Analysis

Semantic Analysis is a method for eliciting and specifying user requirements. One of its theoretical foundations is organisational semiotics (Stamper *et al.* 1997) and the semiotic framework. The method has been

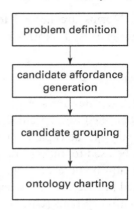

Figure 6.3. Major phases of Semantic Analysis.

applied in many fields such as user requirements for business systems, organisational analysis, legal document design, and analysis and design for computer systems (Ades 1989, Liu 1993, Liu *et al.* 1994, Liu & Dix 1997).

The method of Semantic Analysis can be summarised in a few major phases as schematically presented in Figure 6.3. The first phase is for people involved to receive a document which is sometimes called a problem statement or definition, and for them to understand the problem. The people involved may be a single analyst or, for a large project, often a group of analysts with users' participation. The next phase, *the candidate affordance generation,* is to produce a list of vocabulary of semantic units that may possibly be used in the semantic model to describe agents and their patterns of behaviour. The phase of *candidate grouping* will allow further analysis of the semantic units. Following that, there is *ontology charting*, where a complete semantic model is produced. Finally, *Norm Analysis*, as a separate method, can be carried out to identity norms, and to link the norms with each part of the semantic model. Below, each of these phases will be elaborated. A case study of project management[2] will be used to illustrate the whole process of Semantic Analysis.

6.4.1 Understand the problem domain

A Semantic Analysis exercise always begins with the phase of *problem definition*. In this phase, the assignment of system development is given in the form of a written document where the problem is defined. But the written official definition would normally not be enough to capture a com-

---

[2] After a case study used in a series of lectures and workshops run by the MEASUR team in Utrecht and Twente between 1991 and 1993.

Table 6.2. *Candidate affordances.*

company	charged	department	hourly rate
responsible for	depend on	project	function
budget	total time	employee	spend
work	imputed to	assigned to	total cost
belong to	computed	activity	

plete picture of the problem. Therefore, thorough investigations have to be done by studying the relevant documents. In addition, interviews with potential users of the envisaged system can be carried out for collecting supplementary information.

The following is the *problem statement* of project management with some simplification, which describes the case study that is going to be used to illustrate how to conduct Semantic Analysis. Our task here is to take the problem statement as the basis for producing a semantic model using Semantic Analysis. The result can be used either for understanding the mechanism and practice of project management in the company, or as a basis for designing a computer system for project management purposes.

> In the company, departments are responsible for projects. Each department and each project has a budget.
>
> Employees work in one department but can be assigned to different projects. Projects do not belong to a single department. Work activities are charged at an hourly rate which depends on the function of the employee.
>
> The total time which an employee spends on a project is imputed to it at the hourly rate, and the total cost of the project is computed.

The problem is basically introduced in the problem statement, so by reading it the analyst can gain an overview of the problem. However, sometimes the problem statement may be too vague and the requirements may be fuzzy. In this case, gathering more information about the problem is needed, which is normally done by collecting relevant documents and conducting interviews with the problem-owners. Those documents and interviews, as important supplements to the formal definition, can help the analyst to understand better the words and expressions in the problem statement.

6.4.2 *Generating candidate affordances*

The second phase, *candidate affordance generation*, is to study the collected papers and notes, and to single out the semantic units, for example nouns,

Table 6.3. *Candidate grouping (I).*

company	agent
department	agent, a part of a company
responsible for	affordance (a department)
project	affordance
budget	affordance
amount	determiner of budget (required to add to quantity a budget)
employee	role name (of a person who works in a company)
work	affordance
assigned to	affordance
belong to	affordance (of department and project)
activity	affordance (of employee)
charged	affordance
hourly rate	determiner (of function or activity?)
depend on	affordance (of function?)
function	determiner (of employee)
total time	a derived value as determiner, will not appear in the model
spend	affordance (of employee and project)
imputed to	complex action governed by rules, will capture as norms
total cost	a derived value as determiner, will not appear in the model
computed	complex action governed by rules, will capture as norms

noun-phrases, verbs, verb-phrases, and prepositions, which may indicate possible agents, affordances and other relationships.

In this phase, semantic units are identified from the problem definition as listed in Table 6.2. Every word in the problem definition is in principle useful in analysis; therefore, one has to be careful when a word is going to be ignored. Even an article, a preposition or an auxiliary verb may suggest some additional information to a concept, a relationship, or an intention, though nouns and verbs are more likely to suggest concepts of agent and affordance. The words and phrases that form semantic units are singled out as candidate affordances, and they contain complete concepts. It can be noted that some words are left out but that does not mean they will not be included in the model. Some words are taken in different forms, e.g. from the plural form of nouns to the singular form.

6.4.3 Candidate grouping

The phase of *candidate grouping* consists of a few small steps. First of all, the semantic candidates can be categorised as agents, or affordances. Among affordances, they can be further classified into universal action-types, determiners, role names, and so on. The specific affordances should

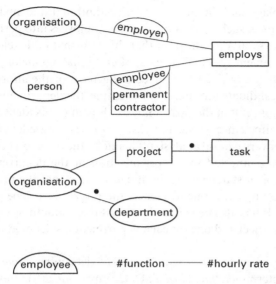

Figure 6.4. Candidate grouping (II).

be grouped into generic families. Dependants will be connected to their antecedents. The work in this step can be seen as a preparation for the next phase.

In this phase, the functions of the semantic units listed are firstly studied by labelling them as agents, affordances, role names, and determiners. They are also classified according to the universal–particular and generic–specific relationships. As shown in Table 6.3, not only are these semantic units classified, but at the same time additional information for explaining the functions is noted, which will be useful for the next step in construction of the whole ontology chart. In the table, one can see that functions of some semantic units are not certain at this stage. For example, the '*hourly rate*' is noted as 'determiner (of '*function*' or '*activity*'?)', showing an uncertainty on which antecedent the semantic unit, '*hourly rate*', will have. Would it be '*function*' or '*activity*'? A few more affordances may be added to the previous list, as they are needed for a sounder representation of the underlying ontologies. Finally, sketches of piecemeal ontological structures are conceived at this stage (see Figure 6.4).

These unconnected pieces of ontology charts help one to see better the effect of the grouping of the semantic units. One can start with the 'easier' pieces, for example an '*organisation*' and a '*person*' jointly afford a dependency '*employs*', in which the '*organisation*' plays the role of '*employer*' and the '*person*' plays the role of '*employee*'. Additional information may be added at this time, such as to categorise the employees into permanent staff and contractors, on a justification that this information is relevant in this project management system. The piece of chart that has an '*organisation*', a '*department*', a '*project*', and so on, contains most of the information produced in the candidate grouping. For example, the department is a part of the organisation. But in the early analysis, though it was identified that the project is an affordance, it was not clear about its antecedent (supposedly owing to a not very careful analysis). Therefore, the question here is: should the project be connected to the organisation or the department? If one reads the problem statement again, it can be seen that the project should not belong to any department. Hence, the project is a dependant of the organisation. It has also been found out that there should be two '*budgets*', one for each project and one for each department, as denoted in Figure 6.5 below.

An '*employee*', as seen in Figure 6.4, has a determiner, '*function*', which itself has a determiner, '*hourly rate*'. Determiners are attributes that enable one to describe an agent or affordance. For example, one can describe an employee with his or her '*function*' which can be further described with an '*hourly rate*' of how much he or she earns per hour. More such pieces can be produced for discussion and verification with the users before a complete ontology chart is produced.

6.4.4 Ontology charting

After the candidate affordances are analysed and grouped into scattered pieces of ontological structures, the fragments will be assembled into an integrated ontology chart. The ontological dependency between the fragments is the key to their connections, and it is constantly checked and maintained. It is unavoidable that some mistakes in the last phase may have been made and they will be corrected at this step. Figure 6.5 is the ontology chart for the project management.

The model exposes a few basic assumptions underpinned by the ontological principles. There is a *root* agent in the chart which functions as the ultimate antecedent for the whole problem domain under study. This root agent is the social community in which all its members share some fundamental concepts and cultures. Without these fundamentals, there would not be agreed meanings of organisation and person. Different social communities may have completely different definitions of an organisation. Differences may even exist in determining the boundaries of a person for its

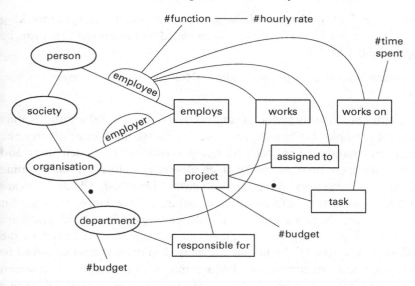

Figure 6.5. Ontology chart for project management.

start and finish, which may be the causes of debates on moral issues relating to abortion and euthanasia.

A project is ontologically dependent on an organisation, but not a department. This suggests that a project exists independently from a department. The relationship between a department and the project is by the department's participation. An employee working in a department may or may not be assigned to a project. An employee who is assigned to a project may work on a certain task, but the actual effort put into the task is measured by the determined '*time spent*'.

This ontology chart must be read many times by the analysts with reference to the problem statement and other business knowledge that is gained through various channels. After the draft of an ontology chart is produced, checks and verifications with input from the users are strongly suggested for maximum support and assurance from them.

6.4.5 *Norm Analysis*

The analysis can then proceed to the application of the method of *Norm Analysis* where norms will be identified and specified as the conditions and constraints for realisations of the affordances. Norms specified here are kinds other than the ontological dependency imposed on the antecedent and dependant. In the case of the project management, everyone working on a task must in the first place be assigned to the project. This can be specified in LEGOL:

assigned_to(*employee, project*) **while** *task*(*project*) → *works_on*(*employee, task*).

A norm has a validity period of time marked by a start and a finish. Norms are, for example, institutional rules such as the age limit for employees, the maximum number of projects an employee is allowed to participate in, and total time spent on a project by an employee. Therefore, the validity time during which the norm can be applied must be identified. All the norms are linked to the relevant affordances as constraints. For example, the age limit for employees is linked with the affordance '*employs*'; and the maximum number of projects for an employee to participate in is linked to the affordance '*assign to*'. Note that normally the norms should be linked to affordances, the patterns of possible actions, rather than agents, because an agent may have a number of patterns of possible actions, each following a set of norms specific to that affordance.

A detailed discussion of the method of Norm Analysis is found in the next chapter.

6.5 Commentary on Semantic Analysis

In an actual practice of Semantic Analysis, the order of the phases is not strictly followed. For example, even when it is in the phase of ontology charting, some new affordance may be identified, and it may then be added to the model. Iterations of the analysis phases may be necessary in order to reach an adequate analysis. Moreover, interactions between the analysts and the problem-owners are essential during the analysis. In this way, opinions and judgements can be inspired by the preliminary results, and comprehensive requirements can be elicited and incorporated into the model well before any system is developed.

There are a number of special features of Semantic Analysis worth noting. The first one is the role of the ontological relationship in modelling. The method always requires one to begin a Semantic Analysis by identifying agents who create the social world around them. An agent has some abilities to accomplish things. These abilities are also identified and put into the analysis model to construct the picture of the world. In doing so, a rigorous analytical principle must be observed, i.e., the existence constraint, or in other words, the ontological constraint. The ontological constraint says that a pattern of behaviour can be described only if the agent who acts is described in the model. So the agent is a kind of ontological antecedent to his actions (the latter being the dependants of the agent). The ontological constraint must be fully observed. That means that the existence of the dependants must be within (or during) the existence of the antecedent. If there are more affordances available when a certain behaviour is realised, they should also confirm the ontological constraint. That is, any added affordance should not exceed the existence of its antecedent affordances already described in the model.

Besides the ontological constraints as a principle for analysis, there is another important principle: it is not allowed for an analyst to invent artificial terms or introduce new concepts when modelling the agent's actions. The purpose of this is to force the analyst to speak the same language as the problem-owners. Any ambiguity in the terms or concepts used in describing the problem should be resolved by putting them into a context of actions which are already described and understood. When doing so, if the problem-owners are inspired with some new terms, they may be used only after a careful justification by the problem-owners and the analyst. The reason for this is that the world to be modelled is constructed by the community of agents, i.e. the problem owners. The agents know the meanings of words in their own world, their interpretations are the only ones justified.

Another feature is the scope of the analysis. Jayaratna (1986, 1990) observes that some methods of systems analysis have a narrow scope of analysis; some issues of enquiry, such as problem-owners' notional systems (i.e. basic assumptions of the focal problem and the environment), tend to be ignored. Some predominantly 'standard' systems development approaches take the physical world as an entry. For example, with Jackson's development method, a physical world is given as consisting of objects in motion from state to state; the task of the systems worker is to build a model which is an abstract description of the real world (Jackson 1983). Semantic Analysis, however, covers both the 'wet' and 'dry' aspects of the problem (Goguen's terminology 1992). It places the problem-owners at the kernel of the total enterprise of analysis. The role of an analyst is only to elicit and specify the business knowledge. The analysis is aimed at producing precise requirement specifications which are intelligible to the users (Liu *et al.* 1994), so the responsibility still remains with the users.

7
Pragmatics and communication

A sign has a meaning, and it can be used intentionally for communication. Pragmatics, as a branch of semiotics, is concerned with the relationships between an intentional use of a sign and the resulting behaviour of responsible agents in a social context. Communication takes place successfully when a meaningful sign is used with an appropriate intention between the two parties involved (e.g. speaker and listener).

This chapter addresses the effects of using signs in organisations. Before introducing the semiotic approach, various approaches to and techniques for analysis of the pragmatic aspect of signs are discussed in the chapter, such as speech act theory, functional grammar, and deontic logic. The semiotic approach distinguishes a number of elements in a communication act: propositions, propositional (or illocutionary) attitudes and perlocutionary effects. A communication act will further result in a variety of commitments and responsibilities. The method of Norm Analysis introduced in this chapter provides a formalism for one to identify and specify these important notions in analysing and modelling social and organisational aspects of communications.

7.1 Human communication

A social community is a purposeful system in which human beings act and interact with each other for achieving goals that may relate to the community or its individuals. 'Doing things with words' in a concerted way becomes a necessity for fulfilling ever more complex objectives of social beings in ever more complex organisations. Communication is the indispensable means by which agents in society coordinate their actions to achieve their goals.

A language–action view of information systems leads one to design information systems as part of the relevant human communication system; analysis of communication, therefore, is the essential entry for information systems analysis and design.[1] This school sees the uses of language as actions. A radical recognition about language and existence – 'Nothing exists except through language', stated by Winograd and Flores (1987) – is a typical representation of this point of view. In addition to this view of *language as actions*, another complementary view should be advocated, that is, the notion of *actions as language*. Actions should be regarded as a kind of language because they manifest ideas, thoughts and propositions. Using non-linguistic means, such as facial expressions, gestures, and other ostensive actions, can also perform communication of messages and intentions. An integrated language–action view has been adopted here for information analysis in the current project. According to this view, speech acts have the capacity not only to represent the relevant social world, including its actions, but also to constitute part of its (social) actions. Accordingly, information communicated through language has its complement in the social world of situations, norms, institutions and cultural patterns; and vice versa.

Theories and formal methods are available for studying language and the use of language in human communication. Speech Act Theory and Functional Grammar provide facilities to analyse the taxonomy and functionality of communication acts which will be discussed in this chapter. In order to analyse the social effects of communication acts, deontic logic will be examined and used to link the linguistic and the social acts. As computer-based systems are introduced into business practice, how to utilise this modern technology to enhance human performance in terms of interaction and communication becomes an important question. In order to answer this question, the modelling of human communication is done in this chapter by analysing communication acts employed and propositional attitudes expressed. This analysis serves as a theoretical basis for the development of a technical information system (e.g. Normbase).

7.2 Other approaches to communication

7.2.1 Speech Act Theory

Speech Act Theory originated in Austin's 1955 William James Lectures at Harvard (Austin 1980) and was further developed by Searle (1969). It

---

[1] Some examples of such a language–action approach can be found in Andersen (1991), Auramäki *et al.* (1988), Dietz & Widdershoven (1991), Flores *et al.* (1988), Lyytinen & Lehtinen (1986), Weigand (1990).

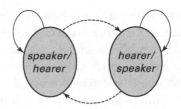

Figure 7.1. Speaker and hearer. Solid line, illocutionary act; dotted line, perlocutionary act.

studies roles of language use in communication and focuses on the performative aspects of language. Searle proposed a classification of four sorts of speech acts: utterance acts, illocutionary acts, propositional acts and perlocutionary acts. An utterance act is simply the act of uttering an expression. An illocutionary act is a basic, meaningful unit of human communication which consists of propositional contents and carries intentions to be perceived by a hearer. A propositional act is a subsidiary act of an illocutionary act. It expresses a propositional content which is realised by uttering the expression. The effects produced on a hearer by an illocutionary act are called perlocutionary effects and the acts of producing them are called perlocutionary acts. Perlocutionary acts, unlike illocutionary acts, are not essentially linguistic, for it is possible to achieve perlocutionary effects without performing any utterance at all.

For the purpose of studying roles of a language in communication, the most relevant acts are illocutionary acts and perlocutionary acts. In the course of a conversation, a complete unit would always be an illocutionary act which is produced by the speaker with certain meanings and intentions incorporated in the utterance. The hearer receives this communication unit and perceives the meaning from his own perspective which may result in a different one from the speaker's. In any case, there may be (or may not be, if the hearer ignores it) effects on the hearer. The effects are in the mental world of the hearer; e.g. he changes his feelings, mental states, etc. In this case, thus, the perlocutionary acts are not overt linguistic acts and not observable. He may also make explicit reactions to the perlocutionary act; e.g. he accepts an invitation and changes his agenda, which is observable. Figure 7.1 illustrates two agents involved in a process of communication to show that the roles of the speaker and the hearer will change in turn. The speaker addresses the hearer with an illocutionary act which produces effects on the hearer; one should be aware that the effect on the hearer may or may not be desirable from the speaker's perspective. However, in a broad sense, the speaker himself is a hearer while he performs the utterance; therefore, there is also a perlocutionary effect on him. The perlocutions are directed to the internal perlocutionary effects on the hearer (Eemeren & Grootendorst 1984). However, consequent behaviour is observable and that indicates the perlocutionary effect. In the above example of issuing an invitation to someone the perlocutionary act that the speaker should perform is that he must make himself physically available and mentally ready for whatever he is inviting the speaker for.

The structure of an illocutionary act consists of propositional content, illocutionary force, and contextual information. The propositional content is contained in the proposition of the message. For example, the two sentences 'You will jump off the car.' and 'Jump off the car!' have the same propositional content – *you will jump off the car*; though the former may be seen as a predication and the latter as a command. The contextual information is concerned with the context in which the speech act is uttered. A context, suggested by Auramäki *et al.* (1988), is delineated by the terms of speaker, hearer, time, place, and possible world. The first four terms simply define a situation in which a speaker utters something to a hearer at a certain time and a certain place. The possible world refers to the 'residual features' of the context which are relevant to the performance of a speech act. The possible world is 'something more than the "actual world", and it enables us to talk about "what could be" (e.g., the future)'. Terms that indicate the jurisdiction (i.e. authority of the speaker over the hearer), presuppositions of the agents involved in the performance of the speech act, and the like are typical constituents of the specification of the 'possible world'.

An illocutionary force is a necessary component of every successful speech act. There are seven illocutionary forces identified by Searle and Vanderveken (1985). They are (1) illocutionary point, (2) degree of strength of the illocutionary point, (3) mode of achievement, (4) propositional content conditions, (5) preparatory conditions, (6) sincerity conditions, and (7) degree of strength of the sincerity conditions.

The most important component of the illocutionary force is the *illocutionary point*, while the rest serve as the further specification and consequences of the illocutionary point. The illocutionary point tells the point or purpose which is internal to its being an act of that type. It determines the direction of fit for the propositional content and the commitments created; and the direction of fit determines the direction of matching between the propositional content and the world (Austin 1980). Searle and Vanderveken (1985) propose the five types of illocutionary points.

Assertive This is to state how the world is (e.g., to claim, to inform, to predict).

Commissive This point makes the speaker committed to doing something (e.g., to promise, to offer, to accept, to refuse).

Directive This concerns making the hearer do things (e.g., to request, to order, to permit).

Declarative This is used when the speaker wishes to change the world through the utterance (e.g., to declare, to appoint, to approve).

Expressive This point is employed by the speaker in expressing feelings and attitudes (e.g., to apologise, to thank, to congratulate).

Degree of strength of the illocutionary point: different illocutionary acts often achieve the same illocutionary point with different degrees of strength.

The propositional content conditions determine if a speech act is non-self-contradictory and feasible. For example, a sentence 'I order you to have finished your homework last week' is self-contradictory; 'Cut a square round shape' is infeasible; that one promises to have done something in the past is both self-contradictory and infeasible.

The *preparatory conditions* specify the states of affairs the speaker must presuppose to exist in the world if an intended illocutionary act is to be performed. For example, to let the hearer do something, the speaker must assume that the hearer is capable of that. This kind of preparatory condition is normally an ontological constraint by which one can distinguish the speech act that may be successful and non-defective from those that are impossible.

A speech act may be successfully performed but defectively so. For example, one may apologise to a hearer for something that one considers disgraceful but the hearer thinks otherwise. Similarly, to issue a command can be successfully done by the speaker; but if the performance is not within the appropriate jurisdiction (e.g., the speaker has no necessary authority), the speech act is defective. Therefore, if one could consider that the success of a speech act is largely dependent on the speaker, the effect of it relies, on the other side, fully on the hearer. In other words, the effect of the speech act is realised through self-adjustment by the hearer, or through the perlocutionary act.

7.2.2 *Functional approach*

The functional view of natural language (typified by Dik (1979, 1989)) regards a language as an instrument which human beings use intentionally to achieve certain goals and purposes. To achieve the goals and purposes, human beings perform linguistic actions following complex, socially established patterns. A *speaker* uses linguistic expressions to communicate messages to an *addressee* so as to construct or modify the state of affairs in a certain way.

According to functional grammar theory (Dik 1989), any natural language text can be divided into clauses and extra-clausal constituents. The clauses follow certain underlying structures and can be mapped onto the actual form of the corresponding linguistic expressions by a system of expression rules. The expression rules determine the form of each part of the expression, their order, and the intonation.

The underlying clause structure is a complex abstract structure that can be analysed at several levels:

clause→speech act,
proposition→possible fact,
prediction→state of affairs,
predicate→property/relation,
term→entity.

The constructions at the lower level are the building blocks of the higher level. A *term* is an expression denoting some entity in some (mental) world. *Predicates* designate types of entities and patterns of actions. A *predication* consists in a few predicates to specify relations between entities and/or actions. A *proposition* is composed of one or more predications; it connotes a possible state of affairs. A *clause* (or *message*) is constituted of a proposition associated with a certain propositional attitude; it normally includes entries of speaker, addressee, speech time, content, etc. (Weigand 1990).

Predicates are organised in *predicate-frames*, the structure that specifies the fundamental semantic and syntactic properties, such as (i) the syntactic category of the predicate (verbal, nominal, adjectival), (ii) the number of arguments, (iii) the semantic functions of the arguments (agent, goal, recipient, etc.). For example, a predicate-frame of 'give' can be specified as follows:[2]

$$\text{give}_V \ (x_1)_{Ag} \ (x_2)_{Go} \ (x_3)_{Re}$$

which states the category of 'give' is 'V'; it has three arguments which play the roles of agent, goal and recipient. Predicate-frames can be extended by *satellites* (non-arguments) which pertain to additional features such as

---

[2] This and the next three examples are based on Groot (1992) and Dik (1989), of which the former is also the source of the syntax used in these examples.

location, speaker's attitude, or character of the speech act. *Terms* are the NPs (noun phrases) to replace the arguments in the predicate-frames and satellites. There are two types of terms to be distinguished: (i) basic terms, which are expressions given as such in the lexicon (e.g. pronouns, proper nouns, question words) and (ii) derived terms (a derived term is a basic term with optional set of restrictors). *Nuclear predications* consist of predicates and terms. A nuclear predication as a whole designates a set of *States of Affairs* (SoA) which is used in the broad sense of 'conception of something which can be the case in some world' (Groot 1992). *Core predications* are obtained by adding *predicate operators and satellites.* The predicate operators relate *aspectuality* information (e.g. perfective/imperfective, quantificational and phrasal descriptions) to the predications; the predicate satellites are terms which specify manner, speed, instrument and the like for the predications. *Extended predications* are further constructed with *predication operators and satellites.* The most important types of predication operators are tense, external phrasal aspect, quantificational aspect, objective mood, and polarity (positive/negative) operators. The satellites are, for example, terms with functions of time and place. Below is an example of extended predication:

$$\text{Past read}_V \text{ (John)}_{Ag} \text{ (the book)}_{Go} \text{ (quickly)}_{Manner} \text{ (yesterday)}_{Time}$$

which reads as 'John read the book quickly yesterday.' Notice that the sequence of the words is supposed not significant either in the sentence or in the predicate-frame, though in an actual use of language the word sequence may have some pragmatic effects. *Propositions* can be built from extended predications by incorporating *proposition operators and satellites.* Proposition operators are employed mainly to distinguish two modalities, subjective and evidential; proposition satellites indicate the attitudes of the speaker. The result of these extensions is called an *extended proposition*, see below for example:

$$\text{Subjunctive Mood [John writes the book] (in my opinion)}_{Attitude}$$

which represents 'In my opinion, he should write the book'. *Clauses* (equally, messages or speech acts) can be composed on the basis of the extended propositions by associating *illocutionary operators and satellites.* Typical examples of the operators are declarative, imperative, and interrogative; and the satellites are terms describing the action of speaking, namely the illocutionary act itself. Below there is an example of a speech act:

$$\text{Decl [he is stupid] (frankly)}_{Illocution}$$

which reads 'Frankly, he is stupid.'

The levels of term, predicate and predication are concerned with representation which is at semantic level; while the proposition and clause levels deal
with interpersonal relationships (in other words, the issues at pragmatic
level).

7.2.3 Deontic logic for communication

A communication act may convey the speaker's intention which is corre-
lated to the illocution of the act. The ultimate purpose of performing a
communication act, in business cases, is to establish or alter social relationships between the agents. This capacity of producing social effects is called
the deontic aspect of the communication act, which can be systematically
studied by means of deontic logic.

Deontic logic

The word 'deontic' is derived from a Greek word which means 'as it should
be' or 'duly'. Deontic Logic (DL) is the study of those sentences in which
only logical words and normative expressions occur essentially (Follesdal &
Hilpinen 1970). Its subject matter is a variety of normative concepts, such
as obligation (prescription), prohibition (interdiction), permission and
commitment. The first concept of these is often expressed by such words as
'shall', 'ought' and 'must'. The second concept is expressed by 'shall not',
'ought not' and 'must not'. The third one is associated with 'may'. The last
notion is related to an idea of *conditional obligation*, expressible by 'if . . .,
then it shall (ought, must) be the case that . . .'.

Standard DL

Von Wright has proposed an 'Old System' or OS (Wright 1951) which has
had an enormous influence on later work. It consists of the following
axioms and rules:

(C0)   All (or enough) tautologies of propositional calculus

(C1) $Op \leftrightarrow \neg P \neg p$

(C2) $Pp \lor P\neg p$

(C3) $P(p \lor q) \leftrightarrow Pp \lor Pq$

(C4) $p \leftrightarrow q > Pp \leftrightarrow Pq$

(C5)   '$O(p \lor \neg \emptyset p)$' and '$\neg P(p \land \neg p)$' are not valid.

Later, it was realised that the system OS is very close to a normal modal
logic. A *von-Wright-type* system of a normal modal logic is presented as a
standard deontic logic OK (Åqvist 1984):

(A0)   All (or enough) tautologies of propositional calculus
(A1)   Pp↔¬O¬p   'Permission is the dual of obligation'
(A2)   O(p→q)→(Op→Oq)   'If p implying q is obligatory, then p being
                                        obligatory implies that q is obligatory'

Rules of proof:

(R1)   p, p→ q>q   (Modus ponens, detachment)
(R2)   p>p   (O-necessitation)

The system OK$^+$ is obtained by adding an axiom:

(A3)   Op→Pp   'Whatever is obligatory is also permitted'

Furthermore, OK (and hence any normal monadic logic) is closed under
the following rules of proof, which means that every OK-theorem can be
derived from the axioms and applications of the rules of proof:

(OKa)   p→q>p→Oq
(OKb)   p↔q>p↔Oq
(OKc)   p→q>p→Pq
(OKd)   p↔q>p↔Pq

Finally, OK$^+$ is closed under the following rule of proof:

(OK$^+$)   p>p

whereas OK fails to be closed under that rule.

Dyadic DL

Meyer and Wieringa (1993) summarise the system NS proposed by von
Wright to cope with conditional obligations, since these gave rise to severe
problems in the standard DL approach. In the system NS the syntax is aug-
mented by the construct O(p/q), meaning that 'p is obligatory under condition q'. The system consists of the following axioms and rules:

(NS0)   All (or enough) tautologies of propositional calculus
(NS1)   O(p∧q/r)↔O(p/r)∧O(q/r)
(NS2)   O(p/q∨r)↔ O(p/q)∧O(p/r)
(NS3)   ¬ (O(p/q)∧O(¬ p/q))
(NS4)   P(p/q)↔ ¬ (¬ p/q)
(NS5)   Pp↔O(p/q→q))
(NS6)   Modus ponens
(NS7)   Substitution rules

Dynamic logic approach to deontic logic

One approach is to develop deontic logic as a variant of dynamic logic first developed by Meyer so as to avoid some paradoxes (Meyer 1988, Wieringa *et al.* 1989). This approach makes a distinction between actions (practitions) and propositions (assertions). It also uses a special violation atom V (a sanction), indicating that in the state of concern a violation of the deontic constraints has been committed. The central notion of the approach is represented by a modal operator $[\alpha]$ associated with an action α. The expression $[\alpha]\phi$ is read as 'the performance (execution) of the action α leads necessarily to a state (possible world) in which ϕ holds'; $[\alpha]\phi$ means the weakest precondition that is required to ensure that ϕ afterwards. $[\alpha]$ will be interpreted as a modal operator of the necessity kind in a Kripke-structure induced by the performance of actions. In this approach, the expressions that α is forbidden (F), permitted (P) and obligatory (O) are reduced to dynamic expressions as follows:

$F\alpha =_{def} [\alpha]V$	'A forbidden action leads necessarily to a sanction – the notation "$[\alpha]$" stands for "necessarily α", "V" for *sanction*'
$P\alpha =_{def} \neg F a \ (=_{def} <\alpha> \neg V)$	'A permitted action is a non-forbidden action, or an action that possibly does not lead to a sanction – the notation "$<\alpha>$" stands for "possibly α"'
$O\alpha a =_{def} F(-\alpha) \ (=_{def} [-\alpha]V)$	'An obligatory action is forbidden not to do, or not performing the action leads necessarily to a sanction'

For the reduction of the obligation operator O, the negation of an action α, denoted by '$-\alpha$', expresses the non-performance of this action.

Formalisation and translation

A system of formal deontic logic can be supplemented with definitions of locutions in ordinary English. The formal language can be conceived of as a structure (Åqvist 1984)

$$L = <Bas, LogCon, Aux, Sent>$$

Where

(i) Bas (= the set of basic sentences of L) is a denumerable set Prop of proposition letters p, q, r, p1, p2, . . . ,

(ii) LogCon (= the set of primitive logical connectives or constants of L) is the set $\{\nabla, \perp, \neg, \wedge, \vee, \rightarrow, \leftrightarrow, O, P\}$,

(iii) Aux (= the set of auxiliary symbols of L) is the set consisting of the left parenthesis and the right parenthesis (thus, Aux = $\{(,)\}$),

(iv) Sent (= the set of all well formed sentences of L) is the smallest set S such that

    (a) every proposition letter in Prop is in S,

    (b) ∇ and $\perp$ are in S,

    (c) if p is in S, then so are $\neg p$, Op and Pp,

    (d) if p, q are in S, then so are $(p \wedge q)$, $(p \vee q)$, $(p \rightarrow q)$ and $(p \leftrightarrow q)$.

Definition:

$$Fp =_{def} \neg Pp \text{ (alternatively: } O\neg p)$$

Intended English readings of the connectives are shown in the following list:

$\neg$:   not (more fully: it is not the case that)
$\wedge$:   and (more fully: both . . . and . . .)
$\vee$:   or (more fully: either . . . or . . .)
$\rightarrow$:   if . . ., then. . .
$\leftrightarrow$:   if and only if (alternative: if and only if . . ., then . . .)
O: it is obligatory that (alternatively: it must be that . . .)
P: it is permitted that (alternatively: it may be that . . .)

The symbols $\neg$, $\wedge$, $\vee$, $\rightarrow$, and $\leftrightarrow$ are for the five best-known so-called truth-functions of classical propositional logic, viz. negation, conjunction, disjunction, material implication and material equivalence, respectively. O and P are to symbolise the normative (or deontic) notions of obligation and permission. There are two other symbols: ∇ (*verum* in Latin) represents some arbitrary but fixed logical truth or tautology, and $\perp$ (*falsum* in Latin) some arbitrary but fixed logical falsehood, contradiction or absurdity.

In order to translate certain English locutions into the formal language L and assign English readings to the connectives in LogCon, the following definitions can serve as equating rules for that purpose, applicable to any L-sentences A and B:

(D1)   'It is not the case that A' $=_{def} \neg A$
(D2)   'Both A and B' $=_{def} (A \wedge B)$
(D3)   'Either A or B' $=_{def} (A \vee B)$
(D4)   'If A then B' $=_{def} (A \rightarrow B)$

(D5) 'If and only if A then B' $=_{def} (A \leftrightarrow B)$
(D6) 'It is obligatory that A' $=_{def} OA$
(D7) 'It is permitted that A' $=_{def} PA$

Impact and applications of deontic logic

Deontic logic has traditionally been used to analyse the structure of norma-tive law and normative reasoning in law. Legal analysis and legal automa-tion were typical areas of application of deontic logic in its early days. Only recently, along with those application areas, has deontic logic been applied to computer applications such as specification of normative security poli-cies, specification of fault-tolerant systems, automation of contracting, specification of normative integrity constraints for databases. Wieringa and Meyer (1991) provide a comprehensive survey of applications of deontic logic, of which LEGOL is one of the examples discussed.

The LEGOL project (Stamper 1980) is one of the examples that adopts the deontic approach to computer assisted applications to legal reasoning. The project, initiated in the middle of the 1970s, was to 'attempt to remedy the present lack of adequate methods for analysing and designing the infor-mation systems'. A quest for a language in which the organisational rules (or norms) can be precisely expressed was formulated, and the language is named LEGOL (LEGally Oriented Language). The basic form of a norm in LEGOL has the following shape:

protasis → apodosis

which contains other components and can be elaborated as

<condition> → *<D> <agent> <action>*

The deontic operator, *D*, can be one of the following: obligatory, permitted and prohibited. A norm expressed in this structure has an intended reading 'if . . . then it is obligatory/permitted/prohibited for some agent to do some action'.

In the four major categories of action norms distinguished, namely standing orders, status norms, powers of legal action, and legislative powers, the first two categories are related to the *right set* of concepts; while the last two categories of norms are associated with the *power set* of con-cepts. Two components take important positions in formulation and appli-cation of a norm in LEGOL, which are jurisdiction and purpose. Jurisdiction is defined as the giver and the receiver of the norm (direct agents involved, or stakeholders). The purpose is the intentional result that the application of the norm brings in. The purpose can be characterised by sorts of actions in relation to some event or state in a social world, for example, to *start*, to *finish*, to *prevent* or to *sustain* an event.

Later on, the LEGOL project has evolved into a larger scale project, MEASUR. The language LEGOL has been developed as a general norm definition and manipulation language, not restricted to legal modelling only. A further discussion on LEGOL will be found in Chapter 10.

7.3 Pragmatic aspect of human communication

Communication is normally a means rather than an end. The means of communication are employed to create, modify, and discharge social commitments. An agent can be in any state as far as a social commitment is concerned, for example, obliged, permitted or forbidden to fulfil it. These kinds of states are associated with the deontic concepts, thus they are called the *deontic states*.

The minimal unit of human communication is the performance of certain kinds of communication acts – language acts. This is the basic assumption of Speech Act Theory and the functional school. A complete communication act can be defined as a structure consisting of three components: performer, addressee, and message (Dietz 1992) (the message is equivalent to a clause, or a speech act, in the functional grammar). The message can be further distinguished as two parts: the function and the content.

The *content* part of a communication act manifests the meaning of the message as it is expressed in the proposition. The meaning (or semantics) of a proposition is fully dependent on the environment in which the proposition is uttered. The interpretation is realised by relating the proposition to the referent which is a universal social construct or a pattern of human behaviour, which is performed by both agents: the speaker and the hearer. Sometimes a proposition's semantics can be obtained by referring to another proposition in the case of indirect speech.

The *function* part of a communication act specifies the illocution which reflects the intention of the speaker. The illocutions can be grouped into three dimensions. In one dimension, there are distinctions between descriptive and prescriptive inventions, whereas, in another, there are denotative and affective modes. Moreover, the illocutions can be associated with different times, namely, now, the future or the past, as they are organised in Figure 7.2. Each cell of the classification framework has been assigned a title and a few representative verbs of that type of illocutions are placed in each cell. The functions of communication are realised through use of signs. If the illocution in a communication act is related to expressing the personal modal state (e.g. feeling and judgement) mood, then it is called

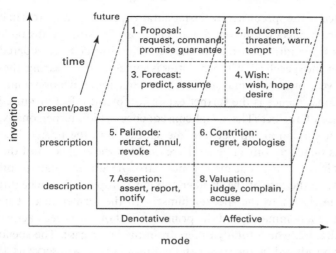

Figure 7.2. Classification framework of illocutions (based on Stamper, (1973)).

affective, otherwise *denotative*. If the illocution used in a communication act has an inventive or instructive effect, then it is called prescriptive, otherwise descriptive. The classification on the time axis is based on the social effects produced by the communication act: whether the effect is on the future or the present/past.

The ultimate consequence of the communication act lies in the social context which the speaker and the hearer both inhabit. At the social level of the semiotic framework issues such as beliefs, expectations, commitments, contracts, etc., are typical examples of social consequences. Table 7.1 shows a preliminary analysis of the types of illocutionary acts and consequences in relation to the propositional attitudes of the relevant parties before and after the acts are performed. The labels in the first column indicate types of illocutions, e.g. 'PDf' means *prescriptive, denotative, future*; 'DAp' means *descriptive, affective, present/past* – as illustrated in Figure 7.2. The symbols 'x' and '~x' appearing in the table represent a proposition or an event and their negations. The illocutionary acts can be viewed as linguistic operators that have certain social and pragmatic functions. The analysis in the table reflects an attempt to articulate their functions. A further attempt to adopt these linguistic operators in studying semantic database operations can be found in Chapter 9.

The above analysis, with much simplification over communications, is based on a supposition that the communication is performed in an honest, sincere and reliable manner. In such cases the speaker's intention will be expressed in the speech act by the illocutions. As a result, there will be a perlocutionary effect on the addressee. The analysis shown in the table distinguishes the addressee from the hearer. The former is considered as the target of the speech act while the latter is someone 'overhearing' the conversation; very often they may all be relevant in communication analysis. The social consequence is the further expansion of the effect produced by the utterance of the act. The social consequence is an interpersonally, jointly established relationship between the speaker and the hearer. The consequences of illocutions in general are on both the speaker and the hearer, though in some cases one may be more strongly affected than the other. For example, in the case of the speaker making a proposal, it can be directed to someone else or to the speaker himself. In the former case, it may be a request or a command, and the primary effect of the speech act will be on the addressee, which totally differs from the latter case. The social consequence, produced by the social and cultural norms, will serve as a kind of 'terms of reference' of socially contracted behaviour for both the speaker and the hearer.

　　Some explanations must be offered on Table 7.1.

(1) There are always consequences to both parties of the communication act. The speaker and addressee each and both have propositional attitudes before and after an illocutionary act. The ones before are conditions, whereas the ones after are consequences. The ones in the table are views from the speaker's perspective.

(2) Directives (not being listed in the table as a basic category) are complex acts that are composed of *proposals* and *inducements*. When a speaker with a proper authority makes a proposal, the inducement is implied, therefore the proposal he makes is in the nature of a directive. Without authority, one can also produce a directive by associating the proposal with an inducement (e.g. threat or reward). It should be noticed that the assumed conditions of honest, sincere and non-defective communications are essential. This implies the communication will always be carried out normally, not taking into account the abnormal disruption.

(3) Some illocutions have stronger illocutionary forces than others which are not taken into account in the classification. For example, the illocutions 'command', 'insist', 'request', 'ask' and 'beg', all create obligations on the addressee; but 'command' and 'insist' have stronger illocutionary force than the rest, and of these the former is even associated with authority. 'Beg' has the weakest illocutionary force, but it still creates obligation on the addressee because of the ideal conditions assumed in the communications.

Table 7.1. *Perlocutionary acts and propositional attitudes.*

Illocution type	Speaker (S)'s propositional attitudes		Illocutionary acts (= operations)	Addressee (A)'s propositional attitudes		Listener (L)'s propositional attitudes
	Before	After		Before	After	
(1) PDf	wish	expectation	proposals (to others)	liberty	obligation	Illocutionary acts also influence propositional attitudes of listeners other than addressees, e.g. a listener may have expectations in the cases of *proposals* and *forecasts*; beliefs in the case of *palinodes* and *assertions*.
	liberty	obligation	proposals (to self)	wish	expectation	
(2) PAf	wish	expectation	inducements	—	expectation	
(3) DDf	expectation	expectation	forecasts	—	expectation	
(4) DAf	wish	wish	wishes	—	belief that S wishes x	
(5) PDp	belief in x then belief in ~x	belief in ~x	palinodes	—	belief in ~x	
(6) PAp	wish ~x	approval of ~x	contrition	wish ~x	approval of ~x	
(7) DDp	belief	belief	assertions	belief	(stronger) belief	
(8) DAp	judgement	judgement	valuations	judgement	judgement to S's	

Denotative scale

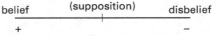

Affective scale

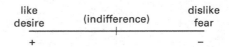

Figure 7.3. Propositional attitude scales.

Propositional attitudes can be roughly indicated by two scales: the denotative and the affective (see Figure 7.3). A propositional attitude can normally be expressed as a position on one of the two scales. The denotative attitudes are related to someone's acceptance of a proposition or event in terms of belief. One can have a strong or weak belief or disbelief, or a neutral position. A supposition is related to a neutral position of belief: the neutral belief may be the condition before and the consequence after the hypothesis is made; very positive or negative beliefs are, for example, related to assertions. The affective scale facilitates one's indicating value judgement such as like and dislike, and aspiring feelings such as desire and fear. Desire, wish, hope and fear are examples of such feelings. Deontic consequences are produced on the basis of mixtures of these two kinds of propositional attitudes.

7.4 The Norm Analysis method

7.4.1 *The concept of norms*

The idea of a norm corresponds at the social level to the idea of an affordance at the individual level. Wright (1963) explains the concept of a norm in this way:

'Norm' has several partial synonyms which are good English. 'Pattern', 'standard', 'type' are such words. So are 'regulation', 'rule', and 'law'.

Norms are developed through practical experiences of agents in a society, and in turn have functions of directing, coordinating and controlling actions within the society. Complex agents can be formed for certain purposes, for example, cultural clubs, political parties, corporate bodies, governments, nations and multi-national alliances. The functions of norms, such as laws and regulations of the organised complex agents, are to determine of patterns of behaviour whether they are legal or acceptable within the social context. Norms also have directive and prescriptive functions, which are sometimes termed *normatives*. When a particular agent is to act, the norms provide guidance for his action. However, in each particular case, the agent will evaluate the situation he is in and find some norms which he thinks relevant to his case. The process of this evaluation and selection of norms may be entirely subjective. In other words, norms do not have predetermined relationship to particular actions, because the norms can be manipulated, applied and disregarded accordingly. Holy and Stuchlik (1983) explain the non-deterministic relationship between norms and particular actions as follows.

(1) A norm has to do with a type of situation, not with one particular situation.

(2) Any action is understandable to at least someone other than the actor, which means that it is performed according to some plan, rule or norm. An action is considered as deviant or norm-breaking, but it is not deviant essentially but only in relation to one particular norm or a cluster of norms; it is, at the same time, performed according to some other norms.

(3) An actor may invoke different norms for deciding on his actions. On whether the action is norm-confirming or norm-breaking, one has to speak from the viewpoint of particular norms.

Nevertheless, norms are developed as collective affordances of the complex agent at social level. The society allows itself or its members to conduct actions on an agreed moral or legal basis. They serve as a standard for the members to coordinate their actions, and this makes it possible for one to expect, predict and collaborate with others in performing coordinated actions. When modelling the agent and the actions, which may reveal the repertoire of available behaviour of the agent, the norms will supply rationale for actions.

There are six components of norms (Wright 1963), as follows.

(1) The *character*: the effect of the norm, typically, 'ought to' for mandatory norm, 'may' for permissive norm, and 'must not' for prohibitive norm.

(2) The *content*: the action or activity prescribed in norms.

(3) The *condition*: the circumstance or the state of affairs in which the norm should be applied.

(4) The *authority*: the agent who gives or issues the norm.

(5) The *subject(s)*: the agent(s) who can apply the norm.
(6) The *occasion*: location (space) or span (time) in which the norm is given.

Von Wright calls the character, the content and the condition the norm-kernel. Behind all these components, there are 'promulgation' and 'sanction' as means of enforcement for application of norms. Brkic (1970) describes such means as 'systems of social control' at multiple levels. Societies employ various systems, such as normative, religio-ideological, educational–cultural–scientific, socio-political, and economic ones, as the primary control. Other systems of organised forces in the form of police can be used as an institutionalised form of coercion, whereas military aggression and blackmail would be non-institutionalised forms of coercion. Other lower-level instruments of control, permitted by the higher-level systems, are, for example, a company's economic means, business organisation policies, employees' codes, etc. All these norms and means of control form a kind of vital force which, formally or informally, explicitly or implicitly, governs all members of the social or cultural community, or business institution. Within the scope of this kind of vital force, people use signs and language to establish commitments, discharge responsibilities, fulfil social obligations.

7.4.2 Norms in business organisations

Norms exist in a community and will govern the members of the community in their behaviour, thinking, making judgements and perceiving the world. The shared norms are what defined a culture or sub-culture. A sub-culture may be a team who know how to work effectively together, and their norms include a solution to their organisational problems. Norms can be represented in all kinds of signs, whether in documents, oral communication or behaviour, in order to preserve, to spread and to follow. However, one cannot always put hands conveniently on a norm, as one might grasp a document that carries information through an organisation. A norm is more like a field of force that makes the members of the community tend to behave or think in a certain way (Stamper *et al.* 1997).

Norms are developed through the practical experiences of people in a culture, and in turn have functions of directing, coordinating and controlling actions within the culture. A research group or a working team may have a sub-culture and therefore may have 'local' norms. The norms will provide guidance for members to determine whether certain patterns of behaviour are legal or acceptable within the given context. An individual member in the community, having learned the norms, will be able to use the knowledge to guide his or her actions, though he or she may decide to take either a norm-conforming or a norm-breaking action. When the norms of an organisation are learned, it will be possible for one to expect and predict behaviour, and hence to collaborate with others in performing coordinated actions. Once the norms are understood, captured and represented in, for example, the form of deontic logic, this will serve as a basis for programming intelligent agents to perform many regular activities.

One way to categorise the norms is according to how norms control human behaviour. Five types of norms can be identified in this way, each of which governs a certain aspect of human behaviour. *Perceptual norms* deal with how people receive signals from the environment via their senses through media such as light, sound and taste. *Cognitive norms* enable one to incorporate the beliefs and knowledge of a culture, to interpret what is perceived, and to gain an understanding based on existing knowledge. *Evaluative norms* help explain why people have certain beliefs, values and objectives. *Behavioural norms* govern people's behaviour within regular patterns. Finally, *denotative norms* direct the choices of signs for signifying; such choices are culture-dependent, e.g. the choice of a colour to signify happiness or sadness.

Another method of classification of norms is based on the effects of the execution of norms. Four types of norms are found in this classification.

Standing orders The execution of a standing order may result in a change in the physical world. Standing orders are commands to perform actions, and are usually expressed as one 'may', 'may not', 'must' and 'must not' do something. Typically, in a business environment, a department manager can give a standing order to the people in the department.

Status norms The execution of a status norm often creates or alters social structure and legal relations. The norm designates one to have liability, immunity, right, or no-right over certain events or actions. Job descriptions and company regulations are examples of these norms.

Powers of intervention The execution invokes or inhibits the use of existing standing orders and status norms. For example, a judge may have the power to decide which law to apply to a case.

Legislative powers These change the other norms. The execution of this type of norms may lead to an alteration of the legislative structure. The agent applying the norm must have the right to modify or create a norm. Normally the board of directors has the powers to alter the company rules and to set up new rules.

Norms can also be classified according to the types of objects that the norms are applied to. Three classes of norms are found.

Substantive norms These norms are concerned with core business functions and operations. These business functions and operations contribute directly to organisational objectives.

Communication norms These norms specify patterns, structure and procedures of communication within an organisation. The role of the norms is to ensure that everyone knows what information should be kept and provided, and what actions should be taken and when. Without these norms, the whole organisation cannot act in a coordinated manner to achieve its objectives.

Control norms These norms introduce sanctions and rewards. They act as a mechanism to reinforce that everyone does what he or she is supposed to do, as prescribed by the other two types of norms.

These classifications do not exclude one another. For example, a standing order can be any of the three types: substantive – if it is concerned with business operations; communication – if it specifies the processes for how the task should be performed; and control – if it informs about the consequence when one fails to complete the task.

7.4.3 Norm Analysis

Norm Analysis is useful for studying an organisation from the perspective of agents' behaviour which is governed by norms. From this perspective, to specify an organisation can be done by specifying norms (Stamper 1992). Norms can be expressed in a natural language and a formal, machine-executable language, and they will be incorporated into the database as integrity and consistency constraints.

A Norm Analysis is normally carried out on the basis of the result of the Semantic Analysis. The semantic model delineates the area of concern of an organisation. The patterns of behaviour specified in the semantic model are part of the fundamental norms that retain the ontologically determined relationships between agents and actions without imposing any further constraints. A pattern of behaviour is available as long as the antecedent behaviour is there as described in the ontology model. However, a realisation (i.e. obtaining an instance) of the antecedent may not necessarily lead to a realisation of the dependent behaviour; there are norms to allow the agent to judge the situation and to decide if a particular action will be taken. Results of Norm Analysis can be written in NORMA, and further in any programming language.

Normally a complete Norm Analysis can be performed in four steps.

1 Responsibility analysis

This analysis enables one to identify and assign responsible agents to each action. The analysis focuses on the types of agents and types of actions. In other words, it would answer the question as to which agent is responsible for what type of actions.

As an instance of behaviour, its lifecycle goes from being realised, through being sustained, till termination. The first and the last states are marked as the 'start' and the 'finish', and in between them the behaviour exists. One should be interested in the agents who bring about changes of behaviour, namely, the agents authorising the start and the finish. This analysis is to define these two kinds of agents who influence the start and the finish, as they are called the start authority and the finish authority of the affordance in NORMA.

In an organisation, responsibilities may be determined by the organisational constitution or by common agreements in the organisation. In the CRIS case (see Appendix B), for example, to decide if a topic should be included in a working conference is the responsibility of the programme committee. More responsibilities are defined by the IFIP organisational rules as follows in NORMA:

working conference	$+@, -@$: IFIP Council;
work	$+@, -@$: Organising Committee;
meeting	$+@, -@$: Programme Committee, Organising Committee.

The above norms detail the responsible agents for the actions. The IFIP Council decides when a working conference starts and finishes; the Organising Committee is the authority to recognise whether or not something is a piece of scientific work (in the IFIP context); the Programme Committee and the Organising Committee can call a meeting.

2 Proto-norm Analysis

Consider the basic structure of a norm:

$<condition> \rightarrow <D> <agent> <action>$.

A norm in this form specifies the circumstances in which the action *may, must*, or *must not* (as indicated by the deontic operator) be performed by the agent. The Proto-norm Analysis helps one to identify relevant types of information for making decisions concerning a certain type of behaviour. After the relevant types of information are identified, they can be used as a checklist by the responsible agent to take necessary factors into account when a decision is to be made. The objective of this analysis is to facilitate the human decisions without overlooking any necessary factors or types of information.

In the CRIS case, for example, the organising committee responsible for assigning priorities to the eligible persons for attending a working conference must know the following types of information:

   name of the person to be possibly invited;
   whether or not this person is a member of a working group or a technical
      committee; and
   whether the invitee is an author or a referee.

3 Trigger analysis

This step of the analysis is to consider the actions to be taken in relation to the absolute and relative time. The absolute time means the calendar time, while the relative time makes use of references to other events. In Proto-norm Analysis there is no mention about when the types of information should be supplied, decisions made, or actions taken. But in actual business practices, all the activities are organised in relation to time.

The results of trigger analysis are specifications of the schedule of the actions. All the actions can be organised in dynamic sequences. By setting up and managing triggers for the actions, the automated system can prompt human agents to respond to the situation in time. The triggers can be first stated in a natural language and later translated into a computable form. The keys to the triggers are the absolute time and relative time linked to the action types contained in the semantic model.

In the example of the CRIS case, determination of applicants' priority must be done a certain time before the invitations for the working conference are due to be sent. Moreover the invitations for the conference must be sent to the participants in time.

4 Detailed norm specification

In this step of analysis the contents of norms will be fully specified in two versions, a natural language and a formal language. The purposes for this are (1) to capture the norms as references for human decision, and (2) to perform actions in the automated system by executing the norms in the formal language. For example, in the CRIS case, the rules of assigning priorities to applicants, written in English, can be recorded and they can be translated into the formal language LEGOL for automatic execution.

Example Box 7.1: Norm Specification

In business, most rules and regulations fall into the category of behavioural norms. These norms prescribe what people *must, may,* and *must not* do, which are equivalent to three deontic operators 'is obligatory', 'is permitted' and 'is prohibited'. The following format is suitable for specification of behavioural norms (the examples are from Liu & Dix (1997)):

whenever <*condition*>
if <*state*>
then <*agent*>
is <*deontic operator*>
to <*action*>.

Adopting this form, a credit card company may state norms governing interest charges as follows:

whenever an amount of outstanding credit
if more than 25 days after posting
then the card holder
is obliged
to *pay the interest*;
whenever an agreement for credit card is signed
if within 14 days after commencing
then the card holder
is permitted
to *cancel the agreement*.

The first norm says that after 25 days of posting the invoice, if there is still an amount of outstanding credit, the card holder will have to pay the interest. The second norm states that the card holder retains the right of cancellation of the agreement within 14 days of commencing. The next norm says that unless there is a special arrangement made, e.g. with the account manager, the card holder is not allowed to spend more than the credit limit:

Example Box 7.1 (*cont.*)

whenever purchasing
if no special arrangement is made
then the card holder
is forbidden
to *exceed the credit limit.*

The card holders are expected to behave according to the norms stated in the agreements. As understood by both the customers and the credit card company, the company may impose sanctions if a customer fails to observe the norms. With this form of specification of norms, a computer program can be written to execute the norms. As long as the norms are specified, computing technologies such as active databases, object technology and artificial intelligence will have different approaches towards software realisation.

7.4.4 Norms in computer systems

A constraint in an information system, according to van Griethuysen (1982), is a 'prescription or prohibition of the behaviour of the Universe of Discourse or parts thereof'. Norms, controlling behaviour of the agents at the social level, will have to be reflected as constraints in the conceptual models and incorporated into the technical information systems. The norms function as *integrity constraints* that safeguard the systems from behaving improperly.

One approach is to classify the constraints into three groups (Weigand 1993).

Analytical constraints, which define the meaning of the objects and operations in a system. For example, a student can attend a class and a teacher can teach.

Empirical constraints, which set the rules for the generalisation of the domain. For example, an age acceptable to a system cannot be negative.

Deontic constraints, which specify the rules that the objects and operations must comply with. For example, a student can take as a maximum five subjects in a semester. The special feature of deontic constraints is that they can be violated. A violation should not lead to an inconsistency in the information system. Instead, the system should incorporate a mechanism to derive corresponding rules of action for sanction and correction.

Norms can be treated as these constraints. In a computer system, these norms are programmed and incorporated into computer operations. These constraints ensure the system behaves 'reasonably' and 'correctly'. The constraints can also function as triggers for the computer system to perform certain actions, such as changing the value of a record or producing a message.

8
The social layer: modelling organisations as information systems

As the semiotic framework shows, the issues at the social level are concerned with beliefs, expectations, commitments, contracts, law and culture, as well as business functions. If a technical information system is to serve the organisation well, to understand the organisational functions at the social level is crucial. Information systems analysis and design must start with understanding and modelling the organisation first. Many information systems methods provide techniques to deal with business analysis and modelling. Olle *et al.* (1991) summarises the situation by saying that the methods and techniques may be characterised by their different perspectives in modelling:

>*data-oriented* perspective,
>*process-oriented* perspective, and
>*behaviour-oriented* perspective.

However, by reading that textbook, one can see that they mostly concentrate on capturing business functions.

The semiotic approach will take one a step further. It will stress the distinctions as well as the interdependent links between the organisation, the business process and the IT system. The notion of human responsibility and possibility of delegation of functions to an IT system is clarified. An organisational morphology presented in this chapter will offer a useful way for one to understand the whole organisation and will help the modelling. Finally it will discuss the characteristics of an effective method for information systems modelling, which suggest necessary considerations in selection of a method.

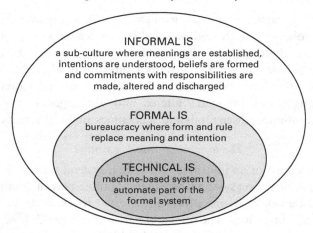

Figure 8.1. The organisational onion.

8.1 Organisations as information systems

An organisation is a social system in which people behave in an organised manner by conforming to a certain system of norms. These norms are regularities of perception, behaviour, belief and value which are exhibited as customs, habits, patterns of behaviour and other cultural artefacts. Teams and organisations exist by virtue of their social norms and cultures. An organisation can be characterised as a structure of social norms, which allows a group of people to act together in a coordinated way for certain purposes. The common purposes may be little more than to maintain the existence of the organisation so that it may serve as an arena for the pursuit of diverse individual and sectional interests of its members (Huang 1998).

An organisation can be seen as an information system where agents employ signs to perform purposeful actions. Some of the organisational functions are of high regularity where rules can be clearly formalised as bureaucracy. Within the formalised part of the job, part of it may be highly repetitive and can be automated where computer-based systems can be introduced. Therefore, the computer-based system is just part of the formal part of the organisation which is, in turn, part of the total organisation. Stamper (1992) names this 'the organisational onion' (Figure 8.1).

The informal information systems

The whole organisation is first of all regarded as an informal information system in which the oral culture plays an important role. The organisational culture, customs and values are reflected as beliefs, habits and patterns of behaviour of each individual member. A healthy organisation would possess a cohesive culture and personal beliefs, whereas, in an unhealthy organisation, there may be considerable conflicts between the organisational and personal levels. This layer is a sub-culture where meanings are agreed, intentions are understood, and beliefs are formed. Commitments and responsibilities are made, altered and discharged in this context through negotiation, discussions and, sometimes, physical actions.

The formal information system

Inside the context of an informal information system, there is the layer of the formal information system where literate culture plays a dominant role. Rules and bureaucratic procedures are created to explicate and replace meanings and intentions. The rules and bureaucracy specify how the work should be carried out and how the tasks should be performed. They are useful when the tasks are mechanistic and repetitive. The rules and procedures can help achieve high efficiency. People involved in the work do not necessarily understand the meaning of the words and numbers they handle, or the purposes for which they are used. People function as 'machines' that transmit and process sign-tokens. This de-skilling is the essential step towards automation. However, such detachment of signs from their meanings in bureaucracy could be dangerous. If the members of the organisation do not understand the meanings of the signs they process, there will be no sound basis for them to check that what they do is what they are supposed to do. An organisation may be detached from its members, or it can run efficiently but not effectively as far as the achievement of its objectives is concerned (Huang 1998).

The technical information system

The technical system, mostly a computer system or an IT system, is placed inside the formal system layer. The technical system can be programmed according to rules. It can automate some of the functions and procedures. The computer system can be developed to read signs, shuffle and re-arrange them, store and retrieve them, and finally present them. Many routine and repetitive tasks can be delegated to the technical system to achieve efficiency. However, to introduce a technical system into an organisation in order to automate some part of the work, there are certain prerequisites that have to be met.

Well-defined work processes The work process and procedures should be clearly defined. There should be clear bureaucracy in place where the technical system can be fitted in.

Clearly defined human responsibility People using the technical system should know clearly about their responsibility. Interfaces between the human system and technical system should be clear as to what a user is supposed to do and what a machine is expected to provide. The purpose of using an IT system is to support the work process, but not to hinder or to provide excuses for not doing the job properly.

Explicitly specified rules for operations Before introducing an IT system, there should be clear specifications of rules for business operations. These rules can then be translated into the IT system or knowledge-based system for automation purposes.

In summary, an IT system presupposes a formal system, just as a formal system relies on an informal system.

8.2 The notion of responsibility

The notion of responsibility is crucial in designing information systems. This has become clear in the above discussion on the relationship between the informal, formal and technical information systems. An understanding of the issue of responsibility may help answer the following two questions. How is one to decide the extent to which human responsibilities should be delegated to an IT system? What are the roles of human users when the IT system does most of the work? An examination of the most fundamental legal conceptions can help us to gain such an understanding.

A legal philosopher, Wesley N. Hohfeld, recognised eight fundamental legal conceptions in two sets (Allen & Saxon 1986). In each set, the paired concepts are 'opposites' in columns and 'correlatives' in rows:

Right Set:	Right	Duty
	No right	Privilege
Power Set:	Power	Liability
	Disability	Immunity

All eight concepts are related to the terms 'must', 'should', 'must not' and more. Each term may involve more than one of these legal concepts. For example, 'a credit card holder *must* pay any outstanding amount of credit within 25 days of posting to avoid incurring interest'. This implies that a card holder has the *rights* to pay, and not to pay till the due day, but a liability of paying interest will occur from the due date if the amount is not paid (Liu & Dix 1997). As pointed out by Allen and Saxon (1986), these terms may also result in multiple interpretations and it is only appropriate to expect a machine to assist the human in interpretation.

The social layer

An IT system should be seen as an assistant to the human, who can delegate some of his or her responsibilities. Only when the human user has the right and power can he or she transfer responsibilities to a machine. It should be noted here that what is transferred are duties or job functions rather than liability. In the same manner the government of a country can delegate responsibilities and functions to an embassy in a foreign country but cannot relinquish the liability for what the ambassador has done. Of course, this does not stop users from attempting to use software to evade responsibility: 'sorry I can't help, the computer says so'!

8.3 An organisational morphology

In systems analysis and design, a first step is to understand the organisation for which the system is developed. This includes the structure and functions of the organisation. A traditional method for organisational analysis is to draw an organisational diagram in a hierarchical structure. The diagram would normally represent the officers in different positions and reporting relationships. This kind of analysis is helpful in understanding the structure, but not what an organisation does.

One approach to understanding an organisation is to focus on the organisational functions (behaviour) rather than just the structure. This approach studies the morphology of the tasks and functions of an organisation. Three areas of organisational functions can be identified, and hence three types of tasks and three types of norms: *substantive, communication* and *control*.

The substantive area The functions in this area contribute directly to the organisational objectives. The tasks are productivity-related. The actions are to realise the essential changes in the physical or social world. For example, in an educational institute, the substantive activities would be teaching and research. In an insurance company, they would be sales of policies, receipt and processing of claims, and payments to customers.

The communication area The functions in this area are about communication. Tasks performed in this category inform relevant people about relevant facts, work procedures, what actions are to be taken, when and by whom. Within a company, such communications are required to coordinate the temporal and spatial use of resources for substantive activities. Typical examples of such activities in this area are communications by sending memoranda, announcements of meetings and events, telephone calls and emails.

The control area The control functions aim at reinforcing the whole business system running properly, particularly the substantive and communication areas. Tasks in this area include monitoring and evaluation of substantive and communication actions, followed by appropriate reward and punishment imposed on the agents responsible. Within an organisation, the power of reinforcement may be informal or it may be explicitly stipulated in rules and regulations. Between organisations, it may be generated by inter-firm agreements or contracts governed by law. But the power of enforcement both within and between organisations ultimately rests upon socially established norms within the business sector and on the wider cultural conventions. The formal control norms supplement the informal norms in cases where they are deemed insufficient to ensure that every relevant agent fulfils his or her duties properly (Huang 1998).

8.4 Modelling the organisation

The substantive, communication and control areas constitute the whole business organisation. A model of organisational morphology (Stamper *et al.* 1994) can be represented as in Figure 8.2. The figure shows that an organisation consists of three sub-areas: the *substantive area x.s*, *communication or message-passing area x.m*, and *control area x.c*. Each of them can be further divided in the same way in more detail, such as *substantive message-passing x.m.s*, *messages about messages x.m.m*, and *control of message x.m.c*. Such a division can continue until the level of detail is sufficient for the purposes of analysis.

In an organisation, all three areas are necessary. The communication functions are required to inform people and coordinate actions. The control functions will ensure the other areas function properly. However, based on this organisational morphology one can see that a 'lean and healthy' organisation should have to consume minimal resources in communication or *message-passing* (**x.m**) and *control* (**x.c**) activities. It should direct most of its resources to building up the organisational platform for *substantive* (**x.s**) activities. An 'unhealthy' or badly designed organisation will have to consume a great deal of its energy in building elaborate communication subsystems and will have to rely largely on formal control subsystems. These two types of subsystems comprise large parts of typical bureaucratic infrastructures. The more elaborate these two subsystems are, the heavier the bureaucratic burden is on the organisation.

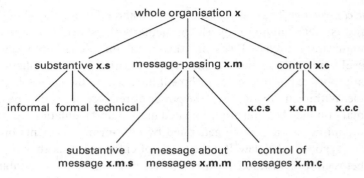

Figure 8.2. Organisational morphology.

8.5 Summary: requirements for an effective information modelling method

To model an information system is to represent, by formal means, an organisation in which people use signs for business purposes. A sound modelling method must cover the issues in semantic, pragmatic and social aspects. Issues at the three semiotic levels are closely related; Figure 8.3 explains the relationship. The left arrow shows that in analysis and representation, the focus must be first on the semantic issues. A model containing a clear description of the organisation, which may be in terms of general patterns of actions, states, etc., is the first basis for further analysis. The model of this kind can be taken as a foundation on which the intentions of actions can be discussed. Furthermore, the rationales, limits and consequences of the actions at the social level can be addressed. But in the case of the 'real-life' operations, as the right arrow indicates, the social concern determines the intentions that the speaker needs to express, and thus decide the words and expressions to be uttered. This is the semiotic approach upheld for understanding information systems.

To clarify the semantic problems and represent a social organisation clearly is regarded as the most critical and difficult task. In a practical situation it is crucial to know how the people are involved in implementing a plan or conducting an activity by translating the words into actions through which they understand their tasks and duties. An effective method must provide techniques for eliciting, clarifying and representing envisaged users' knowledge and requirements. For this purpose, the Semantic Analysis method is advocated for its power in handling the semantic problems. Semantic Analysis focuses attention of analysis on the agents and the actions. The semantic principle for solving business problems and interpreting language in the conduct of practical affairs is that meaning must be

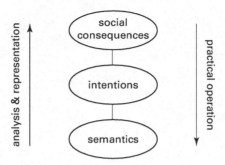

Figure 8.3. Practical operation versus analysis and representation.

created as a relationship between signs and actions. The actions include the physical kind and the uses of signs (semiological kind) for fulfilment of purposes. The semantic model delineates the boundary of concern in the analysis and defines the meanings of the terminology used in the model.

Questions of intentions and social consequences are addressed by means of analysing norms, which govern people's behaviour. The analysis of norms is based on the result of semantic analysis. With the semantically defined words and expressions resulting from the semantic analysis, the intentions and the social consequences can be associated with the actions and the uses of signs in communication. The norms acquired, in addition to the semantic model, serve as some more detailed knowledge of the business organisation. Furthermore, the norms can be used for reasoning and prescriptive analysis of the organisation, for example, planning and behaviour simulation.

Part two
Applications

9

From semiotic analysis to systems design

If the objective of a system analysis is to understand and specify the users' requirements, then the next objective is to produce a design of a computer information system. The core of a computer information system comprises a database and other application programs. This chapter will address the semantic aspect of the computer information systems, and discuss the relationship between semantic models and database design.

9.1 The semantic aspect of databases

Data and code in a database are meaningless until someone assigns a meaning to them and someone is able to interpret them. The meaning of data is rooted in social and cultural conventions and norms. The assignment of meaning to the data and interpretation of the data have to follow the same social and cultural norms. The interpretation is a complex, creative act that relies on personal knowledge and understanding of the norms. A successful use of data and derivation of information meaningful to a user is a key issue in databases. This issue cannot be resolved by technical means alone but requires social and organisational arrangements.

There can be two kinds of meanings distinguished: intension (sense) and extension (or reference). These two notions can be applied to predicates, propositions and sentences. The intension of a predicate, i.e. its sense, is identified with the property it expresses; its extension is the generalised class of referents in the world of affairs that possess the property. The intension of a proposition is determined by the meanings of the predicates used; the extension is its correspondence to the world of affairs. Then the meaning of a sentence is determined by the propositions it contains. People sometimes do not know the extension (reference, denotation) of the components of a sentence, but only their intension (sense, understanding). However, they are

119

able to understand a sentence intensionally without knowing its correspondence to a world of affairs (Thayse 1989). What is critical in modelling is the intensional meaning. The affordances in NORMA that are considered as the foci in modelling are the abilities of sense-making, understanding, or recognising of the intensional meanings. These abilities are generalised patterns of behaviour of the agents that are governed by the social norms.

The semantic database takes an ontology model as the conceptual schema. Affordances can be roughly comparable with entities and relations, and determiners (a specific kind of affordance) with attributes in terms of relational databases. Affordances are defined and organised according to the ontology model. Instances (or particulars of affordances) are called realisations of the affordances and are managed in the databases. Each universal and particular affordance has temporal attributes, for example a *start* and a *finish*, as its intrinsic properties. Each application in such a database will involve both the semantic and temporal operations.

9.2 Capturing the semantic aspect

The ontology model delineates a context which involves concepts and terminology used in a particular problem domain. According to van Dijk (1981), the 'context' is both 'a theoretical and a cognitive abstraction, viz. from the actual physical–biological–etc. situation'. The context in which a certain speech act is performed supplies the more general linguistic and other knowledge in memory, against which the language users match incoming information. The context makes it possible for agents to establish a link between the intensional and extensional meanings. The categorised concepts and terminology according to the ontological relationships provide determined semantics contextually, because every word or expression is linked with its antecedents in the ontology model. For example, a student can be defined in many ways: even someone who follows an evening course of ball-room dancing once a week can be called a student in that context. But, with the help of an ontology model specifying exactly the circumstance, the meaning of 'student' can be uniquely determined by ontologically linking the terms used in the discourse: someone registered in a school, only during his registration period. Thus, the NORMA expressions

(university#employer, person#employee)employs,
and
(university, person#student)registered

constitute a practical circumstance in which the boundaries and semantics of the concepts are settled by linking the dependants to the ontological

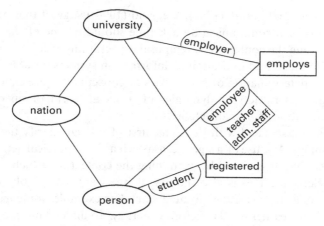

Figure 9.1. Ontological structure and semantics.

antecedents. The antecedents (e.g. in this case, *'university'* and *'person'*), moreover, are ontologically dependent on some other antecedent (e.g. a *'nation'*). The graphic representation may explain better how a 'student' and a 'teacher' are defined (see Figure 9.1). The 'student' and 'employee' are role names for a 'person' who is 'registered' at or employed by a 'university'; A 'teacher' is a specific kind of 'employee'; 'registered' and 'employs' are affordances that are ontologically dependent on the antecedents, the 'university' and the 'person'.

A definition of ontological dependency in NORMA can be given as follows. Given two objects x and y, if y's existence depends on x's, and y only exists during or within the existence of x, then the dependency relationship between x and y is called an ontological dependency. Or it can be said that y ontologically depends on x. The object x is called the antecedent and y is the dependant. The structure constrained by the kind of ontological relationship determines exactly the boundaries of each concept. In the example discussed above, the student never exists beyond the existence of the person, the university and the registration; the same principle applies to the teacher and administrative staff.

9.3 Capturing the time aspect

Winograd and Flores (1987) state that, in communication, 'time is not an incidental condition, but a critical aspect of every speech act'. Therefore they build a mechanism for keeping temporal relations in the computer-assisted communication system, The Coordinator. Many related works (e.g. Auramäki *et al.* (1988), Weigand (1990)) suggest that, regarding the context of a communication act, time should be one of the elements for specifying the context. The temporal aspect is important in relation to the development and utilisation of information systems for at least three purposes: determination of boundaries of concepts that are expressed in language; description of dynamics of a social world or an organisation; coordination of human activities.

Time associated with the signs, first of all, can clarify the actions and meanings. Any use of a sign, i.e. a speech act or a physical act, brings about a meaning determined by examining the context, of which time is one of the elements. This is also the case if one wants to be able to equate the 'morning star' with the 'evening star'. For example, someone says that it was bad weather the day before yesterday. To understand properly what is meant by 'bad weather', someone else must be referred to the time mentioned in the utterance; only then can he understand that the 'bad weather' just means it was a bit too cold, though some people may not think it was bad weather at all.

The use of language enables agents to talk about actions, states and events in the direct environment or at a distance. They may refer to something that happened in the past, or will happen in the future, or something they wish to avoid. Time plays a key role in such uses of language. For example, John informs his boss Mary that his colleague Henry is taking leave. In this case, it is important to know both when Henry left and when John told Mary. Things may get more complicated if John said to Mary that Henry told him to ask Mary for a permit for his leave. Then the time becomes essential, because appropriateness of Henry's and John's behaviour is judged, to a large extent, on whether John's informing Mary took place well in advance of Henry's leave.

The temporal aspect of information has a great importance in coordinating actions in practical affairs. Perlocutionary effects will result in social consequences which have to be expressed in the time horizon. For example, an obligation is established for a certain period of time; a retraction of some speech act is to end the existence of an existing propositional attitude. An illocutionary act may take place at one time; the perlocutionary act may be at another time because of communication delay or time needed for the hearer to take a decision. Interpersonal relationships, e.g. commitment and responsibility, are set up at one time, altered or finished at another time. This kind of beginning and ending processes continues constantly. Every agent in a social and organisational context is involved in a network of constantly changing relationships. Commitments and responsibilities are only sensibly clear when time is taken into account. Time can be useful for checking the sincerity of a speaker and feasibility of actions – if the speaker promises or plans to do too many things at the same time, then either the speaker's sincerity or the feasibility of performing the actions may be questionable. The commitments and responsibilities are normally placed into a temporal framework so that the actions (and the hearer's reactions) can be expected and coordinated.

There are other reasons for arguing that time is an important aspect of information. As a result, the semantic data structure for database design must contain time as an indispensable part. That means every data record in the database comprises times, e.g., the start time and the finish time of the realisation of an agent or an affordance.

9.4 Ontological modelling for conceptualisation

The primary purpose of Semantic Analysis is to assist an analyst and a problem-owner to articulate the requirements by focusing on clarifying the language used in expressing the problem. The ontology model obtained from the Semantic Analysis, however, serves as a database *conceptual schema* (a term defined in Griethuysen (1982)).

A Semantic Analysis is a process of conceptualisation of a business organisation through which the behaviour of the organisation is analysed and captured in the ontology model. The agents and the patterns of behaviour are the focus of representation in an ontology model. The semantic primitives appearing in the model represent possible patterns of actions of a complex agent, which are known as affordances in NORMA. The boundary or existence period of an affordance in NORMA is bound to the agent who possesses it, while, in many other information analysis approaches (e.g. Chen (1976), Verheijen & Bekkum (1982)), *entities* are supposedly observable independently of the agents involved.

The affordances captured in an ontology model compose a conceptual representation according to which the data can be organised in a database. The realisations of the affordances are the instances that are recorded in the database records. For example, an expression in NORMA,

(university person) employs,

defines a part of the conceptual model, which can be represented as an ontology chart (Figure 9.1). The affordances of *'university'* and *'person'* are two antecedents that jointly afford a pattern of action *'employs'*. The particulars of universities, persons and employments will be instances to be stored in the database. Figure 9.2 shows some instances of these three affordances in a database.

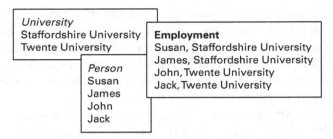

Figure 9.2.   Instances of three affordances.

9.5 Intentions, propositional attitudes and consequent operations

The semantics of language used in the problem domain is handled with NORMA in Semantic Analysis. Semiotic behaviour is expressed in the formula: *B "Ax"*, as discussed in Chapter 6. Using signs enables the agent to talk about actions, states and events at different times with intentions. A proposition can be uttered, for example, as an assertion, a prediction or a hypothesis, which are coined as intentions. An extension is made to the NORMA syntax for the association of the intention with the formula of semiotic behaviour as follows:

B "Ax" α,   where *B* is the agent performing the semiotic action with an illocution *α*, between the quotes are signs employed by *B* in his behaviour. *Ax* is the meaning or referent of the semiotic action. E.g. *'Mary "John happy" assert'*.

The intention operator *α* can be assigned different illocutions for indicating the intentions of the agent in using the signs. The illocutions by the speaker are, as discussed in Subsection 7.2.1, categorised under eight headings. Following the illocutions, there will be consequent actions by the speaker and by the hearer. In the case where a database is involved as a medium of recording and assisting the communication, there will be corresponding operations on the database, as illustrated in Table 9.1.

The directives will bring the hearer into an action, as normally the directives produce social consequences of deontic nature. The types of deontic consequences that are recognised in deontic logic are *obligatory, permitted,* and *prohibited* which are typified by auxiliary verbs in speech acts such as 'should', 'should not', 'may', etc. Another type of deontic consequence that may be produced by the directives is a *liberty* (or *freedom*) (Stamper 1980). This is comparable with Hohfeld's legal concept of *privilege* (or *immunity*), because having a privilege is legally weaker than having a right. The privilege enables an agent to preserve discretion in taking actions. Some of the direc-

Table 9.1. *Illocutions, propositional attitudes and database operations.*

Illocutionary category by speaker (S)	Propositional attitude of addressee (A) (after speech acts performed)	Operation on database (to reflect S's acts)
Proposal	obligation	record (or insertion)
Inducement	expectation	record (or insertion
Forecast	expectation	record (or insertion)
Wish	belief	record (or insertion)
Palinode	retraction	update
Contrition	retraction	update
Assertion	belief	record (or insertion)
Valuation	judgement	record (or insertion)

tives and other illocutions by the speaker generate a liberty. The deontic attitudes of obligation, permission and prohibition can be created by the directives. Some of the illocutions do not involve deontic modalities at all. This can be seen from the fact that if the hearer does not follow the expected pattern of behaviour, there would not be a punishment enforced on the hearer. For example, if a speaker makes an illocutionary act of forecast by uttering 'Mr X will arrive here tomorrow', it is at the hearer's discretion whether to believe or not, though normally the hearer will believe what the speaker uttered if the communication is honest and sincere. Therefore, Table 9.1 only represents some ideal patterns that are based on the supposition that the agents involved in communication 'behave normally' (i.e., obey social norms of sincere, honest communication).

This table attempts to depict a part of a system of social norms of communication, especially focusing on the consequent actions by both speech agents. Operations on the database, which is used to record and assist the communication, are derived as seen from the table. In most of the cases, the operation on the database is to record the speech act except for the illocution of retraction. The illocution of palinode or contrition is used by the speaker when an earlier speech act is to be withdrawn. In this case, an operation of correction is required on the database. All operations on the database comprise three aspects, *semantics*, *intention* and *time*, which will be discussed in more detail after the semantic template is defined in the next chapter.

9.6 Other aspects of databases: facts, beliefs, and knowledge

A database, at the syntactic level, can be viewed as a well organised, but variable, set of data packages, which during a longer period is used in an organisational system as a means of communication (definition of Lindgreen (1990)). The language–action approaches regard a database as a model of some Universe of Discourse for communication (see Weigand 1990)); a database functions as a device for recording, processing, indexing, and transmitting communication acts. From this point of view, what is managed in a database is not the 'recording of facts', as suggested by Nijssen and Halpin (1989), but subjective observations, opinions and beliefs. Based on the two radical subjective axioms adopted, knowledge is bound to the *knower*. To retain the subjectivity, both knowledge and the knower will have representations in a database. Personal value judgements, the speaker's intentions, and differences in perspectives and interests seem no less important than the propositional contents of the utterances, which should be accommodated in the database as well.

From another dimension of database studies, numerous researchers have noticed that, with many databases, information in the system reflects only the current state of affairs (e.g., Clifford & Tansel (1985), Kim *et al.* (1990), Sadeghi *et al.* (1988)). The databases of this kind only provide a snapshot of an organisation. However, in business practice, historical information is important. Based on his historical studies and business experience, Achueler (1977) strongly appeals for a database technique that will be able to keep historical records. He describes the common update technique in the database by erasing the records as like the 'Aton-Update', a 'mass update' of a large Egyptian database pertaining to Aton that was undertaken with hammer and chisel throughout the country in 1347BC. This kind of erasing update is also comparable to the 'update' of a most important database in the year 47BC that the Library of Alexandria was completely 'updated' by a fire. Loss of historical data through such actions on databases may sometimes cause irreversible, disastrous consequences. Meanwhile, the historical information can be useful for businesses. In banking, for example, information about the history of clients can help the banker assess the customer's credibility. Therefore it assists them in making decisions about granting loans. When a company plans to introduce a new product into the market, historical information can help the company do a trend analysis and predict the market for the product. On the other hand, hypotheses and predictions for the organisation are relevant for studying organisational behaviour and performance, for coordinating future actions, and for planning and policy-making purposes.

The semantic temporal database developed in the project aims at accommodating data pertaining to business semantics and intentions. Each particular instance of actions and use of signs is associated with the intention that is expressed by the language user. Moreover, each instance has a pair of times, the start and the finish, to indicate the existence of an action or a state, from the speaker's point of view.

Example Box 9.1: Semantic, intentional and temporal aspects in speech acts

To show the distinctive components of semantic, intentional and temporal aspects that can be considered in the representation with the proposed data structure, the following sentences will be used in discussion (after Searle, 1983, p. 30):

(S1) 'John wants Mary's house in the summer of 1994' (suppose 'now' = summer of 1993).

(S2) 'In 1994, John will want Mary's house.'

(S3) 'John now wants Mary's house in the summer of 1994 though by then he will not want it.'

A semantic analysis of the sentences reveals there are a few universal affordances which should appear in the ontology chart: 'person' and 'house'. 'John' and 'Mary' are instances of the affordance 'person'. The word 'want' seems to be used with mixed meanings. To 'want' may mean to 'want to have'; to 'have' may be more specifically understood as to 'occupy' (or, to 'live in'), to 'rent', to 'buy' or to 'own'. At the same time, to 'want' may indicate an intentional modality. In order to represent the semantic and intentional aspects associated with the word 'want', several possible interpretations are captured in the analysis (e.g., 'occupy', 'rent' and 'own'). The temporal aspect of every affordance is treated as an intrinsic property, that is, every affordance is attached with a *start time* and a *finish time* to delineate its existence. The temporal aspect of every affordance is intrinsically handled by referring to the times defined in a standard time framework. Therefore the time 'now', '1994' and 'the summer of 1994' are not explicitly shown in the chart, but handled as hidden parts in all affordances in the ontology model. Figure 9.3 shows the ontology chart resulting from the semantic analysis of the three sentences.

Some other concepts, such as 'illocution' and 'attitude', are added to the chart in addition to the affordances identified in the early analysis for discussion of the aspects of communication acts. With such an ontology chart, one can represent a fact such as 'John occupies/rents/owns Mary's house (in a certain period)', and all the three sentences (S1), (S2) and (S3)

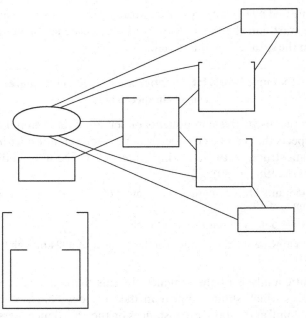

Figure 9.3. Semantic, intentional and temporal aspects in an ontology chart.

(they are either predictions, assertions or requests). The dotted lines linking the illocution and the attitude to the affordance *have* (with three specific kinds of meanings listed under it) can indicate the illocution and the attitude attached to the utterance. As shown in the figure, time is defined in a standard temporal reference system that can be referred to by every affordance. There are some important issues in the chart worth discussing.

To grasp the meanings of the word 'want', several possible interpretations are identified on the chart, which allows the language user to determine the meaning of 'want' between 'occupy', 'rent' and 'own' when the word 'want' is employed in the sentence.

An illocutionary act can be made with or without an illocutionary verb explicitly in a sentence. In the latter case, however, it may require careful analysis to decide to which illocutionary category the sentence belongs. For example, the sentence (S1) ('John wants Mary's house in the summer of 1994') may be regarded as a prediction, an assertion, or a request.

Intentions may be different from propositional attitudes. For example, if one says 'I want your house' it may appear to be analogous to 'I like your house' (Searle 1983). In addition, one may very likely encounter a situation in which a speaker has an unstated, different propositional attitude from the expressed intention. However, in most of the analysis in this book, an assumption is that communication normally takes place in a sincere and honest manner, which means consistency between the intentions expressed in illocutions and the propositional attitudes.

With the chart (Figure 9.3), one can describe the present situation (the house is presently occupied by a person, which is just one of the possible specific forms of 'have') and the different scenarios described by the three sentences. The situation at present can be described as in the following expression:

(B, house)occupy   the house is now occupied by the person B (the person B may be John or Mary, for example).

In steps, the following can be obtained in analysing the sentence (S1):

(R1.1) *(A, house)occupy*   person A occupies a house;
(R1.2) *(A, house)occupy, summer of 1994*   in the summer of 1994, the person A will occupy the house;
(R1.3) *"(A, house)occupy, summer of 1994"*   a semiotic act (i.e. a speech act) with the contents between the quotation marks;

therefore, as a whole, the following is obtained:

(R1) *A "(A, house)occupy, summer of 1994" want*

The expression (R1) represents the sentence (S1). The contents between the quotation marks are propositional contents which are seen as the semantic part of the whole expression 'the person A wants to occupy the house in the summer of 1994'. Note that the time 'summer of 1994' is related to the action '(A, house)occupy' to express that occupation of the house will take place in the summer of 1994.

In steps, the following can be obtained in analysing sentence (S2):

(R2.1) *(A, house)occupy*   person A occupies a house;
(R2.2) *'(A, house)occupy'*   a semiotic act (i.e. a speech act) with the contents between the quotation marks;

130   *From semiotic analysis to systems design*

(R2.3) *A '(A, house) occupy' want*   a speech act performed by the person
                                          A with an illocution 'predict';
(R2.4) *('(A, house) occupy' want),*   the act of wanting will take place in
         summer of 1994   the summer of 1994;
(R2.5) *'('(A, house) occupy' want),*   a semiotic act (i.e. speech act) with
         summer of 1994'   the contents between the quotation
                                          marks;

therefore, as a whole, the following is obtained:

(R2) *A "A "(A, house) occupy" want), summer of 1994)" predict.*

The expression (R2) is from a semantic analysis of the sentence S2. It is a
prediction that in the summer of 1994 the person A will want to occupy the
house.
  The analysis of the sentence (R3) in steps results in the following:

(R3.1) *A "(A, house) occupy,*   same as in (R1);
         summer of 1994" want
(R3.2) *"(A, house) occupy" not*   'not want' is an illocution to indicate
         want   a retraction of the speech act per-
                                          formed earlier which is the content
                                          between the quotation marks;
(R3.3) *("(A, house) occupy" not*   the act of 'not want' will take place in
         want), summer of 1994   the summer of 1994;
(R3.4) *A"("(A, house) occupy" not*   the person A has made a prediction
         want), summer of 1994" predict that in the summer of 1994 A will not
                                          want the house (which is now occu-
                                          pied by B);

therefore, a complete expression by combining (R3.1) and (R3.3) is
obtained as follows:

(R3) *A "(A, house) occupy, summer of 1994' want ,*
(R3) *A" "(A, house) occupy "retract-want, summer of 1994" predict.*

The expression (R3) results from the sentence (S3) which says that the
person A now wants to have the house in the summer of 1994 while it pre-
dicts that in the summer of 1994 he will not want the house. In the expression, the mood 'will not' is represented by the illocution of prediction.
  The three aspects of information can be seen from the above analysis of
the three sentences. The core of the meaning is conveyed by the proposition

which can be interpreted in a semantic sense without there being any intention associated with it. The meanings of the propositions are determined by putting the words in the semantic context in the ontology chart. The intentional aspect of the semiotic act is reflected by the associated illocutions. The time aspect is dealt with as a necessary component in every expression. All these three aspects will have to be accommodated in the semantic template, to be discussed in the next chapter. The semantic template will be defined as a uniform syntactic structure for databases that can handle the semantic, temporal and intentional information.

Example Box 9.2: A speech act in a database

The three aspects of information have been identified to be represented and processed in the semantic temporal database: semantics, intentions and time. A standard record structure based on the elements of a speech act can be derived. Consider the following fragment of an ontology model:

(person#absentee, course)absence

which can be represented in the form of an ontology chart (Figure 9.4). With this ontology model, one can record in a database facts as to who is absent from which course at what time. In addition to that, it is also possible to record in the database the more sophisticated uses of signs, such as hypothetical or declarative uses. The two appearances of 'illocution' in the chart show the possible recursive uses of signs, that is, an illocutionary act can be contained in another, and so on.

Suppose the following speech comprising a piece of knowledge: 'Susan yesterday observed that John had been absent from 1-6-90 till 30-6-90'. This piece of knowledge can be captured in a record as follows:

<Susan, <John, absence, course 123, 1-6-90, 30-6-90>, assert, assert, yesterday, —>.

The explanations below will assist reading of this record and also present considerations of some issues, such as agent, intention and time, in knowledge representation in the database record form.

(1) Susan is the agent who uttered the speech act, the user of sign.
(2) The semantic part of Susan's action resides in the proposition which is abbreviated as '<John, absence, course 123, 1-6-90, 30-6-90>'.

Example Box 9.2 (*cont.*)

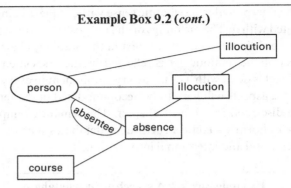

Figure 9.4. A chart of person–course–absence.

The meaning of 'John', 'absence' and 'course 123' is determined by referring to the corresponding part of the ontology chart.

(3) '1-6-90, 30-6-90' refers to the period during which an instance of John's absence is realised.

(4) Both the start mood (i.e. *mood+*) and the finish mood (i.e. *mood−*) of the proposition, found in Susan's action, are assertive. This is because what is represented is an observation, which can be seen from the original sentence (if it is not directly seen from the speech, it is up to the analyst to decide what mood Susan had).

(5) 'Yesterday' indicates the start of Susan's observation. The blank finish time means the assertion is valid till now (a filled finish time would suggest a retraction of the assertion, which would mean Susan had withdrawn the assertion).

10

Semantic temporal databases

The method of Semantic Analysis offers a means of representing information requirements and database modelling. Based on the database theory and semiotic methods, a semantic temporal database is proposed. The semantic temporal database provides a technology of management of the data with semantic and temporal properties. A semantic temporal database language, LEGOL, has been developed for the specification of norms. LEGOL statements can specify constraints and triggers, and can be executed by a LEGOL interpreter.

10.1 Databases

A *database*, from the information technology point of view, can be regarded as a kind of electronic filing cabinet (Date 1995, p. 2). It can be defined as a persistent collection of logically related data that allows shared access by many users. A DBMS (DataBase Management System) is the application-independent software that protects and manages databases. Since the late 1960s when the pioneering DBMS, IMS, was published, the database technology has provided ever improving tools for information management. Since then, the development of new types of DBMS and research into new ways of organising information have been taking place. This section provides a quick review of some major contemporary types of database systems and of the presentation of the semantic temporal databases which are considered highly relevant to business information management purposes.

10.1.1 Developments in database management systems

Relational DBMS is the most widespread and popularly used type of database systems nowadays. Other types of systems are also being introduced to

133

meet diversified application purposes, typically the objected-oriented databases and deductive databases.

A relational database organises data based on a model published by
Codd (1970). A relational DBMS provides the following functionalities
(Loomis 1990) which later become a standard for all kinds of DBMS.

> *Persistence* A database exists outside of the scope of any particular
> program run-unit. It has a complete separation of the data from the
> program that creates and uses them. The data exist on non-volatile
> storage even after the programs terminate.
>
> *Secondary storage management* A DBMS provides efficient ways to rep-
> resent and access small and large volumes of data with the techniques
> from structuring databases, addressing database storage, providing
> 'fast paths' to database contents, clustering portions of a database in
> the physical devices.
>
> *Concurrency* A DBMS allows more than one user to have access to the
> database concurrently without jeopardising the database and the data
> integrity.
>
> *Recovery* This feature enables the DBMS to cope with system failures,
> especially soft crashes, so that it provides a protection of database con-
> tents from destruction.
>
> *Ad hoc query facility* This enables a user to access database contents
> without writing a program.

A relational database design is a process of firstly identifying entities and
attributes that represent application objects and then organising them into
relations (i.e. tables). The relations must conform to formalisation standards for optimisation to achieve performance efficiencies. SQL has
become the *de facto* relational database language. Example methods for
database design can be typified by Chen (1976), and elaborate discussions
can be found in Date (1995).

The deductive, or logic-based, approach sees the database as a set of
axioms. The ground axioms, as well as the deductive rules, are treated as
tuples stored in the database. A formal definition of a deductive database in
Thayse (1989) is given as 'a theory composed of an *extensional database*
and an *intensional database*'. The extensional database is a set of ground
instances (i.e. ground axioms) of atoms defining the extensions of the *base
predicates* (i.e. a relational database). The intensional database is a set of
deduction rules defining the *virtual predicates*. To perform a query in the
database is to prove that some specified formula is a logical consequence of
those axioms; in other words, it is to prove a theorem. This approach can be

seen from Minker (1988), Reiter (1984), Thayse (1989) and Wieringa *et al.* (1989). Propositions about some domains or Universe of Discourse (UoD) are normally the sources of knowledge that will be organised in the database. Such a type of database is sometimes termed a 'logic database', 'inferential database', 'deductive database', 'knowledge base', etc. Language in this approach plays an important role in knowledge acquisition and representation because of the great metaphorical resemblance between the database modelling and natural language uses (see Way (1991) for the notion of metaphor in knowledge representation). One of the advantages of the deductive over the relational database is the declarative operations on the database, both the data input and application: what needs to be specified is concerned with the 'what' rather than the 'how'. However, shortcomings of the deductive database are lack of structure of the data and the shallowness of the semantics of the predicates.

To cope with these problems, Weigand (1990) proposes a linguistically motivated approach to knowledge-based systems. According to his suggestion, a *lexicon can be built* in which the vocabulary of predicates are semantically defined, so that the deep semantic structures can be used by a knowledge engineer in conceptual modelling. In some sense, the ontology model resulting from the Semantic Analysis is actually used as a suitable formalism for organising the deep semantic structures of the vocabulary. It contains certain vocabulary that is relevant to an articulated problem domain. The words reflecting the meaning in human actions are organised in accordance with the ontological dependencies between the actions. In this way the semantics of the words are bound to the context and uniquely defined; therefore, uses of the word in operations on the database can be related to the established structure and will not result in ambiguity.

Another type of database system is the Object-Oriented Database Management Systems (OODBMS). This type of DBMS covers the functionalities listed for the relational DBMS. In addition, they support the object-oriented programming language notions of complex objects, object identity, encapsulation, types or classes, inheritance, overriding and late binding, extensibility, and computational completeness. The incentives for developing an OODBMS come from the application areas of CAD, CAM, CASE, GIS, etc. where complex data types need to be handled and a relational DBMS cannot meet the requirements. Besides, OODBMS can be integrated with an object-oriented programming language, which means a model of representation can be implemented by a programmer consistently in one environment, whereas in a relational database project the application and the database parts are two separate tasks. Standards for OODBMS, or a new generation of DBMS with object-oriented functions, are proposed by Atkinson *et al.* (1990) and Stonebraker *et al.* (1990).

New research directions of DBMS include distributed database systems, federated architecture and integrated heterogeneous databases, client-server architecture of distributed databases, and integration of relational, object-oriented and knowledge databases.

10.1.2 Semantic temporal databases

The appeal of temporal databases comes from various application areas, such as CAD, CAM, software engineering, business data processing, etc. In some areas of business data processing where legal responsibilities are involved and time is a critically important factor in the business transactions, to keep historical images of business becomes essential. Examples of such areas are banking and insurance industries, policing, and government administration systems such as social security. In these applications, a key system requirement may be the ability to make non-destructive, retrospective updates. In the design of the computer system for Income Support (now operational) of the Department of Social Security of Great Britain, a key requirement is to make retrospective update to claimant data, without destroying the original data (Shearer 1992).

Data are neither 'real' actions, events, nor states of affairs, but they are simply a representation of what the business world believed at a given point of time. In other words, data are nothing more than assertions about business reality, which may only temporarily remain 'true' at a specific time. Therefore, one can recognise two types of time: the time referring to the events and states, and the time referring to when the assertions are made. Both kinds of time are sometimes important and many database systems keep records of them.

The evolution histories of entities, actions and states of affairs in the practical world need to be kept in the database. Databases containing these types of data with historical images are called *temporal databases* (Kim *et al.* 1990, Snodgrass 1985).[1] Two types of times associated with each record are kept in the temporal databases: the *event time* and the *transaction time*. The event time indicates the period of the event, action, or state of affairs; the transaction time reflects when the operations of entering and changing data in the databases are actually done. Both types of time are intervals that are marked with a start and a finish.

---

[1] Many research efforts have been put into the temporal databases, see for example Clifford & Tansel (1985), Sadeghi *et al.* (1988), Kim *et al.* (1990).

Table 10.1. *Illustration of functions of time.*

Person	Status	Valid time		Transaction time	
		Start	Finish	Start	Finish
John	student	20/8/86		25/8/86	16/6/92
John	student	20/8/86	15/6/92	16/6/92	—
Paul	student	20/8/86	—	25/8/86	16/12/92
Paul	lab assistant	1/5/89	—	5/5/89	4/1/91
Paul	lab assistant	1/5/89	31/12/90	4/1/91	—
Paul	student	20/8/86	15/12/92	16/12/92	—

The database developed by the MEASUR research team has the features of managing time at different levels. It requires the adoption of the ontology charting as the conceptual modelling so that the semantic richness is captured in the databases. The databases under such a DBMS that handle the temporal features and organise data according to the semantic ontology model are called the *semantic temporal databases*. As to the two types of time managed in the semantic temporal databases – the event time and the transaction time – the former represents the existence of an affordance, the latter the actual time of entering and changing the content of the data record. The event time in business applications tells the state of affairs in relation to time periods, for example the period that one is in a particular salary rank or financial status. This type of time is directly related to the depiction of dynamic pictures of practical affairs. The transaction time registers when an operation on a particular data record is performed. The users of the databases do not have control over this type of time, in the sense that they can only view the time when the data record is put into the database, and when an update is made. But it is not possible for the users to change the transaction time as the time is recorded by the DBMS automatically. Table 10.1 shows the uses of the two types of times and their functions.

When an observation is made explicitly about business affairs, it can be recorded in the database, for example the status of John and Paul as to whether or not they are students. The first observation as seen in the first record in the figure is about John being a student from 20/8/86, which is entered into the database on 25/8/86. The next observation is made to tell that John's studentship is from 20/8/86 till 15/6/92; the time of entering this observation is 16/6/92. At the same time, a finish transaction time 16/6/92 is put onto the earlier record about John for labelling the record as being 'out-of-date'. To read the tuples about Paul, one can also obtain a picture of Paul's movement: he began to be a student from 20/8/86. During his studentship, he was a lab assistant for the period from 1/5/89 till 31/12/90. The finish of his studentship is on 15/12/92.

Several details must be noticed about the semantic temporal databases.

Each tuple records a message which may originally be from a written document, business report or oral notice. This shows a correspondence between the database tuples and semiotic acts.

Values of the transaction time may be different from those of the event time if the database only records what takes place in the business world. However, the more one relies on the database for the business operations, the less the difference will be between the two types of time. For example, if one decides to use the start of the transaction time as the start of the event time, which means the transaction time has a legal effect on determining the period of studentship, then these two types of time will always be the same (therefore, only one type of them is needed).

A tuple with an unfilled finish transaction reflects the current state of affairs; therefore, there is no need to physically remove the out-of-date records to update an observation.

10.2 The semantic templates

The purpose of defining a semantic template is to devise a uniform structure by means of which the semantics and intentions of use of signs can be accommodated and operated with. The semantic template will be the basis for devising a uniform database structure.

10.2.1 Defining a semantic template

The semantic primitives handled in the knowledge representation language NORMA are the words that label the affordances. The words are used to describe practical problems in a business context with intentions. In order to capture the semantics and intentions of the use of words, behind every NORMA expression there is a uniform semantic structure, which is termed the semantic template. A Semantic Template (ST) is defined as follows.

Definition of the semantic template:

ST :   = '<' agent, ST, mood+, mood−, time+, time− '>' '<' agent, action, time+, time− '>';

agent :   = *agent performing the action*;
action :   = *realisation of affordance*;
mood+ :   = mood;
mood−:   = mood;
mood :   = proposal | inducement | forecast | wish | palinode |contrition |
               assertion | valuation;
time+ :   = time;
time− :   = time.

The ST definition is recursive, which means that an ST can be related to an
agent within an ST structure. A minimum ST structure has three parts: an
agent, an *action* and a *time*, to be able to portray 'an agent performing an
action at a certain time'. A minimum, first-order ST normally refers to a
substantive action. It does not contain a modality but normally only a
proposition, and it sets up a direct relation between a sign and a substantive
action. A higher-order ST may have a reference to a lower-order ST; it
establishes a reference between signs. The modalities of a higher-order ST
are associated with the start and the finish at that level. This shows an
analogy with an ordinary use of language, that a speech or quotation can be
embedded into another speech.

The values of each particular *mood* are the illocutions (e.g. request,
command, permit, assert, assume, etc.). The value-types of *time* can be a
point-of-time, a *period-of-time*, and a *relative time* referring to other action.
Further definitions for both the modality and time will be given in
Appendix A, supplemented by examples and explanations. More discussions about use of time can be found later in this chapter where the semantic temporal database language, LEGOL, is presented.

10.2.2 ST for database design

The design of the structure of a database is set to satisfy requirements
derived from philosophical considerations and theoretical discussions.
Semantic properties, subjectivity, intentionalities and temporalities are
some of the most important aspects which should be entertained in the
semantic temporal database. In designing the structure of a database, the
ST has been taken as a basis for construction. Although, during the stages
of representing an informal system and implementing it in a technical
system, a great many properties of the informal systems may be lost, attention in devising the database design method has been paid to minimising
such expenditure.

A database record is called a *surrogate*. At the specification level, a surrogate is described as a tuple:

surrogate := <surrogate-identification, <content>, <antecedents>, authority+, authority−, mood+, mood−, action-time+, action-time−, record-time+, record-time− >

where

surrogate-identification provides a unique key for each realisation of an affordance, by which one can equate the 'morning star' and the 'evening star';

<*content*> corresponds to the semantic part of an ST which represents a semiological action (e.g. a speech act) or a substantive action (e.g. *being absent from school*);

<*antecedents*> establishes links between the surrogate and its ontological antecedent surrogates, which enables the association of the surrogate with the semantic context;

authority+ and *authority−* relate the action to the responsible agents who certify or recognise the start and finish of the action;

mood+ and *mood−* indicate the intentions of the action represented in the surrogate (the mood for start may differ from the mood for finish, e.g., a surrogate may record a course of action started with a mood of assertion and finished with a mood of retraction, in a case where the agent realised what was asserted is a mistake);

action-time+ and *action-time−* denote the start time and finish time of the action;

record-time+ and *record-time−* signify the start time and finish time when the action is reported or observed.

Example Box 10.1: A speech act in a database

To illustrate the construction of a surrogate in a database, it may be convenient to continue with the example used in illustration of ST. The surrogate for that example is specified as follows:

<srg-id123, [absence], John, course123, auth+123,

　　a　　　　　b　　　　c　　　d　　　　　e

　　　　　　　　　　—, assert, —, 1-6-90, 30-6-90, [yesterday], —>.

　　　　　　　　　　f　g　　 h　i　　 j　　　　 k　　　　　l

The explanation of the surrogate is given below (the letters below the surrogate label the items in order to relate to the explanations).

Example Box 10.1 (*cont.*)

The speech-act agent, Susan, is not recorded in the surrogate; but if it is necessary to have information about the agent, Susan can be regarded as an *authority* responsible for recognising the action of John's absence. Normally, the responsible agents to certify or recognise a type of action are generally defined in a problem domain (e.g. in an organisation).

(a)   Firstly, *srg-id 123* is the surrogate identification which is uniquely generated by the database system.

(b)   Next, *[absence]* is a defined action type (an affordance defined in the ontology model) in the database.

(c),(d) Antecedents 'John' and 'course 123' relate the action, *being absent*, with the semantic context by adding the action agent and action object.

(e)   Next, *auth+123* is the authority who recognises that John is absent. The authority, in this case, may be the teacher of John's class.

(f)   The unfilled *authority−* indicates that this record is valid, i.e., no one has considered that this recording is a mistake needing to be corrected. A filled *authority−*, however, would indicate a responsible agent for identifying the recording as an incorrect observation if someone as the agent does so.

(g)   Next, *assertion*, as a *mood for start*, signifies that the surrogate is supposed to contain a reported fact or observation (not a hypothesis or a prediction, for example).

(h)   The unfilled *mood−* (i.e., *mood for finish*) designates that no one disagrees with the surrogate; the observation is considered correct.

(i),(j) Two times, *1-6-90* and *30-6-90*, indicate the period of the action of *being absent*.

(k)   The time, *[yesterday]*, tells when the observation of the action is made. The database system may transform *[yesterday]* into a proper time representation.

(l)   The unfilled *record-finish-time* indicates that the surrogate is still valid. This field of time must be filled in accordance with the *authority−* (the item (f)); that means the item (f) will indicate the responsible agent who decides the record as being incorrect and the item (l) records the time of his making of the decision.

Table 10.2. *Database excerption of the example of university*
administration.

sr9-id	label	ant1	ant2	type	...	action+	action−	record+	record−	...	...
xx1	organs'n	xx0	xx0	u	...	—	—	–	—	...	...
xx2	Staff Uni.	xx0	xx0	xx1	...	19600901	—	19980901	—	...	...
xx3	Twente U.	xx0	xx0	xx1	...	19650901	—	19980901	—	...	...
xx4	department	xx1	—	u	...	—	—	19980901	—	...	...
xx5	Computing	xx2	—	xx4	...	19900901	—	19980901	—	...	...
xx6	person	xx1	—	u	...	—	—	19980901	—	...	...
xx7	Piet	xx2	—	xx6	...	19700203	—	19980901	—	...	...
xx8	Peter	xx3	—	xx6	...	19230205	19921231	19980901	—	...	...

Note:
'action+', 'action−', 'record+' and 'record−' are the start/finish times for
action/record, equivalent to the notions of valid time and transaction time in temporal
databases.
The type having a value 'u' indicates the surrogate to be a universal, otherwise the
surrogate belongs to the type of the surrogate referred to in the field 'type'.

10.3 Systems construction

After systems analysis and design, the next step is system implementation
in which the database records are defined.

A surrogate is a tuple in a database; it is a semiotic representation of an
affordance. A surrogatebase is a semantic temporal database containing
and managing a set of surrogates. A surrogate has a basic structure with a
fixed number of intrinsic properties. Affordances in an ontology chart represent universal types whereas the instances of the affordances are values
of the universal types. Behind the ontology chart, all the universal
affordances have the same number of properties, such as 'surrogate-
identification', 'label', 'antecedents', etc., which correspond to the components indicated in the surrogate definition. For a system design, what is
required is the specification of the property values of each affordance
identified in the ontology chart. Data on the particulars have the same
structure as the universals. With regard to the example of project management (see Figure 6.5), data containing the universals and the particular
instances can be as shown in Table 10.2 which illustrates the major properties of the surrogates.

The implication of this canonical structure is that once a semantic model
is produced, the design of the database is already virtually known because
the components of the surrogate are predefined. If there is a computer
supported environment available for capturing the semantic model and

translating the model into the database design, the implementation of the database can be immediately realised. This would allow one to concentrate on systems analysis, and would make it possible to obtain a prototype system for testing and verifying the result of systems analysis. When the verification is satisfactory, the system can be used as an information system for real business applications.

10.4 LEGOL

The project LEGOL was originated in the early 1970s (see Stamper (1980)), one of the objectives being to develop a language, with the same name as the project title, for specifying legal rules and also for operating on relational databases (Jones *et al.* 1979). Several versions had been developed earlier. LEGOL-3.0, based on the early versions, is devised for two purposes: as a specification language for norms and as an operation language for the semantic temporal databases. This section will give a brief introduction to LEGOL.

10.4.1 Basic syntactic structure

The statements in LEGOL can be seen as norms specified in a formal syntax. The norms can define database constraints, specify applications in the databases, and trigger human actions. The basic structure of a LEGOL statement is the same as that of a norm. There are two parts composing a statement:

<*condition*> <*consequence*>.

The condition part specifies the circumstances in which the actions will be taken, while the consequence part designates the actions. It is possible to have just the condition part, then the statement will be seen as a query in the database.

There are two types of actions defined in LEGOL for the consequences: one type is called substantive and the other semiotic. Two specific actions are defined as the substantive kind, 'start' and 'finish'; and two as the semiotic kind, 'print' and 'report'. They can be schematically grouped as in Figure 10.1. Each tuple stored in the database is a representation of a particular of an affordance which has a start time and a finish time associated with it. The operations of the conventional (relational) databases such as 'insertion', 'update' and 'deletion' can be sufficiently realised by these two operators. The 'start' and 'finish' deal respectively with the start time and

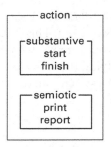

Figure 10.1. Types of the consequent actions.

the finish time of the existence of an affordance: When a tuple is entered as a database record, a start time and a finish time will be filled to indicate the existence of the particular affordance (as the 'event times', see Figure 10.1). The start of the transaction time is filled with the current time of the operation on the database. When a tuple is deleted, the tuple will not be physically erased from the database, but a finish for the transaction time will be filled with the current time of operation on the database. The two operations, to start and to finish, will actually change the states of affordances; that is why they are called substantive actions. The semiotic operations are done by the operators 'print' and 'report'. The former will direct the database output to be displayed onto the screen, and the latter will send information into a disk file to generate a report.

To demonstrate the basic shape of the LEGOL statements and the consequence operations, the following norms for the CRIS case (see Appendix B for the ontology model) are formulated below and the corresponding expressions in LEGOL are supplied in Table 10.3. More examples and query results can be found in Appendix B.

Norm 1: Any contributor of an abstract or member of TC or WG associated with the conference is eligible for the conference.

Norm 2: Any member of the OC, PC or any author of a selected paper has priority 1.

Norm 3: An invitation should be sent to the author within two weeks after his paper is selected.

As can be seen from the examples, the consequence part of the statements contains action operators, e.g. **start, finish,** and **report**; the condition part of the statements may involve many operators such as **while, while-not, or-while,** and so on. Some operators used in the condition part of the LEGOL statements will be discussed in the next sub-section.

Table 10.3. *Examples of LEGOL statements.*

1. (*contribution(person, abstract*) **while** *on(subject(WC#CRIS*-3*), abstract*))
    or-while (*membership(person, TC*) **while** *sponsors(WG(TC), WC#CRIS*-3))
    or-while (*membership(person, WG*) **while** *sponsors(WG, WC#CRIS*-3))
    start *eligible(person, WC#CRIS*-3).

    or   using role names:

    (*contributor(abstract*) **while** *on(subject(WC#CRIS*-3*), abstract*))
    or-while (*member(TC*) **while** *sponsors(TC(WG), WC#CRIS*-3))
    or-while (*member(WG*) **while** *sponsor(WC#CRIS*))
    start *eligible(person, WC#CRIS*-3).

2. *membership(person, OC(WC#CRIS*-3))
    or-while *membership(person, PC(WC#CRIS*-3))
    or-while (*contributes(person, paper*) **while** *selected(paper*))
    while *on(paper, subject(WC#CRIS*-3))
    start *priority(eligible(person, WC#CRIS*-3)) = 1.

3. (*contributor(paper*) **while** *on(paper, subject(WC#CRIS*-3)))
    within 2 *week* **after start-of** *selected(paper*)
    report 'invitation' *person, WC#CRIS*-3.

    and the control norm:

    (*contributor(paper*) **while** *on(paper, subject(WC#CRIS*-3)))
    while start-of *selected(paper*) **while-not** *invitation(person, WC#CRIS*-3)
    report 'invitation-delay' *person, WC#CRIS*-3.

10.4.2 Some important operations

Most of the operators appear in the condition part of LEGOL statements. If the consequence part is not explicitly mentioned, then the statement is a query and the result will be displayed on the default output terminal (i.e. the screen). The LEGOL operators involve two kinds of operations: a selection from the database contents and a calculation on the basis of time. Examples of the operators having explicitly strong relations to time are **while, while-not, after,** '**within** . . . **after**'; the ones having implicit relations to time are **whenever** and **whichever**. Another way to classify the operators is to put them into two groups according to the syntactic features, the unary operators and the binary operators, which will be a line for the following discussion on some LEGOL operators.[2]

Binary operators

The syntax of a binary operator is '<*operand*> <*binary-operator*> <*operand*>'. Only three binary operators will be discussed below; many

---

[2] In fact there are more LEGOL operators in addition to these two categories, e.g. 'between . . . and . . .'.

others, e.g. **when, whenever, whichever, after, before**, may directly appear in the text because they may even be understood without detailed explanations.

operator:	**while**
syntax:	x **while** y
semantics:	The 'x' and 'y' are affordances. The result is a complex type expressed in a tuple (x, y, event-start, event-finish). The interval indicated by the event-start and the event-finish results from the time intersection between x and y.
example:[3]	*person* **while** *membership(person, TC)*
	The question in natural language is 'who, during what period, is a member of a TC'.
	This query will show all the persons who are members of a TC. The event-time for each person will be the period while he is a member of a TC.
operator:	**or-while**
syntax:	x **or-while** y
semantics:	The 'x' and 'y' are affordances. The result is a complex type expressed in a tuple (x, y, event-start, and event-finish). The interval indicated by the event-start and the event-finish results from the time union between x and y.
example:	*membership(person, TC#2)* **or-while** *membership(person, TC#8)*
	The question in natural language is 'who, during what period, is a member of either TC2 or TC8'.
	This query will give a result of the persons who are members of either TC2 or TC8. The result contains the following items: 'person', 'membership', 'TC', 'event-start', and 'event-finish'.
operator:	**while-not**
syntax:	x **while-not** y
semantics:	The 'x' and 'y' are affordances. The result is a complex type expressed in a tuple (x, y, event-start, and event-finish). The interval indicated by the event-start and the event-finish results from the time exclusion of the existence of x by that of y.
example:	*national-org* **while-not** *membership(national-org, IFIP)*
	The question in natural language is 'which national

---

[3] Examples in this sub-section are based on the CRIS case; see Appendix B for more examples.

Temporal location of affordance   Operator

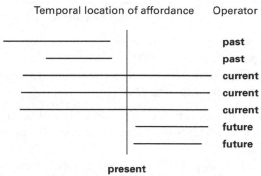

present
(the moment of the operation)

Figure 10.2. Temporal locations of affordances and operators.

(information processing) organisation after its creation, during what period, is not a member of IFIP'.
This query will produce a list containing the national information processing organisations that were not member organisations during certain periods. The listed organisations must now be IFIP member organisations which did not become IFIP members immediately after their creation.

Unary operators

A unary operator has an operand on the right. The syntactic usage of a unary operator is: '*<unary-operator> <operand>*'.

The three operators, **current**, **past** and **future**, select the particulars of the affordances in different states. The event start and the event finish times of a particular instance indicate one of the three states that the particular belongs to (as shown in Figure 10.2). The operator **current** will select the tuples in the database which have a start time in the past and a finish time in the future (with known or unknown exact times). The operator **past** will select the tuples with both a start time and a finish time in the past; and the operator **future** with a start time and a finish time in the future. These operators can be put in different places, hence have different effects. See the following LEGOL statements for examples.

Example Box 10.2: LEGOL statements

membership(national-org, IFIP)   (1)
current membership(national-org, IFIP)   (2)

Example Box 10.2 (*cont.*)

*membership(**current** national-org, IFIP)*   (3)
*membership(**past** national-org, IFIP)*   (4)
***future** membership(national-org, IFIP)*   (5)
*membership(**future** national-org, IFIP)*   (6)

The result of the execution of statement (1) will be all the national organisations which were, are and as far as we know will be IFIP members.

Statement (2) will give all the present membership of the IFIP members.

Statement (3) will show all the periods of membership in past, present and future of the current members (if a national organisation had been expelled from IFIP and then some time later re-admitted, this would appear as two separate instances of membership).

Statement (4) means the memberships of the national organisations which no longer exist.

Statement (5) shows which organisations IFIP expects to admit as members.

The last statement would show, if possible, that IFIP will (or may) admit a national organisation which will (or may) be founded in the future.

The operators of ***start-of*** and ***finish-of*** will produce the event time of the start and the finish of the affordances. For example, '*start-of membership(national-org#NGI, IFIP)*' will return a value of time '1962-01-04' supposing NGI was admitted by IFIP as a member on January 4, 1962. The operators **before** and **after** are defined as unary operators (notice they can be used as binary operators, e.g. '*WG(IFIP) **after** WG#WG8.1*'). If an expression in LEGOL is

***before** start-of membership(national-org#NGI, IFIP)*

the result of this statement can be a time interval up to the time when the organisation NGI became a member of IFIP, i.e. '—, 1962-01-03'.

Functions

There are functions defined in LEGOL such as arithmetical calculations and analytical functions. The analytical functions are grouped into two categories: diachronic and synchronic. The diachronic functions operate

Table 10.4. *LEGOL functions.*

Diachronic functions	Synchronic functions
count	number
accum	sum
highest/greatest	max
lowest/least	min

across the time horizon while the synchronic ones calculate the result with respect to the distribution over time. For example, the use of a diachronic function as in '*count member (IFIP)*' will summarise all the IFIP members over the complete IFIP history. The counted value will not decrease but only increase whenever there is a new member joining IFIP. The counterpart of *count* is the synchronic operator *number*. The use of '*number member (IFIP)*' will produce a list of present IFIP members distributed over the history.

The number will increase whenever there is a new member joining IFIP, and decrease when a member has left IFIP. The time periods in which the two types of functions calculate can be specified by operators associated in the same expressions. Table 10.4 summarises the analytical functions defined in LEGOL.

11

Normbase: a new approach to information management

Normbase is not just a software system. It represents a new way of managing information. It also represents a new approach to the development of information systems using semiotic methods. The chapter will introduce the concept of Normbase, and the Normbase system as a software environment for managing information. It will also discuss how the Normbase system can be used for supporting business management and decision-making.

11.1 The Normbase concept

Norms are parts of business knowledge that determine the meanings of the data in databases. The knowledge serves as a constraint upon the organisation and utilisation of the data. In order to allow only meaningful interpretations of and operations on the data, the knowledge must be consolidated into the technical information systems in a proper way.

The database discipline has established an approach to incorporating business knowledge into the technical information systems following the principle of data independence. Data independence, as one of the objects of database systems, provides an important separation between data and applications. It furnishes an immunity of application programs from changes of the data storage structure and access strategy (Date 1995). Data independence is achieved by isolating the domain-specific (knowledge) parts of the database system from the general (supporting) part. This process of knowledge abstraction can be applied not only to databases, but also to programming techniques. In object-oriented programming languages, the technique of abstract data types allows one to specify certain operations on a data type without having to affect the internal representation of the instances. In databases, the domain-specific knowledge is

150

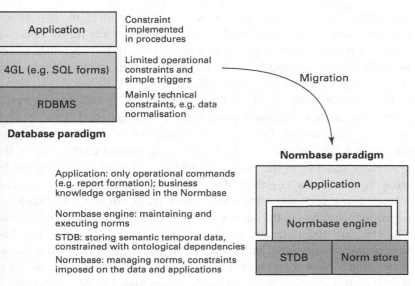

Figure 11.1. From database to Normbase.

represented in a *conceptual model*, which is typically stored in a *data dictionary*. Practice of database development normally follows the principle that the more 'knowledge' is put in the conceptual model, the less remains for the application programs (Weigand 1990).

Stamper *et al.* (1991) advocate a higher-level data and knowledge independence in information systems: a liberation of business knowledge from the application programs. After the evolution of techniques of information systems development being reviewed, a concept of the Normbase has been introduced in their paper. The Normbase structure will be created, as it states in the paper,

. . that will complete the separation of data management from applications programming, extend the distributed systems concepts, and also divide applications programming into parts that focus exclusively on knowledge of the organisation (expressed by the norms of teams, firms, social groups or nation states) or upon knowledge of how to exploit the technology.

The emergence of the Normbase system suggests a strategic advance in information systems development, which can be schematically summarised as in Figure 11.1. With the present database approach, business knowledge is interpreted as program semantics and reflected in application programs. The underlying part, DBMS, is only concerned with syntactic constraints, typically data normalisation. The database approach eliminates the dedication of the data to specific application domains; however, the application programs remain problem-specific. This means that any newly emerging application requirement implies a new application to be programmed; any modification of the requirement embedded in an existing application module may require an alteration in the application software.

This Normbase approach requires, first of all, an information model which reflects the most basic knowledge of the social world. The ontology model describes the most fundamental patterns of behaviour. The scope of the model is determined according to the requirements of the users of the system. In relation to the information model, the norms are elicited by studying the agents in action. The norms will be written formally and managed in a centralised knowledge base, the norm store. The data are organised according to the ontology model and stored in the surrogatebase. The standard database operations are available to the surrogates. The norms centrally managed in the normbase are treated in the same way as data but in a more complex structure. Standard operations, such as insertion, update, etc., are possible on the norms as well. The links between the surrogates and the norms are established and maintained by the Normbase engine. When any operation in the system takes place, the relevant norms will be invoked to check the consistency and validity.

The Normbase approach is not just a modified technical solution. It takes a revolutionary step toward a completely new paradigm of information management. It requires one to adopt the viewpoint that an organisation is an information system where people act within the constraints of norms. The objects managed in the technical information system are not just objective and timeless descriptions of the world, but are representations of agents in action based on subjective viewpoints. The Normbase system is an extension of the capacity of human agents which should always incorporate their changeable personal values and judgements.

11.2 The Normbase system

The Normbase system is a software environment for management of information and norms. These are the major software components of the Normbase system: the Normbase engine, the Semantic Temporal DataBase (STDB) and the norm store.

11.2.1 The Normbase engine

The Normbase engine is composed of a semantic analyser, a Norm Analyser, a LEGOL interpreter and other data management facilities.

Semantic Analyser

Semantic Analysis is the first step in setting up a Normbase for a particular application. The Semantic Analyser is a facility to assist a user to produce an information model and to design the database. The Semantic Analyser provides a knowledge-based semantic charter, which remembers and applies the knowledge of Semantic Analysis. Together with the description of the semantic units generated by a concordance generator, the Semantic Analyser can perform semantic checking on whether a user builds an ontology model correctly. The concordance generator is a specially designed text-processor for Semantic Analysis that takes a piece of text (a problem description) as input to produce a list of semantic units. One can then give descriptions to each semantic unit, for example whether it is an agent or affordance, and whether it is a role and in what relation this role is involved.

The Semantic Analyser opens an ontology chart editor window for a user. With the Semantic Analyser, the user can draw graphic entities on the ontology chart, link the lines between the entities, and modify and move the entities around in the window with the lines connected. The Semantic Analyser can optimise the connection lines if the user wishes. It also allows the user to edit the graphic entities and lines manually. A user can get the ontology chart created previously from the system storage onto the window. The user can also let the Normbase system produce a new ontology chart automatically with optimised positioning of the graphic entities.

Norm Analyser

Norm Analysis is the second important step in setting up a Normbase system for an application. The norms will be captured and represented through the norm analyser. In most cases, the norms are linked to the *universals* (universal concepts), though sometimes norms will have to be linked to *particulars* (particular instances). The norms to be captured in the normbase system are classified into three kinds.

  Constraint: defining status or relations other than ontological dependency. These norms specify the data consistency and legitimacy from the business point of view.

  Authority: defining authorities for the start and the finish of an affordance. The concepts of responsibility and authority are closely related. Unless the responsibility and authority are clear, a business can hardly be managed successfully.

Trigger: defining conditions and actions to be taken by responsible agents. Actions will be taken by the Normbase system as soon as the conditions are met, or messages will be produced to call for human actions.

LEGOL interpreter

The interpreter accepts LEGOL statements and translates into a series of appropriate actions. A LEGOL statement usually contains two parts. The first part supplies the conditions and the second part specifies a consequent which often results in an action. The actions can be as follows.

Retrieval of information according to requirements stated.

Evaluation of the state of affairs The interpreter takes into account the facts supplied in the statement and records in the system. The result of evaluation can be advised to the user immediately or recorded in the system.

Generation of an event The event can be producing an email message and sending it over the network, or sounding an alarm.

Notification, i.e. a message displayed on the user's screen.

11.2.2 The semantic temporal database

The Semantic Temporal DataBase (STDB) manages the data for the Normbase. It performs standard database operations, such as insertion, retrieval and update, and other services to the Normbase.

Generation of a database structure from a semantic model The semantic model generated by the semantic analyser is usually in the form of an ontology chart, though sometimes it can be a schema (a textual description). Once the semantic analyser has produced an ontology chart, it will be used as the conceptual model from which a database structure is generated automatically. The STDB has a uniform record structure, as discussed in Chapter 10. An illustration is given in Example Box 11.1.

Data management. STDB manages data according to the semantic models. The ontology chart defines ontological relationships between antecedents and dependants. This ontological consistency will be all the time maintained by STDB, and will be used to check every database operation, e.g. insertions and updates. All updates are non-destructive, which is achieved by using the concepts of action times and record times.

Example Box 11.1: Generation of an STDB from an ontology chart.

This example box shows a simple ontology chart (Figure 11.2). The ontology chart is then used as the basis to generate a STDB structure. See Table 11.1.

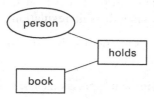

Figure 11.2. From database to Normbase.

Table 11.1.

srg-id	label	ant1	ant2	type	sort	act+	act−	...	...
1	person	0	0	u	a	0		...	...
2	book	0	0	u	af	0		...	...
3	holds	1	2	u	af	0		...	...

Only certain fields are shown in the database for illustration purposes. The surrogate identities (sur-id) are generated by the STDB as unique keys to each record. The labels contain the three concepts in the ontology chart. All three records are universals, indicated by 'u' in the field *type,* one agent – person– and two other affordances, as indicated in the field *sort* by 'a' and 'af'. The *antecedent* fields (ant1 and ant2) tell that the concept *holds* ontologically depends on *person* and *book*. All start times of action *(act +)* are zero, which means these concepts came into existence a long time ago. The unmarked finish times of action *(act −)* indicate these concepts are still valid (as opposed to a known finish time which means an invalidity).

11.2.3 *The norm store*

The norms are kept in the norm store. The same as the data in the STDB, each norm has a unique identity number. Each also has a start time and a finish to identify the validity period. Norms can be inserted and updated, in a non-destructive way, as data. Norms function as conditions and constraints for the system operations. All the norms are coupled with appropriate affordances in the STDB. The functions of the norm store are to maintain the consistency of the norms and invoke appropriate norms whenever the Normbase performs an action.

Example Box 11.2: Norms in the norm store.

Suppose we are in the context of a person borrowing books from a library, this is a norm (a membership regulation).

If a person already holds ten books, then that person is not allowed to borrow more.

This can be translated into an expression close to LEGOL:

Whenever *count(holds(person, book))* >= 10,
The person is not allowed to borrow.

In LEGOL, it reads like this:

Whenever count(*holds(person, book)***))** >=10
Forbidden *to start holds(person, book)*

The boldface words are LEGOL operators or system reserved words. The LEGOL operator *count* is a synchronous operator which will check at this point of time how many instances of *holds(person, book)* a particular person has. If it reaches 10, then the system will forbid us to insert (i.e. *to start*) a new record of *holds(person, book)*.

This norm is coupled with the concept *holds* in STDB. This entails that every time there is an operation *to start holds(person, book)* in the STDB, this norm will be invoked to check the legality.

11.3 Information management with the Normbase system

The Normbase system is a software environment to support the semiotic approach to information systems development. It enables one to conduct activities at all stages of the development of an information system.

Semantic modelling and Norm Analysis The semantic analyser assists the user to conduct a Semantic Analysis, starting from a problem description, to an ontology chart. The semantic analyser, following the principles and steps of the method of Semantic Analysis, prompts appropriate templates and questions to guide the user through an analysis. It performs all kinds of checking during the analysis, such as ontological consistency, generic–specific, role, and so on.

The norm analyser provides an environment for specifying norms and entering norms into the norm store. It also enables one to specify the coupling between the norms and relevant agents and affordances in the STDB.

Populating STDB Once a Semantic Analysis is completed, a STDB will be generated from the ontology chart. To populate the STDB, the Normbase system provides a multifunctional browser by which one can enter instances of affordances into the STDB. As determined by the nature of the STDB, to insert a record of a particular affordance is *to start* an instance of that affordance, while to delete a record is *to finish* an instance of an affordance.

Information retrieval One can retrieve information from the Normbase system with the multifunctional browser. The browser can be used for data entry as well as data retrieval. Another way to get information is to write commands in LEGOL. In this case, one can write very sophisticated expressions using time-bounding operators such as *while, or-while, while-not*, and other functions. However, for users who do not wish to write queries in LEGOL, there is a query-by-table facility where the users can select items and then specify criteria in a user-friendly manner.

Management and decision support The norms in the system can function as triggers; therefore the system can proactively support management and decision-making activities. The Normbase checks every operation, internal and external event. The events include input from a user or from another connected system, advance of a time clock, and change of the value of a record. The system evaluates the norms against the current state of affairs in an organisation, and can take actions or prompt relevant agents to act if necessary. In this way, the Normbase can be used as an assistant to a manager, or can be delegated to control some business processes.

11.4 Using semiotic methods with other approaches

In a project of information systems development, one can use the semiotic methods presented in this book in conjunction with other methods and approaches. As one may have experienced with object-oriented methods, a project can use methods of OO analysis and design, but use non-OO programming languages to implement the system (for example, C). The reasons for doing this may be that these OO methods bring some benefit in analysis and design, but a non-OO programming language may result in operational efficiency. Nevertheless, most of the OO methods are language independent, which lends the possibility of choosing any conventional language for implementation.

Table 11.2. *Combining semiotic and other methods.*

IS development activities	Option 1	Option 2	Option 3	Option 4
Requirement analysis	SAM, NAM	SAM, NAM	SAM, NAM	SAM, NAM
Systems analysis	SAM, NAM	SAM, NAM	SAM, NAM	other methods, e.g. OO or structured analysis
Systems design	SAM, NAM	SAM, NAM	other methods, e.g. OO or structured design, E–R	other methods (see the entry on the left)
Systems implementation	NB	other methods, e.g. OO or other languages, CASE tools	other methods (see the entry on the left)	other methods (see the entry on the left)

The semiotic methods can be used for systems analysis and design, and then followed by other approaches. Or, even, one adopts the semiotic methods for analysis only, then applies OO or other approaches. If a process of IS development is identified as activities in four stages, these are viable permutations (Table 11.2).

Option 1 adopts semiotic methods to cover all the stages of IS development, which involves the Semantic Analysis Method (SAM) and Norm Analysis Method (NAM) in the analysis and design stages and the Normbase system in the implementation. Other options involve semiotic methods in various early states and other methods later. It is worth mentioning that the semiotic methods such as Semantic Analysis and Norm Analysis will give a great added value to an information system project even if they are only used in the analysis stages. This is because these semiotic methods can help one to understand and articulate the requirements better, and produce systems analysis in a more rigorous way. The requirements and systems analysis are essential to the success of an information system project, as discussed early on in this book.

11.4.1 Relational database for implementation

The function of a semantic model is not only for constructing an information system. The main strength of the semantic modelling is to represent the user's requirements in a precise and formal way so that the undesired omission and misunderstanding of the requirements can be detected and avoided. After an information model is obtained with the help of Semantic Analysis, one of the most critical parts of a system development project is completed. Therefore, a significant benefit is still gained even if one continues the design and implementation with other methods.

For demonstration purposes, a computerised prototype information system has been built using ORACLE *forms* for the CRIS studies. Surprisingly, the semantic model could be almost directly implemented with the relational database tools though some slight modifications were needed. The database of the prototype was composed of five relational tables (Thönissen 1990) so that the features of the canonical surrogatebase are accommodated. Four tables out of the five are worth mentioning below:

the *surrogates* – containing the intrinsic properties;
the *relations* – retaining the ontological dependencies between the affordances;
the *norms* – storing the norms specified in English and LEGOL;
the *agenda* – holding the triggering norms for actions to be taken in the future.

Another example of using relational database technology in combination with the Semantic Analysis is the administration system in the University of Qatar (Ades 1989). The systems analysis work on the computerised administration system was done with Semantic Analysis and the implementation was fully on a relational database language of WANG. One of the advantages of the approach adopted in the project is reportedly the complete coverage of the requirement and the clear specification.

11.4.2 Object-oriented methods for design and implementation

A natural alternative way of systems construction is the object-oriented (OO) approach because of the similarities in viewing objects in the OO approach and in handling affordances in the other.

Object-oriented design

Principles of object orientation were first conceived in programming languages for systems implementation, and they have been further adopted into the areas of analysis and design. The advantages of object orientation in systems design and implementation have been clarified in many works (e.g., Booch (1994), Coad & Yourdon (1990), Micallef 1988)). But as pointed out by van de Weg and Engmann (1992), the techniques and underlying principles of object-oriented analysis and design are not well understood and are still at an immature stage. To an extent, this observation still remains valid, although there have been some new developments in analysis and design methods recently (Booch 1994, Coad & Yourdon 1990, Embley *et al.* 1992, Shlaer & Mellor 1988, 1992). A recent most exciting OO method is UML (Booch *et al.* 1998). As a result of combined work from a number of authorities in the OO field, UML offers a set of comprehensive techniques and supporting tools for object-oriented systems design. But UML never claims to be particularly strong in user requirements analysis.

Some insufficiencies in analysis methods have been observed in the OO methods. For example, Coad and Yourdon (1990) offer a clear method of analysis which consists of five major steps: identifying objects, identifying structures, defining subjects, defining attributes and instance connections, and the last step, defining services and message connections. But the method does not give a sufficient account of how to elicit and represent user requirements in a concise and understandable form for the user. Most analysis methods are based on an assumption that there is a given list of user requirements, so the task of analysts is to represent the requirement in data models. The most often used modelling methods for object-oriented systems development are the extended E–R method and structured method.[1] These approaches to requirement analysis and modelling put a lot of emphasis on logical data organisation. But they do not question at all these important issues: Are the requirements 'given' by the user correct? Is what is said what is really wanted? Is the understanding of what is said correct? Is there is a twist or distortion that may be caused by the analyst's misinterpretation?

The Semantic Analysis method takes especially into account the problem of language semantics that may arise during the requirement elicitation and analysis. The method provides a formal way of representing user requirements in a succinct form which can be easily understood by the user and subjected to the user's critical examination. Therefore, verification at the analysis stage can be realised and this will, to a large extent, guarantee a fundamentally sound basis for the rest of the work in the system development lifecycle. The object-oriented design can be made on the basis of the analysis result. For this purpose a set of transformation rules is provided so that an object-oriented design can be smoothly derived from the result of analysis, and further constructed using object-oriented programming tools.

---

[1] The E–R method can be best represented by Chen (1976), the structured method by Yourdon & Constantine (1979) and Yourdon (1989).

From Semantic Analysis to OO design

To conduct a Semantic Analysis is to capture and articulate user requirements. The semantic model produced from the analysis tells what objects are needed and the semantics of the objects. However, the model does not readily lend itself to implementation. It needs a transformation in order to derive an object-oriented design.

The three principles of transformation from a semantic model to an OO design are as follows:

Principle 1: *All information in a semantic model must be used in derivation of a design. Any alteration of the semantic model must be approved by the user.*

The semantic model reflects a conceptualisation of the problem. It results from the consensus between the analysts and users. Sometimes there may be more than one user group involved in the project coming from different professional backgrounds. Therefore, the semantic model serves as a kind of document with authority for the following system development activities.

Principle 2: *There are mapping rules between terms in the semantic model and the object-oriented design:*

agents, entity-like affordances	*→ objects;*
determiners	*→ attributes;*
action–like affordances	*→ communications between objects;*
roles	*→ attributes and static subset constraints;*
whole-part relation	*→ nested or separate objects (depending on the programming language);*
generic–specific	*→ object inheritance.*

The semantic definition of each affordance is determined in the semantic model. The definition includes attributes and actions of an object, and interactions between objects. All information contained in the semantic model can be useful in producing the design model. For example, a role name in the semantic model would suggest a synonym; in an OO design, it can be treated as an attribute if the synonym is required. It also suggests a subset of the role-carrier, because, e.g., teachers consist of a subset of persons. Roles are defined by certain rules and are represented in the OO design as constraints.

Principle 3: *Norms associated with the semantic model must be satisfied as conditions and dynamic constraints for actions between objects.*

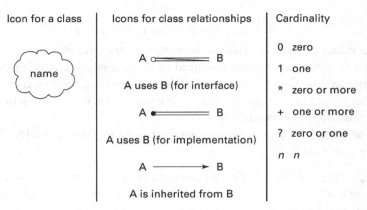

Icon for a class	Icons for class relationships	Cardinality
name	A ⊸══════ B A uses B (for interface) A ●══════ B A uses B (for implementation) A ─────→ B A is inherited from B	0 zero 1 one * zero or more + one or more ? zero or one *n* *n*

Figure 11.3. Design notations (based on Booch (1994)).

Some actions should be taken if the conditions are met. These conditional norms are called triggers. The norms are prescriptive in the sense that they instruct agents when and what actions 'must', 'may', and 'may not' be performed. These norms will be used as constraints incorporated into objects for controlling their behaviour.

The design of the system is basically meant here as the design of a single program which is similar to an Ada or VMS task or a Unix process, as the same definition is used by Shlaer and Mellor (1992). They suggest that there are four significant aspects of design which are class diagram, class structure, class dependency, and class inheritance. This general direction has been followed in developing this design method. However, much simplification has been made for practical purposes. In the proposed design method, three major aspects are defined, which are *class description*, *inter-class communication*, and *inheritance*. An introduction to these three aspects will be given in this section (illustrations of the application of the method will be found in Chapter 13 on the CONTEST system development).

A class description consists basically of *logical components*, *functions*, and *state transitions*. The *logical components* of a class are defined using the class template which is composed of a class-name, brief explanation of the functions, visibility (exported/private/imported), cardinality (0/1/*n*), hierarchy (super-classes, meta-class), interface, implementation, lifecycle, etc. The specification of the interface must indicate authority over the attributes and member functions by specifying whether they are public, protected or private, and stating the clients and servers of the classes. The *functions*

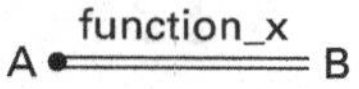

function_x
A •————————— B

Figure 11.4. Class A uses Class B.

are specified with the following elements: name, nature of the function (public, protected or private), input and its data-type, output and its data-type, the states of the class before and after the invocation of the function, other classes involved in performing the function (client and server classes), etc. The *states* of a class are specified by the state transition diagrams on which a class can be led from one state to another by invoking associated actions. The actions are normally reflected in functions, either the member functions of the class or friend functions of other classes.

There is a variety of relationships that are meaningful among classes, including inheritance, using, instantiation, and meta-class relationships (Booch 1994). The most important relationship is communication which can be modelled with inter-class communication diagrams. Figure 11.3 shows some example notations for modelling relationships. In an inter-class communication diagram, the two 'A uses B' notations are employed to indicate the using relationship in terms of sending messages by invoking certain functions. The function names will be placed along the linkage lines. For example, the diagram in Figure 11.4 means class A uses class B by invoking function_x, and B is used in A's implementation. The ways of invoking functions should be specified in the class description.

The class inheritance is illustrated by diagrams to show inheritance relationships between the parents and children classes, for which the arrow is used, as in the notation shown in Figure 11.3. Logical components of both the parents and children classes designed with the class template should be used in association with the class inheritance diagram in order to know exactly the inherited part.

Once an object-oriented design is completed, the implementation can be done in any object oriented, or even any conventional, programming language.

12

Case study: development of a land resources information system

In this chapter, the application of Semantic Analysis, Norm Analysis and the Normbase system in the development of a land resource information system offers an example of adopting the semiotic approach to cover activities of all stages of information systems development.[1]

12.1 Background

The assignment was originally for students in a postgraduate GIS (geographic information systems) course at the International Institute for Aerospace Survey and Earth Science, the Netherlands. The course participants, after having worked in different disciplinary fields for many years, came from all over the world. They were supposed to use some structured method to carry out the systems analysis and design. The purpose of applying the semiotic methods was originally for a simple comparison between different approaches. However, for the purposes of this chapter, the analysis and design with the other approach will not be presented.

The objective of the case is to develop an information system for management of land resources, for an imaginary country, Snake Island. This project represents a typical type of information systems that are currently in high demand in many countries, especially the developing countries. Developing such a system requires tremendous effort, because very often such a system involves a heavy investment on expressive GIS hardware and software, and a costly multidisciplinary team of experts. On the other hand, such a system normally has a significant political, economic or other impact on the region that the system is supposed to serve. Therefore it is important to have an effective methodology for system development, cover-

[1] Part of this chapter was presented by Liu and Stamper in a workshop in GIS in Wuhan, 1991.

ing requirement analysis and specification, system design and implementation.

Brief description of the problem

Snake Island is an imaginary beautiful country situated in the middle of the South Pacific. It has bare mountains, green hills, agricultural plateaux, flood hazard areas, and smooth beaches. The land resources are mainly used for urban, agricultural, and tourism purposes.

Due to the fast rate of economic development, the Land Register offices encounter great difficulties in timely and correct registration of rights on land and buildings for planning, management and taxation. Therefore the central government of Snake Island formed an inter-departmental commission to develop a 'Multi-purpose Cadastral Information System'. The proposed information system has the following objectives:

(1) to help the Land Registers to keep the information about the ownership of land and buildings up to date;
(2) to automate the preparation of 'homogeneous zoning maps' for the Department of Valuation of Agricultural Land;
(3) to help the Land Tax Department in preparing the 'tax bills' to be sent to all owners of the land to be taxed;
(4) to assist in preparing information for the Warning and Evaluation plans required by the 'Safety and Emergency Department'.

12.2 Semantic Analysis for requirements modelling

The Semantic Analysis method is used to produce semantic models (or ontology charts).

Starting point – the problem definition

The analysis normally begins with a written problem definition. The problem definition may sometimes just be written not precisely enough. It will be partial, usually with a measure of vagueness, and not infrequently containing contradictions. A set of techniques for 'problem articulation' can be employed to extend the problem definition (see Kolkman (1995)), if it is necessary. It is rare to find a satisfactory problem definition in a written document.

Study problem definition

Semantic Analysis must begin with such a defective problem definition as an input file. But it is recommended in this step to have sufficient assistance from users for understanding the problem. The method of analysis systematically leads to the clarification of the problem and it increases the mutual understanding among the users. There are criteria for identifying progressively larger swathes of the problem for analysis. For example, initially attention is focused on the substantive aspects of the problem, that is, excluding the issues of control and message passing. The whole procedure will be iterated, gradually increasing the scope of the problem being examined.

In our study case, the case document was the problem definition, where the nature of the problem, system users, and requirements are stated.

Identify semantic units

This step is something like lexical analysis on the problem definition. In this step, the problem definition is taken as input; the output is a list of phrases having specific meanings in their context. This is the list obtained after having conducted the analysis at this stage:

province
district
village
person
owner
ownership
land   (incomplete knowledge)
tax   (incomplete knowledge)
Department of Valuation of Agricultural Land
Safety and Emergency Department
Cadastral Survey Department
Department of Land Tax
. . .

As listed, there is incompleteness of knowledge about some semantic units, which suggests some more effort on eliciting knowledge in these aspects. For example, 'land' is such an item on the list. It seems obviously important. But the precise meaning of 'land' is not so clear; what information about 'land' should be modelled may not be fully understood. To know these, more knowledge about 'land' should be obtained either from studying available documents or from interviewing the problem-owner.

After some more effort, more knowledge about 'land' is gained. Therefore, the following list of semantic units can replace 'land' on the previous list:

land-unit
parcel
agricultural parcel
urban parcel
. . .

And the following list can replace 'tax':

tax-rate
tax-bill

Classify semantic units

The terms on the list can be analysed in several categories.

Agent–affordance In a social system, all phenomena can be classified into two categories: agents who can do actions themselves, and affordances which are actions or results of actions of those agents. The agents construct the whole social world; the agents can hold responsibilities for their actions.

Universal–particular The concept of universal–particular is similar to type–instance in other analysis methods. In an information analysis, one should describe properties of a type of things, rather than a particular instance, unless some particulars are so nearly unique and so important that they have to be described specially. In our case study, the departments, such as Land Tax, Valuation of Agricultural Land, etc., are particulars, but they have to be treated specially in the model.

Generic–specific Many phenomena in a social world may fall into a generic–specific structure. The specifics then inherit properties of the generics. For example, in our case, the land parcel is a generic concept, while the agricultural parcel and urban parcel are specifics of the generic concept 'parcel'. The same kind of structure applies to various departments.

Whole–part Some phenomena only exist as parts of a whole, through which we come to know them. This is the whole–part relationship. For example, in the case of an administrative structure, a district is a part of a province and a village is a part of a district. Similarly, a street exists as part of a settlement but not independently. However, in the case of geographical areas, the parts pre-exist the administrative areas to which they are allocated and, in this case, we do not have the whole–part relationship but simply an assembly of components.

Role-carrier–role-name Some agents may be involved in certain actions, where the agents are the role-carriers and have certain role-names. For example, a person may own one or more land parcels, and then he is an owner of the parcel. The relationship between the person and the owned parcel is called ownership.

After having classified the semantic units, the following list is produced:

administration	universal	agent	generic for province etc
province	universal	agent	whole for district
district	universal	agent	part of prov., whole for village
village	universal	agent	part of district
person	universal	agent	
owner		role-name	person & land ownership
ownership	universal	affordance	
land-unit	universal	affordance	
parcel	universal	affordance	generic for agri. & urban parcels
agricultural parcel	universal	affordance	a kind of parcel
urban parcel	universal	affordance	a kind of parcel
tax-rate	universal	determiner	
tax-bill	universal	affordance	
Department of Valuation of Agricultural Land		particular	agent
Safety and Emergency Department		particular	agent
Cadastral Survey Department	particular	agent	
Department of Land Tax		particular	agent

. . .

Identify ontological dependencies

The ontological dependencies between phenomena are essential conceptually in Semantic Analysis. If one thing y exists only while x does, then the dependence between them is defined as an ontological dependency. In NORMA, it is denoted by

x —— y

indicating y ontologically depends on x. Note the relative positions of x and y: the right item is a dependant, whereas the left item is an antecedent.

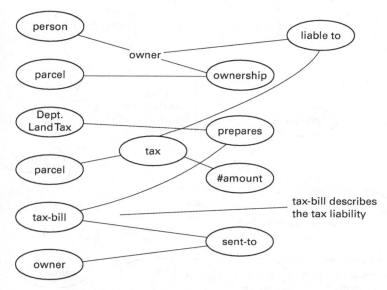

Figure 12.1. Ontological dependencies in fragments.

Using NORMA syntax, the ontological relationships between the semantic units can be modelled as many fragments, as illustrated in Figure 12.1.

The process of constructing these fragments is actually to put each term in its context with respect to ontological constraints. In this way each term has to be assigned a clear meaning. The meanings of the terms are not only clear to the analyst, but also clear to the problem-owner. If there is any misunderstanding of the meaning of a term, it can be easily identified by the problem-owner. Therefore both the analyst and the problem-owner can cooperatively improve the problem definition or clarify the semantics of the terms used in defining the problem through more interactions.

Complete the semantic model

The activity in this step is to assemble the fragments of knowledge into a complete picture. The complete picture, a semantic information model, describes the users' requirements in a formal NORMA syntax, which in itself is a design of the database, and can be directly put into implementation (see the section on design and implementation). The semantic information model of Snake Island is presented in Figure 12.2.

The model is not claimed to be complete in covering all requirements given by the problem definition. Some parts are not detailed enough, e.g.,

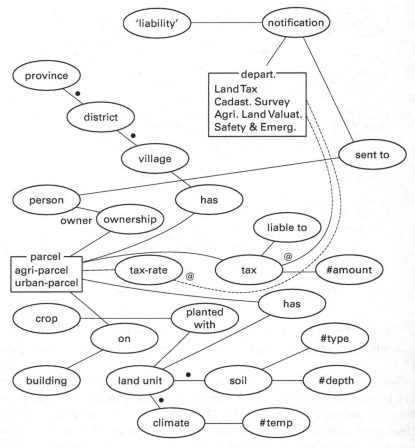

Figure 12.2. The semantic model of Snake Island.

land unit properties, information about parcels. They can be easily added to the model. However, a substantial part of the requirements is covered in this model.

To guide readers to read the essential parts of the model, an explanation of some parts of the model is given as follows.

A district is a part of a province; a village is a part of a district (indicated by a line with a dot attached).

All the four specific departments belong to the generic type of 'department'; but a specific department of Land Tax prepares the tax bills, and another one, Agricultural Land Valuation, determines the tax-rates of land parcels.

A person, as an owner, may have ownership of a parcel which may specifically be an agricultural parcel or an urban parcel. An agricultural parcel (but not an urban parcel) may have several land units; a land unit may be planted with many kinds of crops, and so on. The affordance 'liability' is a sign representing the legal liability and, of course, a tax-bill is just a sign to notify a person of his liability.

Check the model

This is a task for both the analyst and the user. The analyst should present the model and explain what is meant by the model to the user. Very often, the semantic problems may still be discovered in this step, therefore this step serves as not only a simple logic check, but also a continuation of the knowledge elicitation and semantic clarification. Be prepared for the possibility that this step may lead to a modification of some results of previous steps.

12.3 Norm Analysis

The semantic model describes the agents and their possible actions in terms of ontological dependencies, which are a kind of fundamental relationships. Norms, in addition to the knowledge represented in the semantic model, specify the details of these possibilities of behaviours; e.g., the conditions where the actions must happen or where they are actually impossible. The norms are less stable than the ontological relationships because they are determined less by the underlying culture established in the community or organisation, and more by organisational expediency.

Types of norms

Norms can be categorised in a variety of ways (Stamper 1980). We distinguish, for example, between action norms, which direct or permit action, and structure norms, which define the hierarchical norm structure and say when the different branches should be applied.

The action norms subdivide into five main types which control very different kinds of actions:

standing orders	change the physical world
status norms	change the social world
powers of intervention	invoke or inhibit the use of existing norms
powers of legislation	change the norm structure itself
structure norms	define the relationship between norms

Standing order Standing orders state the conditions under which some concrete action *should, should not* or *may* take place. A computer can perform the action if it has the appropriate electro-mechanical devices but, normally, a person will have to do the job. In the case of sending messages we can use the computer to implement the standing order.

Example norm 1:

'The owner or principal owner of a parcel of land should be sent a bill for the tax on that parcel at least four weeks before the tax becomes due.'

Such a norm can be almost totally automated by the selection of relevant people, parcels, and tax liabilities and by reference to the clock. The bill is just a document that contains these details with a request for payment. Someone will probably have to put the bills into the post when the computer has printed them! The action involved is semiological and computers are primarily devices for processing signs.

Status norms Status norms define the legal and social status of the agents and the actions. These norms give the conditions in which certain kinds of legal status exist. Examples for this kind of norms are given below.

Example norm 2:

'If a parcel is owned by more than one person, the owner having the largest share shall be the principal owner, otherwise any one of them may be so designated.'

This norm defines the status of a person to whom the tax-bill should be sent in cases where there might be confusion. Nothing happens until the status constructed is employed in a standing order.

Example norm 3:

'If a parcel is owned by more than one person, each one shall be liable to pay the whole of the tax on the parcel until full payment has been received by the relevant authority.'

This creates a number of liabilities, which will normally be discharged by the principal owner collecting the shares of the tax and paying the bill. It creates a social structure that will simplify the administration and generate pressures among the relevant group to solve their problems of jointly administering their shared ownership in whatever way they choose. The formal system involves no concrete action.

Powers of intervention Powers of intervention allow parts of the law to be brought into action or taken out of operation. They are like substations on an electrical power-distribution grid, enabling parts of the network to be 'switched off' and 'switched on'.

Example norm 4:

'Agricultural parcels which are in erosion or flood hazard areas, upon application by the owner, may be exempted from land tax at the discretion of the District Land Tax Inspector.'

This norm creates discretionary power to be exercised by a person in a designated role. A land parcel may be exempted from being taxed, though the principle remains that every parcel should be taxed.

Example norm 5:

'A claim for exemption from land tax under norm 4, if not allowed, may be submitted on appeal to the District Land Tribunal.'

This safeguards against a corrupt tax official by creating a supervisory power of intervention.

Powers of legislation The powers of legislation define the powers of changing or creating laws and legislative procedures.

Example norm 6:

'A District Land Tribunal shall specify locally appropriate procedures for the conduct of appeals concerning exemptions from tax liability.'

They have to perform an action of making norms, an action that is several steps removed from concrete acts for which standing orders will generate the necessary commands.

Example norm 7:

'The Minister of Land Resources shall inspect the appeals procedures of the various District Land Tribunals and issue any necessary regulations concerning the conduct of appeals in order to maintain administrative efficiency.'

Here the minister is empowered to make norms within constraints that, in principle, the courts could impose if he made norms that did not help to maintain efficiency.

Structure norms are the norms about norms. The structure norms consist of a condition clause determining when a set of norms should be applied. Unlike powers of intervention, structure norms are categorical and do not introduce discretion; they function simply to represent a logical feature of the norm hierarchy.

Example norm 8:

'For the purposes of assessing liability to land tax, the extent and location of erosion or flood hazard areas shall be determined in accordance with the provisions of the Agricultural Development (Marginal Areas) Act 1976.'

Locus of structure – semantic model versus norm structure

Many conventional information systems built upon the foundation of a relational database prove to be uncomfortably rigid in practice, when faced by organisational changes. One of the commonest reasons for this is the tendency to incorporate into the database schema features that are relatively superficial. These flexible features are norms rather than semantic structures. For example, Example norm 3 above establishes, in effect, that a liability to land tax cannot be subdivided into parts but it is not inconceivable that the law could be changed in order to allow this. The problem for the designer is whether to treat the individuality as a feature for the schema or as one to be handled by the application programmes. Decisions of this kind are not always easy but the preferred solution is always to treat constraints that are not ontologically necessary as being defined by norms. In the Snake Island problem we are studying here there is a case in point.

Example norm 9:
'No building shall be erected on an agricultural parcel of land.'

This may be incorporated into the model by giving a building a relation 'on' that is confined to urban parcels, and not to the other kinds of parcels.

Identification of norms

Sometimes we can build computer systems to support the administration of existing legislation, codes or regulations. This gives us an obvious way of identifying the norms that must be built into the system. However, it does not guarantee that the norm system will be complete. Here the semantic model gives us valuable support as a checklist. Once the semantic model is obtained, the boundary of the requirements is clear but, also, the items specified in the semantic model identify all the norms required for their regulation. This is because the norms are the elements of the system specification that define the dynamics and we can associate with each element in the model the start and finish events. Every one of these events must have its (formal or informal) governing norm. These norms can be as complex as the problem domain requires.

12.4 System design and implementation in the Normbase approach

The Normbase system can assist one to achieve the following:

accepting a semantic model as an input,
automatically turning the model into a time-based database design,

helping users to capture data with a user-friendly interface and consistency checking,

offering users standard application tools, e.g., query and report,

simplifying system maintenance.

12.4.1 From semantic model to database design

In the Normbase system, there are predefined meta-classes. Each meta-class has a standard data structure. As soon as the semantic model is input into the Normbase system, all the agents and affordances have their predefined data types. The ontological dependency relationships in the model are also captured in the system. The ontological dependencies are established between particulars as well as between universals. For example, in the land resources information system, there are universal relationships between the universals 'person' and 'parcel'. And, at the particular level, there are particular persons and particular parcels between which there are particular ownerships.

STDB

The STDB as a kernel part of the Normbase system handles data in a structure that incorporates periods of existence (*start time* and *finish time*) as their attributes. For data manipulation purposes, a time-based language, LEGOL, is employed. It can be used for two purposes: to write queries and to write norms.

Queries

Most LEGOL operators are time related, for example, the operators **while**, **or-while**, and **while-not**. When these operators are used, they perform operations in two aspects, i.e. set operation and time operation. The following examples will illustrate how the LEGOL operators work in performing queries on the database.

Based on the semantic model in Figure 12.2, suppose the user has the following questions:

<u>Question 1</u>: Who owns at least both one agricultural parcel and one urban parcel at the same time?

<u>Question 2</u>: Which parcels did/do not have buildings on?

<u>Question 3</u>: Which urban parcel had the highest tax-rate last year? And any time up till this year?

<u>Question 4</u>: Has anyone been notified of their tax liability more than three months after becoming liable?

These questions can be translated into queries in LEGOL as follows.

Query for the question 1:

ownership(person, agri-parcel) **while** *ownership(person, urban-parcel)*

Or using role-names in the query,

person **while** *owner(agri-parcel)* **while** *owner(urban-parcel)*.

These two queries will return the following information:

the persons who own at least one agricultural parcel and at least one urban parcel at the same time;

the particular agricultural parcels and urban parcels those persons own; and

the periods of these ownerships over the parcels.

Query for the question 2:

urban-parcel **while-not** *on(building, urban-parcel)*

This query will tell which urban parcels, in which time periods, did/do not have buildings on them.

The query below, however, can generate the answer to a question like 'Which urban parcels have never had buildings on?':

urban-parcel **where-never** *on(building, urban-parcel)*

Query for the question 3:

highest *tax-rate(parcel)* **while last** *year*

The last query will tell us the parcels with the highest tax-rate last year. But the next one,

highest *tax-rate(parcel)*,

will tell us the parcels with the highest tax-rate over the whole recorded history of the tax regime.

Notice, in the semantic model in Figure 12.2, there are hash signs before *amount, type, depth* and *temp.* to indicate they are determiners (i.e., a generalisation of the measurement concept). With a numerical determiner, it is possible to use the functions like **highest, max**, etc.

Query for question 4:

start-of *sent-to(owner, notification("liability"))* **after** (3 *month* + **start-of**(*liability*)

In the LEGOL expression, **start-of** is an operator which gets the start time of its operand, i.e. 'sent-to', and 'liability'. Also **after** is an operator which produces a valid time period after a given time point, and then performs a joint operation on its left and right operands.

Norms

Norms can be written in LEGOL. These norms are then stored in the Normbase system and they are linked to the relevant agents and affordances in the database. The linked norms can serve two purposes:

As constraints to check operations on the data items. For example, Example norm 4 listed earlier should be linked to the agricultural parcel. When the tax-rate is determined on the parcels, that norm 4 has to be evaluated to see if the parcel has an exemption from tax or an outstanding application for exemption.

As triggering norms to prompt actions. These actions may be of two kinds. One is automatic change of data in the database, which is done by the norm triggering mechanism within the Normbase system. For example, if there is a tax-calculation norm written in LEGOL attached to the tax-rate, the tax-rate can then be calculated automatically according to the updated information about the parcel, which is kept in the system. The other kind of triggering action is to produce messages to users, prompting them to perform the necessary action in the business world.

Generation of a STDB

In the Normbase system, the records that keep information about agents and affordances are called surrogates. All the surrogates have a uniform data structure. Below there is a definition of the surrogate as it is implemented in the existing version of the system.

$$surrogate := \;< surrogate\text{-}identity, type, sort, label, antecedent\text{-}1,$$
$$antecedent\text{-}2, start\text{-}time, finish\text{-}time >$$

Keeping historical data

Sometimes to keep historical data in databases has significance, especially in the application domains where legal responsibility is much concerned. These are domains like banking, contracting, government affairs, as well as land resources management. The Normbase system offers a kind of database able to keep all the historical data. This is realised as in the example demonstrated below.

Suppose in the database there are three surrogates as follows, in which x1, x2 and x3 are values of the tax-rates for land parcel p0:

<201, *<particular>*, *<tax-rate>*, x1, *<parcel#*p0>, 1-7-1988, 30-6-1989>
<502, *<particular>*, *<tax-rate>*, x2, *<parcel#*p0>, 1-7-1989, 30-6-1990>
<803, *<particular>*, *<tax-rate>*, x3, *<parcel#*p0>, 1-7-1990, 30-6-1991>

These surrogates will give historical information on the tax-rate for the land parcel p0 over the last few years.

Non-destructive update

The Normbase system adopts a non-destructive way of updating. Two kinds of time are recognised and treated in the Normbase system, the event time and the transaction time. The event time is to record the existence of a happening in a real world, such as the start time and finish time used in the surrogates. The transaction time is to indicate when a surrogate is inserted into the database and when it is updated. But the surrogate to be updated will not be removed from the database.

The Normbase system realises this non-destructive updating by attaching a transaction time tuple to each surrogate, as illustrated below.

data-record := <surrogate, transaction-time >,   where
transaction-time := <transaction-start, transaction-finish>.

Suppose there are the following data records in the database about a land parcel p0.

<201, *<particular>*, *<tax-rate>*, x1, *<parcel#*p0>, 1-7-1988, 30-6-1989>
   <1-7-1988, ->
<502, *<particular>*, *<tax-rate>*, x2, *<parcel#*p0>, 1-7-1989, 30-6-1990>
   <1-7-1989, 2-7-1989>
<502, *<particular>*, *<tax-rate>*, x3, *<parcel#*p0>, 1-7-1989, 30-6-1990>
   <2-7-1989, ->
<803, *<particular>*, *<tax-rate>*, x4, *<parcel#*p0>, 1-7-1990, 30-6-1991>
   <1-7-1990, ->

Notice the second and the third data records are almost the same, but with different values of tax-rate and transaction time. The reason for this may be that the tax-rate for the parcel p0 for the period 1-7-1989 till 30-6-1990 was first entered into the database on 1-7-1989, but it was discovered it should be x3 and corrected on 2-7-1989. So the valid data records have a null value for transaction-finish time; the data records with filled values of transaction-finish time are not applicable, and possibly there are updated data records for them.

12.5 Discussions and conclusions

Using Semantic Analysis, much more attention is required for the analysis and requirement specification than in the other approaches. One has to follow the analysis formalism to undergo a rigorous process in order to produce a stable model. After having obtained the semantic model, the Normbase system tools can turn the model directly into a database implementation. Meanwhile there will be standard application tools provided. Therefore the emphasis is shifted to the analysis stage from a user's point of view. Because not so much designing and programming is required, the cost of system development can be dramatically reduced.

Semantic Analysis offers a powerful analytical method for information analysis. Together with the Normbase system, it suggests a new way of information system development. This new approach demonstrates how to capture application semantics in an information model, and suggests a complete solution for system development which is more flexible and economical in meeting users' requirements. The time-based DBMS, the time-based database language and the non-destructive updating method adopted in the Normbase system also support, in a practical way, the management of information in the legally oriented areas where it provides a virtually perfect audit trail on account of the non-destructive update.

Finally, it should be noted that in countries that are rich in competent people but short of foreign exchange to buy costly technology, these methods allow careful analytical thought to be substituted for redundant technology.

13
Case study: development of a test construction system

This case study demonstrates how semiotic methods can be used for systems analysis, and the other stages of systems development are covered by other approaches. The chapter also discusses why, after having tried other systems analysis methods, the Semantic Analysis method was chosen for the project.

13.1 Background

CONTEST (COMputerised TEST construction system) is a software engineering project which started from research and then evolved into a commercial project.[1] In this project, Semantic Analysis has been applied for requirement analysis. An object-oriented system design has been produced based on the semantic model, and, further, the system construction has been carried out using object-oriented programming languages and tools.

The project commenced from two doctoral research projects, in which the major theoretical investigation and some experiments were conducted (Adema 1990, Boekkooi-Timminga 1989). A system analysis and design were performed which led to a prototype. The research project has been continued and expanded with input of more resources. The current objective of the project is to produce a practical, useful, computerised system for automatic management and production of tests.

13.1.1 CONTEST project

Tests are traditionally managed and produced manually. The questions (or the *items* as termed by the educational professionals) are written by the item

---

[1] CONTEST was a joint project of the University of Twente, the University of Groningen and the Inter-university Expertise Centre ProGAMMA in the Netherlands. The development of the first version of CONTEST was completed in mid 1994, which is the basis for this chapter.

composers, and centrally collected and stored with their attributes in an item bank in a test agency. These test agencies are specialised in managing and providing tests for all kinds of examinations. Examples of such agencies are the Educational Testing Service (ETS) and American College Testing program (ACT) in the USA, and the National Institute for Educational Measurement (CITO) in the Netherlands. Nowadays several agencies are building item banks in the form of computerised databases. However, in most of the cases item indexes are still used for assembling tests.

The goal of CONTEST is to function as an interactive system for the storage of items, the construction of tests, and the editing and printing of tests. Test construction is the process of selecting items for a test from an item bank in such a way that the test fits the specified requirements (i.e., test specification) formulated by the test constructor. A test specification consists of two parts: an objective function to be optimised and a series of constraints. The test specification is formulated in relation to the examination purposes. CONTEST aims to aid the users formulating specifications by building a knowledge base from which the expertise and experience of making proper specifications can be made available. With reference to the test specification, tentative selections of items must be checked against the specified conditions, and modifications on these tentative test proposals will be adjusted until the conditions posed in the test specification are fully satisfied. Afterwards, the test will be printed for use in examinations and educational quality analysis and for other purposes.

13.1.2 User requirements

The beginning of 1990 can be seen as the beginning of the project in which the computerised test construction system CONTEST became the objective. The knowledge gained in previous years had laid a foundation from which more sophisticated requirements on CONTEST were derived. The following system components and their functions were formulated as preliminary requirements, though some of them were not fully articulated.

An item bank Seven different data sets are considered in CONTEST: persons, items, tests, graphics, auxiliary materials, ability scale, and populations. Besides the contents of the items, characteristics of each item have to be described. In Table 13.1 an overview is given of some possible item characteristics that are stored for each item.

Information about the uses of an item must be kept in the item bank. Information on the tests already constructed from an item set includes, for example, test specification used, items selected, date of

Table 13.1. *Item attributes.*

1. General attributes:
Item ID
Item description
Item text
Length of item text
Word count
Item graphic ID
Item answer
Item format
Item type
Author of the item
Date the item was written
Gender orientation of the item (male/female/neutral)
Ethnic orientation of the item (black/white/Hispanic)
Response time
2. Subject matter attributes:
Content descriptions
Cognitive level
Relation to textbook(s)
Auxiliary material ID
3. Psychometric attributes:
Classical item parameters:
p-value (= item difficulty)
Item test correlation (= item discrimination)
Item criterion correlation
Item reliability
Item validity
Item response model (Rasch, 2- or 3-parameter model)
Difficulty
Item discrimination
Item fit
Differential item functioning
Item guessing

test administration, and group of students to which the test was administered. The graphical parts of the items are stored in the set of graphics. In the set of auxiliary materials information on auxiliary material belonging to (some of) the items is stored. For example, for a reading comprehension item with text passages as auxiliary material, for instance the length of the text passage and/or its required reading time can be stored for each item of auxiliary material. Furthermore, information on possible student populations or abilities for which tests can be constructed is stored.

A test construction mechanism An essential component of CONTEST is the mechanism for constructing tests. A new test specification is formulated, or an existing test specification can be loaded from the test specification storage and adapted if desired. The test specification contains the practical requirements for the test. With the help of mathematical optimisation techniques (e.g., linear programming), items are selected such that all requirements are met. If no solution is found, the system can check which requirements are likely to cause the problem. Otherwise the characteristics of the test and the items selected are shown to the test constructor. It is possible to compare the characteristics of this test with other existing tests. The test selected, its specification, and its attributes are stored in the system. Finally, the test layout is edited and the test is printed together with its answer sheet.

A mathematical optimisation module In the mathematical optimisation module, an objective function maximises or minimises the goal value subject to a number of constraints. For example, a mathematical optimisation model can be to minimise the test administration time subject to the constraint that at least 40 multiple choice items be included in the test. Linear programming models can be used to solve specific types of test construction problems which assume that both the objective function and the constraints are linear expressions in the decision variables.

A package for handling test specifications This module simply must have functions of storing all the test specifications that have been used for constructing tests. These specifications may be useful references for later applications.

A knowledge base assisting elicitation of test specifications The users of CONTEST do not have to be familiar with the mathematical models. A knowledge base which supports the elicitation of the test specification should be provided. The knowledge base contains the knowledge needed for eliciting the test specification, such that the corresponding linear programming model can be derived without involving mathematical notation. The use of this knowledge base makes it possible to elicit test specifications from a test constructor for all kinds of item subsets with their own specific structures. The test specification depends on the item characteristics stored in the specific item subset and the desires of the test constructor. Both influence the possible objective functions and constraints. Besides the assistance for choosing an objective function and constraints, the knowledge base supports formulating test specifications for constructing special types of tests, for example parallel tests. For each special type of test to be constructed, knowledge is stored in the knowledge base that helps the choice of objective function and constraints.

13.1.3 Why choose Semantic Analysis

The reasons for choosing Semantic Analysis came from the special requirements of the project, summarised as several challenges to the conventional methods for analysis, design and implementation.

The challenge can first be attributed to the fact that there are many stakeholders in different states of the system development lifecycles. The project is conducted by a multidisciplinary team. The researchers are the people who have knowledge about the subject matter of the system. They have been generating ideas and producing requirements. However, they are not the real users of the system. The ultimate 'real users' are test agencies and educational institutions. There are several groups of users working with the system. Item composers produce items and store them in the item banks. Test constructors specify the kind of tests to be constructed out of the items available in the item bank, by detailing the purposes of the test and all kinds of constraints. The test constructors then produce test proposals and finalise the test. During the system development, the educational researchers in the project team have played a leading role in deciding the functional requirements. In addition to these knowledgeable people, there are systems analysts, designers and programmers who have been involved at different stages in different tasks, though some of them played more than one role in the project. The complication caused by this situation is that people from various backgrounds have seen the problem from different angles and also presented it differently. Jargons and specialised terms were used in interdisciplinary communications which created many misunderstandings. Many crucial terms for the description of the subject needed to be clarified. A question for the project team was how to use words and terms to formulate requirement specification. To state the question more directly: whether new languages which may be suitable for system development (particularly analysis, design and implementation, etc.) should be created, or at least some new terms, because one does not understand the technical dialects of others. For example, the concept *item* is crucial in the CONTEST system; the educational professionals speak about an 'item' for a question to be used in a test or examination, which was a surprise to the system development people. On the other hand, the documentation of

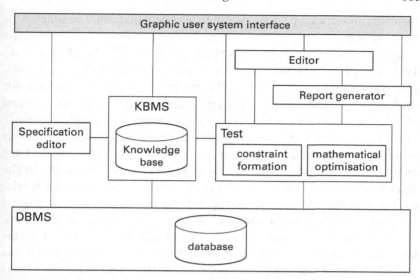

Figure 13.1. The CONTEST system architecture (Boekkooi-Timminga & Sun 1991).

requirement modelling and system design was difficult for the educational experts to judge whether the representations correctly reflected their wishes and desires.

The second challenge came from the ambitious and complex requirements. In the early phase of the project, there was a desire to develop a comprehensive system based on the available theoretical work and experiences. However, difficulties were encountered when the desire had to be expressed as a formally articulated requirement. In addition, the original requirement possibly continued to evolve as the educational researchers had some new inspirations or some new theoretical discoveries.

The third difficulty lies in the technicality. The data objects to be handled in the item bank will include simple data types, mathematical formulae, text and graphs. In the test specification part, specifications must be stored for re-use and knowledge for formulation of specifications must be kept available. In the test construction process, there will be mathematical optimisation and human interactive intervention involved. In summary, what has been required is actually a comprehensive system which comprises a knowledge-based and an object-oriented database as well as a mathematical optimisation mechanism. The system's overall architecture, as illustrated in Figure 13.1, was gradually envisioned during the project (Boekkooi-Timminga & Sun 1991). However, according to the study of the market, there was no software package or database system that could be adapted for these purposes.

At an early stage of the CONTEST project, ISAC (Lundeberg *et al.* 1981) as well as the entity–relationship method (Chen 1976, Howe 1989) was applied for systems analysis. But the project could not continue, for several reasons. The methods do not put emphasis on the semantic problem of concepts and terms, which is typically required in a multidisciplinary project such as CONTEST where some terms are used with several different meanings. The second problem that occurred was that the results of the analysis were difficult to comprehend by the team members except for the analysts themselves. The large volume of documentation created a barrier to comprehension so that the colleagues from the educational background were not able to confirm whether the analysis met their requirements. However, the project went into the design phase with these problems unsolved. In design the entity–relationship method was applied, and it was planned to use a relational database package for implementation. It was also discovered that the use of a standard relational database was not suited for CONTEST for several reasons.

(1)　At that time standard relational database packages could not store graphs.
(2)　The structure of the items to be stored is not fixed.
(3)　The lengths of the data cannot always be fixed (e.g. the item texts can vary very much in length), resulting in memory problems if a relational database is used.
(4)　Eliciting and storing test specifications would be very problematic, because it would be very difficult to store all possible constraints and objective functions for each characteristic of an item in the database for an arbitrary test.

After all these trials, Semantic Analysis was applied. Semantic Analysis immediately seemed to be suitable because it represented the knowledge of the universe of discourse with clear meanings; the model is easy for the professional colleagues to comprehend and they were then able to criticise and make improvements on the model.

13.2　System analysis

The method of Semantic Analysis has been chosen and applied to the CONTEST system. Two major benefits have been experienced from the application of the method of Semantic Analysis. The first one is that a principle of Semantic Analysis is to require analysts to adopt the user's language. The creation of new words or names only for representation purposes is virtually forbidden. Even the use of abbreviations in the semantic chart is not recommended. This will reduce not only the language distance between the problem-owner (or project-owner, in this particular case) and the analysts, but also the psychological barriers. The problem-owners do not have to use a 'data dictionary' to read the requirement documentation as long as the rules of representation are explained. However, there is a cost involved. The analysts must make an effort to understand the problem and to learn to speak the problem-owners' language. They are discouraged from inventing names and labels in representation. No ambiguity in documentation is allowed to hide behind invented jargon and technical terms.

The second benefit from adoption of Semantic Analysis is the minimal volume of the documentation. Previously the large quantity of documentation of analysis was a barrier for the educational experts examining the result of analysis produced by other methods. With Semantic Analysis, the major documents produced from analysis were three pages of ontology charts. One leading educational researcher has actually been able to take part in the construction of the semantic model. Other educational professionals were able to appreciate the complete semantic model because it is clear and concise. Therefore, there have been iterative and critical examinations of the result of Semantic Analysis by the problem-owners. Finally, an approval by the problem-owners of the system requirement model was given on the basis of a full understanding of the analysis, which offers a reliable ground for further steps in the system development.

The system analysis was carried out in the following phases.

1 Study problem description

A description of the problem was obtained during several discussions within the project team. The description was circulated to a wider circle of people concerned with the system in one way or another for criticisms and suggestions. Furthermore, theoretical work was studied and existing test construction systems were evaluated. In this phase, the task of the whole team was to formulate the user requirements at a global level. For the analysts it was, at this phase, the first opportunity to learn the problem, therefore they had to grasp the concepts and terminology.

The user requirement formulated in the problem description was not detailed and precise, but it was not necessary for it to be so. The next phases would provide chances for improvements.

Table 13.2. *Some candidate affordances.*

person
writes [an item or test question]
writes [a test specification]
writer
institute
school
item [a test question]
gender
response time
ability scale
population
test
composed-of [a test] . . . .

2 Identify semantic units

In this phase the semantic units were identified. The focus at this stage was on the identification of the agents and affordances. The semantic units contain specific meanings in terms of describing the agents and the possible actions in the problem domain. In other words, they are candidates which may be put into the information model to represent the perceived object world. Some of the semantic units identified were listed as in Table 13.2.

While identifying these units no attention was paid to the proper grouping of them. Some of the terms were just listed, without knowing whether they would be useful for describing the problem. However, all the terms which seemed to be relevant in defining the problem should be listed as the semantic units. They provided a basis for a formal requirement formulation in the next two steps.

3 Group semantic units

In this phase the semantic units were grouped: the agents and their affordances, and the ontological antecedents and their dependants. The agents and their affordances were related in such a way that ontological consistency was obtained. For example, an agent *person* has an affordance *write* an *item*; a piece of knowledge 'a group of students from a certain school are administered a test'; and 'a test is composed of certain items' are represented as in Figure 13.2. Several such scattered groups of semantic units were the result of this phase, which are to be assembled into a complete ontology model in the next phase.

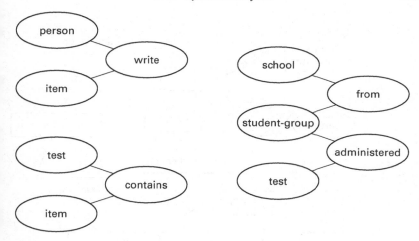

Figure 13.2. Grouping semantic units.

4 Construct the semantic model

In the final phase a complete knowledge model, or ontology model, was derived by collecting all the groups of semantic units obtained in Phase 3. This was not a simple matter of assembling the pieces of knowledge, but a process of putting fragments of knowledge into a large semantic context in which all the pieces must be ontologically and semantically consistent.

Critical evaluation of the model during and after completion is very important. The problem definition was carefully studied again and the ontology model was cautiously checked. During the whole analysis the professionals and analysts carried on the review continuously for some time. In fact the evaluation was a continuing process of knowledge acquisition.

The professionals often use specialised terminology that they perhaps mistakenly expect others to understand. Such terms need to be clarified; otherwise, serious problems can arise later and a system can be built that does not fit the requirements of the problem-owners. Semantic Analysis produces the ontology chart as a platform for the professionals and analysts to reach an agreement on the terminology used; it does not allow the analyst to make arbitrary assumptions about the meanings of words.

Leaving out the many determiners that describe the attributes of the affordances attached, a major part of the semantic model obtained is presented in Figure 13.3. In the figure a line along with a dot represents a part–whole relation, for example, the part–whole notation shows that an item can contain a graph and a text. A person can write items and write a test specification; in both cases they have a role name 'writer' but are

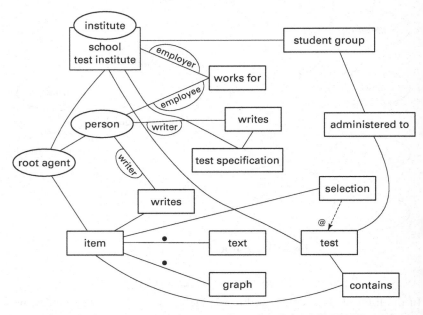

Figure 13.3. An excerpt from the semantic model of the CONTEST system.

involved in different actions. The action of 'selection' is actually a complex process including the generating of a constraint matrix, optimally selecting items according to the constraints, etc. For simplicity of illustration, the details are not shown on the figure. The automatic selection process may lead to the existence of a test if the process is satisfactory according to the test constructor's judgement; therefore, a dotted line along with an 'at-sign' ('authority sign' in NORMA) is used to indicate that the 'selection' determines the start for the 'test'. After the test is constructed, it is reviewed, edited and printed. The final test is administered to a specific student group.

Once the semantic model has been obtained and approved by the problem-owners, it serves as a formal description of system requirements. Moreover, it has been a basic documentation for system design which will be discussed in the next section.

13.3 System design

The semantic model preserves ontological dependencies between agents and actions. Ontological relationships between agents and actions described in the ontology chart reveal that there are usage (e.g. client/server) relationships between them. Actions that are afforded by

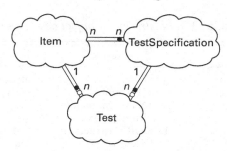

Figure 13.4. Part of the CONTEST class diagram.

agents suggest functions to be performed by objects in the object-oriented paradigm. For example, in Figure 13.3, between the '*item*,' '*test-specification*' and '*test*' there are ontological relationships and actions (e.g. the action of selection of items by a mathematical optimisation procedure). An important task at this stage is to transform the relationships and actions in the ontology chart to the form of system design.

The object-oriented approach has been chosen for the design and construction of the CONTEST system. The rationale for the choice is that first of all the Semantic Analysis itself lends the result of analysis readily to the object-oriented design. There are principles for transformation from a semantic model to an object-oriented design. Identifications of objects, attributes and functions of the object, and relationships between the objects are obtainable from the semantic model. The second reason for using this design method is that the path from the object-oriented design to the object-oriented programming is smoother than if other design methods were used. These implementation decisions, based on the feasibility study of the software tools and packages on the market, were taken at the same time as the design method was chosen.

The design process can be presented in four aspects: class diagrams, object specifications, object lifecycle diagrams, and class inheritance diagrams.

As an example, the part of the semantic model containing the four affordances '*item*', '*test-specification*', '*test*', and '*selection*', is used to show the transformation into a class diagram (Figure 13.4). Three objects are obtained after the transformation with the same names as they have on the ontology chart. The affordance '*selection*' is transformed into the communication action between the objects because it is an 'action-like' affordance. This part of the design also shows that one object uses another in certain ways. The dependency relationships are treated as attributes, while the actions in the semantic model are turned into functions and procedures in

Table 13.3. *Illustration of object descriptions.*

Test specification	Test	Item

attribute:
TestSpec_ID:number;
Test_ID:number;
ConstraintSet: set;
Operator: string;
Bound: real; ... ...
function:
initialise; add; update;
delete;
   view_constraint; ... ...
	attribute:
	Test_ID: number;
	TestName:character;
	Description: text;
	DateOfConstruction:
	   date; ... ...
	function:
	initialise; add; update;
	test_construct;
	   matrix_input; ... ...
		attributes:
		Item_ID:number;
		Description:text;
		AuxiliaryMaterial:
		   composite;
		DateOfCreate: date;
		Content: set;
		CognitiveLevel:set;
		TextBook: booktitle;
		Author: name;
		Difficulty: real;
		Guessing: real;
		... ...
		function:
		initialise; add;
		update; delete;
		View_on_text;
		View_on_barchart;
		select_on_characteristic;
		count_item;
		... ...

object-oriented Pascal (or called *member functions* in C++). A cloud represents a class. The class has a name which is placed inside the cloud. The usage relationships are the most important kind between classes. They are indicated by the double lines with circles placed at one end. For example, the double line between the classes of '*Item*' and '*TestSpecification*' is used and then a filled circle is placed near the class of the '*TestSpecification*', asserting that the class of '*TestSpecification*' uses the resources of the class of '*Item*' in its implementation. A filled circle and an unfilled circle are placed close to the class of '*Test*', asserting that the class of *Test* uses the resources of the class of '*Item*' in its implementation and interface as well. The notation for cardinality among the objects is used. As shown in the figure, for every test object, there is exactly one instance of the class 'TestSpecification' and for every instance of the 'TestSpecification', there is also exactly one 'Test'. There may be many instances of the class of 'Item' associated with each test, also many tests for every item.

Object specifications are formal descriptions of the objects. In the CONTEST project, a special structure was invented for documenting the composition of the object. Each structure consists of three parts: the

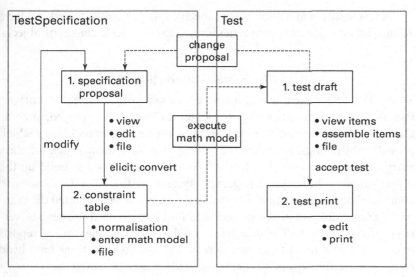

Figure 13.5. Object state transitions.

heading on which the name of the object is placed, the attributes, and the functions (or actions that the object can perform). Table 13.3 presents examples of object specifications for three objects: '*TestSpecification*', '*Item*', and '*Test*'.

The lifecycle of objects is described with state transition diagrams. Figure 13.5 illustrates the state transitions of two objects: '*TestSpecification*' and '*Test*'. The object '*Test*', for example, has two states: 'test draft' and 'test print'. Below the state boxes, possible actions in those states are listed, each preceded by a dot. These actions are the functions that have appeared in the structure of the object specification. Events that bring objects from one state to the other are placed along the transition lines; for example, the events 'modify', 'elicit' and 'convert' change the states of the object 'TestSpecification'. During their lifecycles there are interactions between objects which are caused by the external events. These external events are placed in dotted boxes, e.g., 'execute math model' and 'change proposal'. This kind of event sometimes synchronises states in the lifecycles of both objects.

Another aspect of the design is the class inheritance, for which the class inheritance diagrams were used. This aspect shows that the parent object classes have common structures and properties, and the children classes can have some added, specific functions and properties based on the parent classes. For example, an institute, as a parent, has a name, can employ staff, etc. A test institute and a school are specific types of institute and can have additional functions and properties unique to the specific classes of objects.

13.4 System construction

The CONTEST system was constructed using an object-oriented Borland Pascal. In addition, other object-oriented utilities are employed, such as Object Professional and B-Tree Filer. The former is a class library which provides object implementations for screen, windows, menus, pick list, data entry screen, and so on. The latter, B-Tree Filer, was used to build up the object-oriented database management system for the large database with complex data types, because there was no suitable object-oriented database package available when the project was initiated. Several pre-release versions of the CONTEST system had been developed by the time of report; in each of them, more functions were added. Positive reactions have been received when the system was demonstrated to some potential users.

13.5 Discussion and conclusions

In the case study of the CONTEST project, in which a multidisciplinary team is engaged to develop the information system for computer-assisted education, an emphasis has been put on analysing and specifying user requirements. Semantic Analysis and an object-oriented approach have been chosen to cover the whole process of the system development, namely, analysis, design and implementation.

Application of Semantic Analysis has brought several advantages to the project. The method takes the user's language as the starting point to describe the agents and actions in practical affairs. First of all, the semantic model is a result of articulation and clarification of meanings of the user's conceptualisation represented with a few formal constraints (e.g. ontological dependency). This lends the model itself to be easily understood by the project participants (specifically, the educational professionals) who should actually be in control of the project (or project-owner, in other words).

The second advantage of the use of Semantic Analysis is that the result of analysis was presented in a precise and small volume of documentation, which allows the educational professionals to have the courage to 'walk through' the documents with the analysts. Therefore, the 'project-owners' were able to understand, and criticise and make corrections to the model.

Another positive aspect is that the ontology chart served as a conceptual basis for the object-oriented design. The principles of transformation from a semantic model to an object-oriented design ensure the design quality to a very large extent. Adopting rigid object-oriented disciplines also secures the quality of the product as a whole. Having applied this set of approaches, the whole team, both the 'project-owners' and the system developers, feel confident to commit themselves to put resources into the project. This has been considered as one of the most significant contributions of the Semantic Analysis to such a large-scale, complex system development project.

However, one unsatisfactory aspect was experienced in the project. In application of the system development approach which is based on Semantic Analysis and supplemented by the object-oriented technology, the transformation from an ontology chart to an object-oriented design was not straightforward. The transformation principle could not fully help the exercise because the distinction between the 'agent/entity-like' affordances and the 'action-like' affordances is not explicitly made in Semantic Analysis in the first place. Therefore, as compensation to the problem, the designers had to learn Semantic Analysis and the ontology chart. The ideal solution would be to provide a highly formalised specification technique for representing the result of analysis with which the design process can proceed without having to know the details of the semantic modelling.

Appendix A Semantic templates and surrogate specification

This appendix, as a supplement to section 10.2, supplies further details of Semantic Templates (ST) and the use of ST for database design.

A.1 Definition of ST

The definition of ST, basically following a syntax of Backus–Naur form, describes the structure of a semantic template.

ST := '<' agent, ST, mood+, mood−, time+, time− '>' | ST := '<' agent, action, time+, time− '>';
agent := *agent performing the action*;
action := *realisation of affordance*;
mood+ := mood;
mood− := mood;
mood := proposal | inducement | forecast | wish | palinode | contrition | assertion | valuation;
proposal := 'request'|'ask'|'beg'|'command'|'insist'|'suggest'|'promise'|'guarantee';
inducement := 'reward'|'threaten'|'warn'|'tempt';
forecast := 'predict'|'assume'|'plan'|'accept';
wish := 'want'|'hope'|'expect'|'desire';
palinode := 'retract'|'annul'|'revoke'|'deny';
contrition := 'regret'|'apologise';
assertion := 'assert'|'claim'|'report'|'notify'|'affirm'|'assure'|'argue'|'declare';
valuation := 'judge'|'appraise'|'blame'|'criticise'|'accuse'|'object';
time+ := time;
time− := time;
time := *absolute time or relative time (by reference to another action)*.

The right-hand phrases in italics are explanations of the possible value types of the left-hand items. For example, the 'agent' is defined as 'agent performing the action', which refers to the agent appearing on the ontology chart and relating to the action as the antecedent. The 'action' is defined as 'realisation of affordance'; the affordance should also be predefined on the ontology chart so that there can be a realised instance of the affordance. This can be illustrated by relating to the example shown in Figure 9.4, and it will be used throughout this appendix. In that figure, a person, John, is the agent; a particular case of John's being absent is a realisation of the affordance 'absence'.

The moods are categorised into eight headings. Under each of them, there are some typical illocutionary words. This organisation offers an opportunity for further analysis of the generalised communication patterns. For example, a projection may lead to an anticipation by the hearer; a directive will need a semiological or substantive action by the hearer while an assertion may need no action at all (except the hearer changes his belief, for example). This kind of categorial analysis can be helpful for building an engine into a technical information system for automatic assistance to communication.

A.2 Examples of using ST in discourse modelling

In this section, more examples of using ST in modelling knowledge expressed in language will be given. An ontology chart resulting from a semantic analysis is a basis for ST modelling. The illustration in this section can be seen as a continuation of section 9.5, using the same case (shown in Figure 9.3).

The following passage tells six stories about John's leave. Afterwards, these stories will be represented in ST form, with an intent to capture semantics, intentions and subjectivity of the discourses. Each of the STs represented will be supplied with explanations.

Narrative 1: John was absent from 1-6-90 till 30-6-90.
Narrative 2: John started to take leave from 1-6-90 and planned to be back on 30-6-90.
Narrative 3: Susan thinks (assumes) that John may be off from 1-6-90 till 30-6-90.
Narrative 4: Susan thought (assumed) 31-5-90 that John may be off from 1-6-90. John planned on 15-5-90 to leave from 1-6-90 till 30-6-90. But actually he left on 2-6-90 (discovered on 5-6-90). Finally it is observed that John took leave from 2-6-90 till 20-6-90.
Narrative 5: Peter said today that yesterday Susan asked if John takes leave from 1-6-90 till 30-6-90.

These five stories will be described in the ST form in the following five episodes.

Episode 1: $<$—, $<$John, absence, course 123, 1-6-90, 30-6-90$>$, assert, assert, —,—$>$

Remarks: (a)   This first item in the tuple is the agent who performed the speech act. The agent in this case is not specified for some reason. The agent may be the teacher of John or an officer of student affairs who reported this.

(b)   The semantic content $<$John, absence, course 123, 1-6-90, 30-6-90$>$ is determined by relating it to the corresponding part of the ontology chart, which virtually specifies who John is, what is meant by 'absence', and what the 'course 123' is.

(c)   The start time and finish time '1-6-90, 30-6-90' represent the period of the action 'John's being absent'.

(d)   Both the start mood and the finish mood are 'assert', which means the two dates for start and finish of John's being absent are asserted observations. In other words, the speech act represented in this episode is an asserted (or reported, observed) 'fact'.

(e)   The two dashes in the tuple represent the fact that the times of the performing of the speech act are unknown. With an unknown start time, this means the time when the speech act was performed is not recorded (it might be irrelevant to the subject). The unfilled finish time indicates that the speech act is still considered valid (a filled finish time would signify that the speech act is no longer valid as it might be a retracted error).

Episode 2: <John, <John, absence, course 123, 1-6-90, 30-6-90>, assert, assume, —, —>

Remarks: (a) Generally speaking, the agent who performs the speech act and the one who does the action may be different. However, in this particular example, John is the agent for both.

(b) John actually left on 1-6-90 (indicated by the start mood 'assert'), but intended to come back on 30-6-90 (by the finish mood 'assume').

(c) The time of the performance of the speech act is not recorded, and it is still a valid act (seen from the two unfilled times).

Episode 3: <Susan, <John, absence, course 123, 1-6-90, 30-6-90>, assume, assume, now, —>

Remarks: (a) Susan makes a hypothesis now about John's absence in the future because it can be seen that both the start mood and the finish mood are 'assume'.

(b) The time of 'now' must be earlier than 1-6-90 because the assumption can only be made about the future, though there is no other sign to prove the exact time in the speech.

Episode 4: <Susan, <John, absence, course 123, 1-6-90, —>, assume, —, 1-6-90, —>

<John, <John, absence, course 123, 1-6-90, 30-6-90>, plan, plan, 15-5-90, —>

<John, <John, absence, course 123, 2-6-90, 30-6-90>, assert, plan, 5-6-90, —>

<—, <John, absence, 2-6-90, 20-6-90>, assert, assert, 21-6-90, —>

Remarks: (a) Susan made an assumption about John's leaving date, and she did not make any guess about his return date.

(b) John planned his leave from 1-6-90 till 30-6-90. Though he might not be able to follow it, it should still be kept as a valid record in the memory.

(c) The third expression says that though John did not leave as he planned, he still planned to be back on 30-6-90.

(d) The last ST tells the actual period of John's leave.

(e) The start times and finish times of performances of speech acts in the four ST expressions are significant; they record when the speeches were uttered and whether or not they are still valid.

Episode 5: <Peter, <Susan, <John, absence, course 123, 1-6-90, 30-6-90>, question, question, yesterday, —>, assert, —, today, — >

Remarks: (a) Susan enquired as to both the start time and the finish time of John's leave, which was done 'yesterday'.

(b) Peter reported the start time of Susan's speech act, which was done 'today'.

(c) If an ST is like:

<Peter, <Susan, <John, absence, 1-6-90, 30-6-90>, question, question, yesterday, —>, assert, —, this morning, this afternoon>

then it means this morning it was recorded that Peter reported

Susan's enquiry, but this afternoon it was found out that it was a mistake – Peter did not say anything about Susan's question. In short, the filled finish time 'afternoon' would set the ST record invalid.

A.3 Examples of surrogates

The surrogate structure is the basic record structure of the semantic temporal database. The examples here show how the specifications in ST can be translated into surrogates in the semantic temporal database. The surrogate is defined as a tuple as follows (it is firstly defined in section 10.2 in which one example of surrogate representation with detailed explanations can be found):

surrogate := <surrogate-identification, <content>, <antecedents>, authority+, authority−, mood+, mood−, action-time+, action-time−, record-time+, record-time− >

All five examples given below are translations of the corresponding episodes in ST form in the last section into the surrogate representation (that is, Examples 1, 2, 3 and so on below correspond to Episodes 1, 2, 3 and so on of the last section).

Example 1:
Surrogate: <srg-id1, [absence], John, course 123, —, —, assert, assert, 1-6-90, 30-6-90, [today], —>
Remarks: (a)   The surrogate identification, 'srg-id1', is supposed to be uniquely generated by the technical database system.
      (b)   the item *[absence]* is a defined action type (an affordance defined in the ontology chart) in the database.
      (c)   Antecedents 'John' and 'course 123' relate the action 'being absent' to the context for determination of semantics.
      (d)   The two dashes represent the unknown *authority for start* and *authority for finish* who reported or recognised the action 'John's absent from the course 123'.
      (e)   Both the *mood for start* and *mood for finish* are assertive ('assert') which means the semantic content in this surrogate is a reported observation.
      (f)   Two times '1-6-90' and '30-6-90' are the *start action time* and *finish action time* to indicate the period of John's absence.
      (g)   The item *[today]* is the *start record time*, which means the recording of the speech act is 'today'; [today] will be converted into the date of the day when the surrogate is entered into the semantic temporal database.
      (h)   The unfilled *finish record time* signifies the surrogate is still valid. If the finish record time is filled, then it means the surrogate is marked as an obsolete record.

Example 2:   <srg-id2, [absence], John, course 123, —, —, assert, plan, 1-6-90, 30-6-90, [today], —>
Remarks: The values filled in the surrogate that the *start action time* is 'assert' and the *finish action time* is 'plan' indicate that the start of John's leave on 1-6-90 is an observed fact and the finish of the leave is a projected plan.

Example 3:   <srg-id3, [absence], John, course 123, Susan, Susan, assume, assume, 1-6-90, 30-6-90, [now], —>

Remarks: Susan is the responsible person who assumed the start and finish times
            of John's absence, therefore 'Susan' has been put in the fields of start
            authority and finish authority.

Example 4: <srg-id41, [absence], John, course 123, Susan, —, assume, —, 1-6-90,
            —, 1-6-90, —>
            <srg-id42, [absence], John, course 123, John, John, plan, plan, 1-6-90,
            30-6-90, 15-5-90, —>
            <srg-id43, [absence], John, course 123, —, John, assert, plan, 2-6-90,
            30-6-90, 5-6-90, —>
            <srg-id44, [absence], John, course 123, —, —, assert, assert, 2-6-90,
            20-6-90, 21-6-90, —>

Remarks: Particular person names filled as authorities indicate who made the
            observations or assumptions (to read this example in connection with
            Narrative 4 and Episode 4 will enable the reader to understand the
            example).

Example 5: <srg-id5, [absence], John, course 123, Susan, Susan, question, ques-
            tion, 1-6-90, 30-6-90, [today], —>

Remarks: Susan questioned whether or not John was off from 1-6-90 until 30-6-
            90, which can be seen from the *mood for start* and *mood for finish*, both
            being filled with 'question'.

One of the purposes of discussing these examples is to illustrate a complete process,
which ranges from semantic analysis and modelling to semantic temporal database
design of a technical information system.

Appendix B LEGOL applications in the CRIS case

The CRIS case was invented by IFIP (the International Federation for Information Processing) for the comparative review of information systems design methodologies. The case definition can be found in *Information Systems Design Methodologies* (Olle *et al.* 1982).

In this appendix, the CRIS case is studied using the method of Semantic Analysis which results in an ontology chart (Figure B.1). In order to test LEGOL language and the interpreter, questions are made and then translated into LEGOL expressions. The LEGOL statements were executed by the LEGOL interpreter, a part of an early prototype of the Normbase run on a VAX station, and the results were produced based on some imaginary data stored in the Normbase. Section B.1 contains some questions and the LEGOL statements, and section B.2 presents the corresponding output from the Normbase version.

B.1 Questions and LEGOL statements

In this section, there are questions concerning the CRIS case, and statements in LEGOL that will produce the answers, printed below each question.

(1) What are the Technical Committees of the various learned societies on our records?
TC
(2) Who are the current member organizations of IFIP?
current membership(national-org, IFIP)
(3) What Working Groups now exist?
WG
or
WG(TC)
(4) When was WG8.1 started?
start-of WG# "WG8.1"
(5) Which are the newly created Working Groups after 1980?
start-of WG after @1980
or
start-of WG after start-of WG# "WG8.1"
(Note: the 'at sign' (i.e. @) is an *ad hoc* solution for making that version of the compiler distinguish what after the 'at sign' will be a number for 'year'.)
(6) Who were eligible to attend the Working Conference CRIS-3?
eligible(person, WC#CRIS-3)

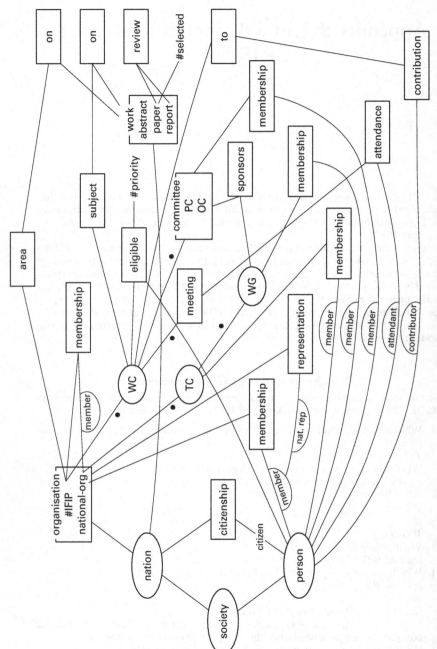

Figure B.1. Ontology chart of the CRIS case. WC—working conference; TC—technical committee; WG—working group;

(7) Who has ever contributed a paper in any area of interest to an IFIP conference?
contribution(person, paper) **where** *on(paper, area)*
(8) Who has ever contributed a paper on the subject of CRIS?
contribution(person, paper) where on(paper, subject#CRIS)
(9) Who has actually contributed a selected paper to a conference?
to(contribution(person, paper), WC#IFIP) where selected(paper)
(10) Who have the highest priority to attend the conference CRIS-3?
high priority(eligible(person, WC#CRIS-3))
(11) Who has ever attended an IFIP conference?
attendance(person, meeting)
(12) Who attended the working conference CRIS-3?
attendance(person, meeting#CRIS-3)
(13) Is there anyone who attended, but did not have the first priority for the Working Conference CRIS-3?
attendance(person, meeting#CRIS-3) **while** *highest priority(eligible(person, WC#CRIS#3))*
(14) Who are the sponsors of the Working Conference CRIS-3?
sponsorship(WG, WC#CRIS-3)
(15) Who are members of sponsoring working groups but did not attend the conference?
membership(person, WG) **while** *sponsorship(WG, WC#CRIS-3)* **while-not** *attendance(person, meeting#CRIS-3)*

B.2 Output from the Normbase

This section shows the output of the Normbase prototype which runs on a VAX station. The results listed below answer the questions of section B.1 with the corresponding numbers.

1.
Legol>TC

TC	start	finish
TC8	1974-01-01	-
TC7	1972-01-01	-
TC2	1965-01-01	-

2.
Legol>current membership(national-org, IFIP)

membership	national-org	IFIP	start	finish
-	NGI	IFIP	1962-01-01	-
-	RSA	IFIP	1979-01-01	-
-	DVI	IFIP	1990-10-06	-
-	Nsk Dataforen.	IFIP	1975-01-01	-
-	BCS	IFIP	1960-01-01	-
-	A.F. Cyb Econ.	IFIP	1960-01-01	-

and
Legol>past membership(national-org, IFIP)

membership	national-org	IFIP	start	finish
-	DVI	IFIP	1960-01-01	1990-10-05

3.
Legol>WG

WG	start	finish
WG2.1 (Algol)	1960-06-01	-
WG8.4	1958-01-01	-
WG8.3 (DSS)	1981-01-01	-
WG2.4	1973-01-01	-
WG2.3	1969-07-01	-
WG2.2	1965-05-01	-
WG2.5	1974-07-01	-
WG8.1	1976-01-01	-
WG7.1	1972-01-01	-
WG2.6	1974-01-01	1985-12-31

or
Legol>WG(TC)

WG	TC	start	finish
WG2.1 (Algol)	TC2	1960-06-01	-
WG8.4	TC8	1985-01-01	-
WG8.3 (DSS)	TC8	1981-01-01	-
WG2.4	TC2	1973-01-01	-
WG2.3	TC2	1969-07-01	-
WG2.2	TC2	1965-05-01	-
WG2.5	TC2	1974-07-01	-
WG8.1	TC8	1976-01-01	-
WG7.1	TC7	1972-01-01	-
WG2.6	TC2	1974-01-01	1985-12-31

4.
Legol>start-of WG#'WG8.1'

WG	start	finish
WG8.1	1976-01-01	1976-01-01

otherwise
Legol>WG#'WG8.1'

WG	start	finish
WG8.1	1976-01-01	-

5.
Legol>start-of WG after @1980

WG	start	finish
WG8.4	1985-01-01	1985-01-01
WG8.3 (DSS)	1981-01-01	1981-01-01

6.

Legol>eligible(person, WC#CRIS-3)

eligible	person	WC	start	finish
-	L. Penedo	CRIS-3	1988-05-01	-
-	R. Piloty	CRIS-3	1988-05-01	-
-	A. Finkelstein	CRIS-3	1988-05-01	-
-	J. Hagelstein	CRIS-3	1988-05-01	-
-	J. Fourot	CRIS-3	1988-05-01	-
-	Alex V. Stuart	CRIS-3	1988-05-01	-
-	A. Bertztiss	CRIS-3	1988-05-01	-
-	Bill Ollie	CRIS-3	1988-05-01	-
-	R.K. Stamper	CRIS-3	1988-05-01	-
-	B.L. Sendor	CRIS-3	1988-05-01	-

7.

Legol>contribution(person, paper) where on(paper, area)

contribution	person	paper	on	area	start	finish
-	L. Penedo	EDI & Groupware	-	Groupware	1990-06-01	-
-	J. Hagelstein	Groupware	-	Groupware	1990-06-01	-
-	J. Fourot	Prog. in Algol	-	Struct. Prog.	1985-01-01	-
-	Alex V. Stuart	Temporal DBMS	-	Temp. databases	1980-07-01	-
-	A. Bertztiss	Time in Data	-	Temp. databases	1986-06-01	-
-	Bill Ollie	New IS Analysis	-	CRIS	1988-06-01	-
-	R.K. Stamper	LEGOL 2.1	-	Temp. databases	1976-01-01	-
-	R.K. Stamper	DB vs Normbase	-	Groupware	1990-05-10	-
-	B.L. Sendor	CRIS Review		CRIS	1989-12-15	-

8.

Legol>contribution(person, paper) where on(paper, subject#CRIS)

contribution	person	paper	on	subject	start	finish
-	Bill Ollie	New IS Analysis	-	CRIS	1988-06-01	-
-	R.K. Stamper	LEGOL 2.1	-	CRIS	1976-01-01	-
-	R.K. Stamper	MEASUR	-	CRIS	1976-01-01	-
-	R.K. Stamper	DB vs Normbase	-	CRIS	1990-05-10	-
-	B.L. Sendor	CRIS Review	-	CRIS	1989-12-15	-

9.

Legol>to(contribution(person, paper), WC(IFIP)) where selected(paper)

contri-bution	person	paper	WC	IFIP	selected	start	finish
• -	L. Penedo	EDI & Groupware	COCIS-91	IFIP	-	1990-06-01	-
• -	J. Hagelstein	Groupware	COCIS-91	IFIP	-	1990-06-01	-
• -	J. Fourot	Prog. in Algol	Structured Prog.	IFIP	-	1985-01-01	-
• -	Alex V. Stuart	Temporal DBMS	Temp. asp. IS	IFIP	-	1980-07-01	-
• -	A. Bertztiss	Time in Data	Temp. asp. IS	IFIP	-	1986-06-01	-
• -	Bill Ollie	New IS Analysis	CRIS-3	IFIP	-	1988-06-01	-
• -	R.K. Stamper	LEGOL 2.1	Temp. asp. IS	IFIP	-	1976-01-01	-
• -	R.K. Stamper	DB vs Normbase	COCIS-91	IFIP	-	1990-05-10	-
• -	B.L. Sendor	CRIS Review	CRIS-3	IFIP	-	1989-12-15	-

10.
Legol>priority(eligible(person, WC#CRIS#3))

priority	eligible	person	WC	start	finish
2	–	R. Piloty	CRIS-3	1988-05-01	-
1	–	Alex V. Stuart	CRIS-3	1988-05-01	-
1	–	J. Fourot	CRIS-3	1988-06-01	-
1	–	R.K. Stamper	CRIS-3	1988-06-01	-
1	–	Bill Ollie	CRIS-3	1988-05-01	-

and
Legol>lowest priority(eligible(person, WC#CRIS-3))

priority	eligible	person	WC	start	finish
1	–	Alex V. Stuart	CRIS-3	1988-05-01	-
1	–	J. Fourot	CRIS-3	1988-06-01	-
1	–	R.K. Stamper	CRIS-3	1988-06-01	-
1	–	Bill Ollie	CRIS-3	1988-05-01	-

11.
Legol>attendance(person, meeting)

attendance	person	meeting	start	finish
–	F. Bodart	CRIS-3	1990-11-26	1990-11-30
–	A. Finkelstein	CRIS-3	1990-11-26	1990-11-30
–	B.L. Sendor	CRIS-3	1990-11-26	1990-11-30
–	R.K. Stamper	COSCIS-91	1991-08-27	1991-08-29
–	G. Bracchi	CRIS-3	1990-11-28	1990-11-30
–	E. Falkenberg	CRIS-3	1990-11-26	1990-11-27
–	R.K. Stamper	CRIS-3	1990-11-26	1990-11-30
–	H.W. Le Roux	CRIS-3	1990-11-26	1990-11-30
–	Bill Ollie	CRIS-3	1990-11-26	1990-11-30
–	R. Piloty	CRIS-3	1990-11-27	1990-11-30
–	J. Fourot	CRIS-3	1990-11-26	1990-11-30
–	A.A. Dorodnicyn	Parallel Proc.	1986-03-04	1986-03-05
–	A. Bertztiss	Temp. asp. IS	1988-09-12	1988-09-16
–	A. Finkelstein	Temp. asp. IS	1988-09-12	1988-09-15
–	O. Longe	Parallel Proc.	1986-03-04	1986-03-03
–	L. Penedo	Parallel Proc.	1986-03-04	1986-03-03
–	F. Bodart	Parallel Proc.	1986-03-04	1986-03-05
–	H.W. Le Roux	Temp. asp. IS	1988-09-13	1988-09-16
–	B. Gunadi	Parallel Proc.	1986-03-04	1986-03-05
–	H.W. Le Roux	Parallel Proc.	1986-03-04	1986-03-05

12.
Legol>attendance(person, meeting#CRIS-3)

attendance	person	meeting	start	finish
–	F. Bodart	CRIS-3	1990-11-26	1990-11-30
–	A. Finkelstein	CRIS-3	1990-11-26	1990-11-30
–	B.L. Sendor	CRIS-3	1990-11-26	1990-11-30
–	G. Bracchi	CRIS-3	1990-11-28	1990-11-30
–	E. Falkenberg	CRIS-3	1990-11-26	1990-11-27
–	R.K. Stamper	CRIS-3	1990-11-26	1990-11-30
–	H.W. Le Roux	CRIS-3	1990-11-26	1990-11-30
–	Bill Ollie	CRIS-3	1990-11-26	1990-11-30
–	R. Piloty	CRIS-3	1990-11-27	1990-11-30
–	J. Fourot	CRIS-3	1990-11-26	1990-11-30

13.
Legol>attendance(person, meeting#CRIS-3) while highest
priority(eligible(person, WC#CRIS-3))

attendance	person	meeting	priority	eligible	WC	start	finish
–	R. Piloty	CRIS-3	2	–	CRIS-3	1990-11-27	1990-11-30

14.
Legol>sponsorship(WG, WC)

sponsorship	WG	WC	start	finish
–	WG8.1	Temp. asp. IS	1986-06-01	1989-01-01
–	WG2.1 (Algol)	Structured Prog.	1984-01-01	1988-01-01
–	WG8.1	COSCIS-91	1990-01-01	1992-12-31
–	WG8.1	CRIS-3	1988-01-01	-

and
Legol>sponsorship(WG, WC#CRIS-3)

sponsorship	WG	WC	start	finish
–	WG8.1	CRIS-3	1988-01-01	-

15
Legol>membership(person, WG) while sponsorship(WG, WC#CRIS-3) while-not
attendance(person, meeting#CRIS-3)

member-ship	person	WG	spon-sorship	WC	atten-dance	meeting	start	finish
–	F. Bodart	WG8.1	–	CRIS-3	–	CRIS-3	1990-11-26	1990-11-26
–	F. Bodart	WG8.1	–	CRIS-3	–	CRIS-3	1990-11-29	1990-11-30
–	Bill Ollie	WG8.1	–	CRIS-3	–	CRIS-3	1990-11-26	1990-11-26
–	Bill Ollie	WG8.1	–	CRIS-3	–	CRIS-3	1990-11-29	1990-11-30
–	R.K. Stamper	WG8.1	–	CRIS-3	–	CRIS-3	1990-11-28	1990-11-30

Bibliography

Achueler, B.-M., 1977, Update reconsidered. In Nijssen, G. M. (ed.), *Architecture and Models in Data Base Management Systems*. North-Holland, Amsterdam.

Ackoff, R., 1967, Management misinformation systems. *Management Science*, **14** (4), B147–56.

Adema, J. J., 1990, *Models and Algorithms for the Construction of Achievement Tests*. Doctoral Thesis, University of Twente, Enschede.

Ades, Y. M., 1989, *NAMAT System User Manual*. SIS project, University of Qatar.

Aho, A. V., Sethi, R. and Ullman, J. D., 1986, *Compilers: Principles, Techniques, and Tools*. Addison-Wesley, Reading, Massachusetts.

Allen, L. E. and Saxon, C. S., 1986, Analysis of the logical structure of legal rules by a modernized and formalized version of Hohfeld's fundamental legal conceptions. In Martino, A. A. and Natali, F. S. (eds.), *Automated Analysis of Legal Texts: Logic, Informatics, Law*. Elsevier Science, Amsterdam, 385–451.

Andersen, P. B., 1990, *A Theory of Computer Semiotics: Semiotic Approaches to Construction and Assessment of Computer Systems*. Cambridge University Press, Cambridge.

Andersen, P. B., 1991, A semiotic approach to construction and assessment of computer systems. In Nissen, H. E., Klein, H. K. and Hirschheim, R. (eds.), *Information Systems Research: Contemporary Approaches and Emergent Traditions*. Elsevier Science, North-Holland, 465–514.

Åqvist, L., 1984, Deontic logic. In Gabbay, D. and Guenthner, D. (eds.), *Handbook of Philosophical Logic, Volume II*. D. Reidel Publishing Company, Dordrecht, Netherlands, 605–714.

Atkinson, M., Bancilhon, F., DeWitt, D., Dittrich, K., Maier, D. and Zdonik, S., 1990, The object-oriented database system manifesto. Proceedings of DPPD Conference, Kyoto, Japan, December 1989, 40–57.

Auramäki, E., Lehtinen, E. and Lyytinen, K., 1988, A speech-act-based office modeling approach. *ACM Transactions on Office Information Systems,* **6** (2), 126–52.

Austin, J. L., 1980, *How to Do Things with Words, the William James Lectures delivered at Harvard University in 1955*. Oxford University Press, Oxford.

Avison, D. E. and Fitzgerald, G., 1995, *Information Systems Development: Methodologies, Techniques and Tools*. McGraw-Hill, London.

Avison, D. E. and Nandhakumar, J., 1995, The discipline of information systems:

208

let many flowers bloom. In Falkenberg, E. D., Hesse, W. and Olive, A. (eds.) *Information Systems Concepts: towards a Consolidation of Views* (Proceedings of the IFIPWG8.1 International Conferences), Chapman and Hall, London, pp. 1–17.

Barbic, F. and Pernici, B., 1985, Time Modelling in Office Information Systems. In *Proceedings of ACM-SIGMOD, International Conference on Management of Data.*

Beck, K. and Cunningham, W., 1989, A laboratory for teaching object-oriented thinking. In Megrowitz, N. K. (ed.), *OOPSLA'89 Proceedings*, New Orleans, Oct. 1–6.

Benyon, D., 1994, A functional model of interacting systems: a semiotic approach. In Connolly, J. H. and Edmonds, E. A. (eds.), *CSCW and Artificial Intelligence*, Springer-Verlag, London.

Bickerton, M. and Siddiqi, J., 1993, The classification of requirements engineering methods. *Proceedings RE'93, IEEE International Symposium on Requirements Engineering.* San Diego.

Boehm, B., 1981, *Software Engineering Economics.* Prentice-Hall, Englewood Cliffs, New Jersey.

Boekkooi-Timminga, E., 1989, *Models for Computerised Test Construction.* Doctoral dissertation, University of Twente. Academisch Boeken Centrum, De Lier, Netherlands.

Boekkooi-Timminga, E. and Sun, L., 1991, Contest: a computerised test construction system. In Hoogstraten, J. and Linden, W.J. v., (eds.), *Proceedings of Dutch National Conference on Educational Research 'Onderwijs-researchdagen'91'.* Stichting Centrum voor Onderwijsonderzoek van de Universiteit van Amsterdam, Amsterdam, 69–76.

Booch, G., 1994, *Object Oriented Design, with Applications.* The Benjamin/Cummings Publishing Company, Redwood City, California.

Booch, G., Rumbaugh, J. and Jacobson, I., 1998, *Unified Modelling Language User Guide.* Addison-Wesley, Reading, Massachusetts.

Boustred, C., 1997, ATSI Seminars, http://www.strategize.com/presentations/paradigm/sld014.htm (accessed on 28 February 1998).

Brachman, R. J., 1979, On the epistemological status of semantic networks. In Findler, N. V. (ed.), *Associative Networks: Representation and Use of Knowledge by Computers.* Academic Press, New York, 3–50.

Brachman, R. J. and Levesque, H. J. (eds.), 1985, *Readings in Knowledge Representation.* Morgan Kaufmann, Los Altos, California.

Bradley, R. and Swartz, N., 1979, *Possible Worlds: an Introduction to Logic and Its Philosophy.* Basil Blackwell Publisher, Oxford.

Brkic, J., 1970, *Norm and Order – an Investigation into Logic, Semantics, and the Theory of Law and Morals.* Humanities Press, New York.

Burrell, G. and Morgan, G., 1979, *Sociological Paradigms and Organisational Analysis.* Heinemann, London.

Checkland, P. B., 1981, *Systems Thinking, Systems Practice.* Wiley, Chichester.

Chellas, B. F., 1980, *Modal Logic: an Introduction.* Cambridge University Press, Cambridge.

Chen, P. P., 1976, The entity–relationship model, towards a unified view of data. *ACM Transactions on Database Systems*, **1** (1), 9–36.

Clifford, J. and Tansel A. U., 1985, On an algebra for historical relational databases: two views. In *Proceedings of ACM-SIGMOD, International Conference on Management of Data.*

210 *Bibliography*

Coad, P. and Yourdon, E., 1990, *Object-Oriented Analysis*. Prentice-Hall, Englewood Cliffs, New Jersey.
Codd, E. F., 1970, A relational model of data for large shared data banks. *Communications of the ACM*, **13** (6), 377–87.
Cunningham, Donald J., 1992, Beyond educational psychology: steps toward an educational semiotics. *Educational Psychology Review*, **4**, 165–94.
Date, C. J., 1995, *An Introduction to Database Systems, Volume I (Fifth Edition)*. Addison-Wesley, Reading, Massachusetts.
Devlin, K., 1991, *Logic and Information*, Cambridge University Press, Cambridge.
Dietz, J. L. G., 1992, Subject-oriented modelling of open active systems. In Falkenberg, E.D., Rolland, C. and El-Sayed, E. N. (eds.), *Information System Concepts: Improving the Understanding*. Elsevier Science, Amsterdam, 227–338.
Dietz, J. L. G. and Widdershoven, G. A. M., 1991, Speech acts or communicative action? In Bannon, L., Robinson, M. and Schmidt, K. (eds.), *Proceedings of the Second European Conference on Computer-Supported Cooperative Work (CSCW'91)*. Kluwer Academic Publishers, Dordrecht, Netherlands, 235–48.
Dijk, T. A. v., 1981, *Studies in the Pragmatics of Discourse*. Mouton Publishers, The Hague.
Dik, S. C., 1979, *Functional Grammar*. North-Holland, Amsterdam.
Dik, S. C., 1989, *The Theory of Functional Grammar, Part 1: the Structure of the Clause*. Foris Publications, Dordrecht, Netherlands.
Eemeren, F. H. v. and Grootendorst, R., 1984, *Speech Acts in Argumentative Discussions*. Foris Publications, Dordrecht, Netherlands.
Embley, D. W., Kurtz, B. D. and Woodfield, S. N., 1992, *Object-Oriented Systems Analysis, a Model-Driven Approach*. Prentice Hall, Englewood Cliffs, New Jersey.
Falkenberg, E.D., Hesse, W., Lindgreen, P., Nilsson, B.E., Oei, J.L.H., Rolland, C., Stamper, R.K., Assche, F.J.M.V, Verijn-Stuart, A.A., Voss, K. 1998, A framework of information system concepts, The FRISCO Report (Web edition), ftp://fip.leidenuniv.nl/pub/rul/fri-full.zip (accessed 10/12/1998).
Fiske, J., 1990, *Introduction to Communication Studies*. Routledge, London.
Flores, F., Graves, M., Hartfield, B. and Winograd, T., 1988, Computer systems and the design of organisational interaction. *ACM Transactions on Office Information Systems*, **6** (2), 153–72.
Follesdal, D. and Hilpinen, R., 1970, Deontic logic: an introduction. In Hilpinen, R. (ed.), *Deontic Logic: Introductory and Systematic Readings*. D. Reidel Publishing Company, Dordrecht, Netherlands, 1–35.
Franke. R., 1987, Technological revolution and productivity decline: computer introduction in the financial industry. *Technological Forecasting and Social Change*, **31**, 143–54.
Gadia, S. K. and Vaishnav J. H., 1985, A query language for a homogeneous temporal database. In *Proceedings of the Fourth ACM SIGACT-SIGMOD Symposium on Principles of Database Systems*.
Galliers, R. (ed.), 1987, *Information Analysis – Selected Readings*. Addison-Wesley, Wokingham, Berkshire, and Sydney.
Gibbs, J. P., 1981, *Norms, Deviance, and Social Control – Conceptual Matters*. Elsevier, New York.
Gibson, J. J., 1968, *The Ecological Approach to Visual Perception*. Houghton Mifflin Company, Boston, Massachusetts.

Goguen, J., 1992, The 'Dry' and the 'Wet'. In Falkenberg, E. D., Rolland, C. and El-Sayed, E. N. (eds.), *Information System Concepts: Improving the Understanding.* Elsevier Science, Amsterdam, 1–18.

Gonzalez, R., 1997, Hypermedia data modeling, coding, and semiotics. *Proceedings of the FEEE,* **85**(7), 1111–40.

Griethuysen, J. J. v. (ed.), 1982, *Concepts and Terminology for the Conceptual Schema and the Information Base,* ISO/TC97/SC5-N695.

Groot, C. de, 1992, Pragmatics in functional grammar. *Proceedings of Workshop of TWLT 4.* University of Twente, Enschede.

Haack, S., 1978, *Philosophy of Logics.* Cambridge University Press, Cambridge.

Hawkes, T., 1977, *Structuralism and Semiotics.* Routledge, London.

Hilpinen, R. (ed.), 1971, *Deontic Logic: Introductory and Systematic Readings.* D. Reidel Publishing Company, Dordrecht, Netherlands.

Hirschheim, R., 1985, *Office Automation: a Social and Organizational Perspective.* John Wiley and Sons, Chichester.

Hirschheim, R. and Klein, H. K., 1989, Four paradigms of information systems development. *Communications of the ACM,* **32** (10), 1199–1216.

Hirschheim, R., Klein, H. K. and Lyytinen, K., 1995, *Information Systems Development and Data Modelling: Conceptual and Philosophical Foundations.* Cambridge University Press, Cambridge.

Hoede, C., 1986, *Similarity in Knowledge Graphs.* Department of Applied Mathematics, University of Twente, Enschede.

Holy, L. and Stuchlik, M., 1983, *Actions, Norms and Representation, Foundations of Anthropological Inquiry.* Cambridge University Press, Cambridge.

Howe, D. R., 1989, *Data Analysis for Database Design.* Routledge, Chapman and Hall, London.

Huang, K., 1998, *Organisational Aspect of EDI: a Norm-Oriented Approach.* PhD thesis, University of Twente, Enschede.

Jackman, M. and Pavelin, C., 1988, Conceptual graphs. In Rinland, G. A. and Duce, D. A. (eds.), *Approaches to Knowledge Representation.* Research Studies Press Ltd, Taunton, Somerset, and John Wiley and Sons, New York, 161–74.

Jackson, M. A., 1983, *Systems Development.* Prentice Hall, Englewood Cliffs, New Jersey.

Jayaratna, N., 1986, Normative Information Model-based Systems Analysis and Design (NIMSAD): a framework for understanding and evaluating methodologies. *Journal of Applied Systems Analysis,* **13**, 73–87.

Jayaratna, N., 1990, Systems analysis: the need for a better understanding. *International Journal of Information Management,* **10**, 228–34.

Jones, A. J. I., 1983, *Communication and Meaning, an Essay in Applied Modal Logic.* D. Reidel Publishing Company, Dordrecht, Netherlands.

Jones, S., Mason, P. and Stamper, R., 1979, LEGOL 2.0: a relational specification language for complex rules. *Information Systems,* **4**, 28–48.

Kim, J., Yoo, H. and Lee, Y., 1990, Design and implementation of a temporal query language with abstract time. *Information Systems,* 15 (3), 349–57.

Klarenberg, P., 1991, *Issues on Design and Implementation of the Normbase Systems.* Thesis, University of Twente, Enschede.

Klein, H. K., 1996, Preface: the potential contribution of semiotics and systems theory to the continuing evolution of information systems research. In Holmqvist, B., Andersen, P. B., Klein, H. and Posner, R. (eds.), *Signs of Work: Semiosis and Information Processing in Organisations.* Walter de Gruyter, Berlin, v–viii.

Kolkman, M., 1993, *Problem Articulation Methodology*. Doctoral Thesis, University of Twente, Enschede.

Kolkman, M., 1995, Managing ambiguity and change with the problem articulation methodology. In Pettigrew A. and Hines D. (eds.), *Globalisation and Process Analysis of the Organisation*. Sage, 000–00.

Kolkman, M. and Liu, K., 1991, Systems physiology: an approach of norm-governed action. In Harten, A. V. and Pol, B. G. F. (eds.), *Proceedings of Dutch National Conference of Business Research (NOBO)*. Enschede. Febodruk, 275–84.

Kotonya, G. and Sommerville I., 1998, *Requirements Engineering: Processes and Techniques*. John Wiley and Sons, New York.

Kuhn, T. S., 1962, *The Structure of Scientific Revolutions* (2nd edition). University of Chicago Press, Chicago.

Lacey, A. R., 1976, *A Dictionary of Philosophy*. Routledge and Kegan Paul, London.

Lakatos, I., 1970, Falsification and the methodology of scientific research programmes. In Lakatos, I. and Musgrave, A. (eds.), *Criticism and the Growth of Knowledge*. Cambridge University Press, Cambridge, 91–196.

Lee, R. M., 1988, Bureaucracies as deontic systems. *ACM Transactions on Office Information Systems*, 6 (2), 87–108.

Leslie, R. E., 1986, *Systems Analysis and Design*. Prentice-Hall, Englewood Cliffs, New Jersey.

Lindgreen, P. (ed.), 1990, *A Framework of Information Systems Concepts (interim report)*. FRISCO Task Group, IFIP WG 8.1.

Liu, K. 1993, *Semiotics Applied to Information Systems Development*. PhD thesis, University of Twente, Enschede.

Liu, K., Ades, Y. and Stamper, R., 1994, Simplicity, uniformity and quality: the role of Semantic Analysis in systems development. In Ross, M., Brebbia, C. A., Staples, G. and Stapleton, J. (eds.), *Software Quality Management*. Computational Mechanics Publications, **2**, 219–35.

Liu, K. and Dix, A., 1997, Norm governed agents in CSCW. *The First International Workshop on Computational Semiotics*. Paris. University of De Vince.

Liu, K. and Gao, Z. L., 1997, A problem articulation method for information systems: planning for responsive information management infrastructure. In Avison, D. (ed.), *Key Issues in Information Systems*. McGraw-Hill, Maidenhead, Berkshire, 353–62.

Loomis, M. E. S., 1990, OODBMS vs. relational. *Journal of Object Oriented Programming*, July/August, 79–82.

Loux, M. J., 1978, *Substance and Attribute – a Study in Ontology*. D. Reidel Publishing Company, Dordrecht, Netherlands.

Lundeberg, M., Goldkuhl, G. and Nilsson, A., 1981, *Information Systems Development: a Systematic Approach*. Prentice-Hall, Englewood Cliffs, New Jersey.

Lyons, J., 1977, *Semantics, Volume I*. Cambridge University Press, Cambridge.

Lyytinen, K., 1987, Two views of information modeling. *Information and Management*, **12**, 9–19.

Lyytinen, K. and Lehtinen, E., 1986, Action based model of information system. *Information Systems*, **11** (4), 299–317.

Machlup, F., 1980, *Knowledge: Its Creation, Distribution, and Economic Significance – Volume I: Knowledge and Knowledge Production*. Princeton University Press, Princeton, New Jersey.

Macro, A. and Buxton, J., 1987, *The Craft of Software Engineering*. Addison-Wesley, Wokingham, Berkshire.
Masterman, M., 1970, The nature of a paradigm. In Lakatos, I. and Musgrave, A. (eds.),*Criticism and the Growth of Knowledge*. Cambridge University Press, Cambridge, 58–89.
McCarty, L. T., 1986, Permissions and obligations: an informal introduction. In Martino, A. A. and Natali, F. S. (eds.), *Automated Analysis of Legal Texts: Logic, Informatics, Law*. Elsevier Science, Amsterdam, 307–37.
Meyer, J.-J. C., 1988, A different approach to deontic logic: deontic logic viewed as a variant of dynamic logic. *Notre Dame Journal of Formal Logic*, **29** (1), 109–36.
Meyer, J.-J. C. and R. J. Wieringa, 1993, Deontic logic: a concise overview. In Meyer, J.-J. C. and Wieringa, R. J. (eds.), *Deontic Logic in Computer Science*. John Wiley and Sons, Chichester, 3–16.
Micallef, J., 1988, Encapsulation, reusability and extensibility in object-oriented programming languages. *Journal of Object-Oriented Programming*, April/May, 12–34.
Michaels, C. F. and Carello, C., 1981, *Direct Perception*. Prentice-Hall, Englewood Cliffs, New Jersey.
Minker, J. (ed.), 1988, *Foundations of Deductive Databases and Logic Programming*. Morgan Kaufmann, Los Altos, California.
Mishra, G. N., 1982, *Ontology*. Shri Maheshwari, Varanasi.
Morris, C. W., 1938, Foundations of the theory of signs. *International Encyclopedia of Unified Science*, **1** (2). University of Chicago Press, Chicago.
Morris, C. W., 1946, *Signs, Language and Behaviour*. Braziller, New York.
Mumford, E. and Weir, M., 1979, *Computer Systems in Work Design – the ETHICS Method*. Associated Business Press, London.
Nachmias, C. and Nachmias, D., 1981, *Research Methods in the Social Sciences*. St Martin's Press, London.
Nauta, D., 1972, *The Meaning of Information*. Mouton, The Hague.
Nijssen, G. M. and Halpin, T. A., 1989, *Conceptual Schema and Relational Database Design*, Prentice-Hall, Sydney.
Olle, T. W., Sol, H. G., and Verrijn-Stuart, A. A. (eds.), 1982, *Information Systems Design Methodologies: a Comparative Review*. Elsevier Science, Amsterdam.
Olle, T. W., Hagelstein, J., Macdonald, I. G., Rolland, C., Sol, H. G., Assche, F. J. M. v. and Verrijn-Stuart, A. A., 1991, *Information Systems Methodologies: a Framework for Understanding*. Addison-Wesley, Wokingham, Berkshire.
OSW, 1995, The circulation document. *Organisational Semiotics Workshop*. Enschede.
Pavelin, C., 1988, Logic in knowledge representation. In Ringland, G. A. and Duce, D. A. (eds.), *Approaches to Knowledge Representation: an Introduction*. Research Studies Press, Taunton, Somerset, 13–44.
Peirce, C. S., 1931–58, ed. Hartshorne, C. and Weiss, P., *Collected Papers of C. S. Peirce*. Harvard University Press, Cambridge, Massachusetts.
Polovina, A. and Heaton, J., 1992, An introduction to conceptual graphs. *AI Expert*, May.
Popper, K., 1970, Normal science and its dangers. In Lakatos, I. and Musgrave, A. (eds.), *Criticism and the Growth of Knowledge*. Cambridge University Press, Cambridge, 51–8.
Porat, M. U., 1977, *The Information Economy: Definition and Measurement*. US Department of Commerce, Washington DC.
Randal, D. M., 1988, Semantic networks. In Ringland, G. A. and Duce, D. A.,

Bibliography

(eds.), *Approaches to Knowledge Representation: an Introduction.* Research Studies Press, Taunton, Somerset, 45–80.

Reiter, R., 1984, Towards a logical reconstruction of relational database theory. In Brodie, M. L., Mylopoulos, J. and Schmidt, J. W., (eds.), *On Conceptual Modelling: Perspectives from Artificial Intelligence, Databases, and Programming Languages.* Springer-Verlag, New York, 191–233.

Ringland, G. A. and Duce, D. A. (eds.), 1988, *Approaches to Knowledge Representation: an Introduction.* Research Studies Press, Taunton, Somerset.

Ryle, G., 1949, *The Concept of Mind.* Hutchinson of London, London.

Ryu, Y. U. and Lee, R. M., 1993, Defeasible deontic reasoning: a logic programming model. In Meyer, J.-J. C. and Wieringa, R. J. (eds.), *Deontic Logic in Computer Science.* John Wiley and Sons, Chichester, 225–41.

Sadeghi, R., Samson, W. B. and Deen, S. M., 1988, HQL – a historical query language. In *Proceedings of the South British National Conference on Databases (BNCOD6).* University College, Cardiff, 69–86.

Sarda, N. L., 1990, Algebra and query language for a historical data model. *The Computer Journal, 33* (1), 11–18.

Schank, R. C., 1972, Conceptual dependency: a theory of natural language understanding. *Cognitive Psychology*, 3 (4).

Schank, R. C., 1975, *Conceptual Information Processing.* North-Holland. Amsterdam.

Searle, J. R., 1969, *Speech Acts – an Essay in the Philosophy of Language.* Cambridge University Press, Cambridge.

Searle, J. R., 1979, *Expression and Meaning.* Cambridge University Press, Cambridge.

Searle, J. R., 1983, *Intentionality – an Essay in the Philosophy of Mind.* Cambridge University Press, Cambridge.

Searle, J. R. and Vanderveken, D., 1985, *Foundations of Illocutionary Logic.* Cambridge University Press, Cambridge.

Shannon, C. E. and Weaver W., 1949, *The Mathematical Theory of Communication.* University of Illinois Press, Urbana, Illinois.

Shearer, I., 1992, Retrospective update: data as it was believed to be. *The Computer Journal, 35* (2), 184–6.

Shlaer, S. and Mellor, S. J., 1988, *Object Oriented Analysis, Modelling the World in Data.* Yourdon Press, Englewood Cliffs, New Jersey.

Shlaer, S. and Mellor, S. J., 1992, *Object Lifecycles, Modelling the World in States.* Yourdon Press, Englewood Cliffs, New Jersey.

Smit, H. J., 1991, *Consistency and Robustness of Knowledge Graphs.* Doctoral thesis, University of Twente, Enschede.

Snodgrass, R., 1985, A taxonomy of time in databases. *Proceedings of ACM-SIGMOD, International Conference on Management of Data.*

Snodgrass, R., 1987, The temporal query language TQUEL. *TODS, 12* (2), 247–98.

Sowa, J., 1984, *Conceptual Structures: Information Processing in Mind and Machine.* Addison-Wesley, Reading, Massachusetts.

Stamper, R. K., 1973, *Information in Business and Administrative Systems.* John Wiley and Sons, New York.

Stamper, R. K., 1980, LEGOL: modelling legal rules by computer. In Niblett, B. (ed.), *Computer Science and Law; an Advanced Course.* Cambridge University Press, Cambridge, 1–27.

Stamper, R. K., 1985, Knowledge as action: a logic of social norms and individual affordances. In Gilbert, G. N. and Heath, C., (eds.), *Social Action and Artificial Intelligence.* Gower Press, Aldershot, Hampshire, 172–91.

Stamper, R. K., 1992, Language and computer in organised behaviour. In Riet, R. P. v. d. and Meersman, R. A., (eds.), *Linguistic Instruments in Knowledge Engineering*. Elsevier Science, Amsterdam, 143–63.

Stamper, R. K., 1993, Social norms in requirements analysis – an outline of MEASUR. In Jirotka, M., Goguen, J. and Bickerton, M. (eds.), *Requirements Engineering, Technical and Social Aspects*. Academic Press, New York.

Stamper, R. K., Althaus, K., Backhouse, J., 1988, MEASUR: Method for Eliciting, Analyzing and Specifying User Requirements. In Olle, T. W., Verrijn-Stuart, A. A. and Bhabuts, L., (eds.), *Computerized Assistance During the Information Systems Life Cycle*. Elsevier Science, Amsterdam, 67–116.

Stamper, R. K., Liu, K. and Huang, K., 1994, Organisational Morphology in Re-engineering. The Second European Conference on Information Systems, Nijenrode, 729–37.

Stamper, R. K., Liu, K., Kolkman, M., Klarenberg, P., Slooten, V. F., Ades, Y., and Slooten, V. C., 1991, From database to normbase. *International Journal of Information Management*, **11**, 62–79.

Stamper, R. K., Liu, K., Hafkamp, M. and Ades, Y., 1997, Signs plus norms – one paradigm for organisational semiotics. The First International Workshop on Computational Semiotics, Paris.

Stamper, R. K. and Nauta, D., 1990, *Information in a Semiotic Framework*. FRISCO Task Group of IFIP WG 8.1.

Stonebraker, M., Rowe, L. A., Lindsay, B., Gray, J., Carey, M., Brodie, M., Bernstein, Ph. and Beech, D., 1990, *Third Generation Data Base System Manifesto*. The Committee for Advanced DBMS Function, Memorandum No. UCB/ERL M90/29, College of Engineering, University of California, Berkeley, California.

Stowell, F. (ed.), 1995, *Information Systems Provision*. McGraw-Hill, London.

Strassmann, P., 1980, The office of the future: information management for the new age. *Technology Review*, December/January.

Strassmann, P., 1990, *The Business Value of Computers: an Executive's Guide*. The Information Economics Press, New Canaan, Connecticut.

Thayse, A. (ed.), 1989, *From Modal Logic to Deductive Databases*. John Wiley and Sons, Chichester.

Thönissen, K., 1990, *Semantic Analysis: a Study and Comparison*. MSc Thesis, University of Twente, Enschede.

UKAIS, 1996, *UK Academy for Information Systems Newsletter,* 2 (1).

Verheijen, G. and Bekkum, J., 1982, NIAM: an information analysis method. In Olle, W., Sol, H. and Verrijn-Stuart, A. (eds.), *Information Systems Design Methodologies: a Comparative Review*. Elsevier Science, Amsterdam, 537–90.

Way, E. C., 1991, *Knowledge Representation and Metaphor*. Kluwer Academic Publishers, Dordrecht, Netherlands.

Weg, R. v. d. and Engmann, R., 1992, A framework and method for object-oriented information systems analysis and design. In Falkenberg, E. D., Rolland, C. and El-Sayer, E. N. (eds.), *Information System Concepts: Improving the Understanding*. Elsevier Science, Amsterdam, 123–46.

Weigand, H., 1990, *Linguistically Motivated Principles of Knowledge Base Systems*. Foris Publications, Dordrecht, Netherlands.

Weigand, H., 1993, Deontic aspects of communication. In Meyer, J.-J. Ch. and Wieringa, R. J. (eds.), *Deontic Logic In Computer Science*. John Wiley and Sons, Chichester, 259–73.

Wieringa, R., Meyer, J.-J. C., and Weigand, H., 1989, Specifying dynamic and deontic integrity constraints. *Data and Knowledge Engineering*, **4**, 157–90.

Wieringa, R. J. and Meyer, J.-J. C., 1993, Applications of deontic logic to computer science: a concise overview. In Meyer, J.-J. Ch. and Wieringa, R. J. (eds.), *Deontic Logic in Computer Science*. John Wiley and Sons, Chichester, 17–40.

Wilks, Y. A., 1978, Primitives. In Shapiro (ed.), *Encyclopedia of Artificial Intelligence*. John Wiley and Sons, New York.

Wilson, B., 1984, *Systems: Concepts, Methodologies, and Applications*. John Wiley and Sons, Chichester.

Winograd, T., 1975, Frame representations and the declarative/procedural controversy. In Bobrow, D. G. and Collins, A. M. (eds.), *Representation and Understanding: Studies in Cognitive Science*. Academic Press, New York, 185–210.

Winograd, T., 1983, *Language as a Cognitive Process (Volume I: Syntax)*. Addison-Wesley, Reading, Massachusetts.

Winograd, T. and Flores C. F., 1987, *Understanding Computers and Cognition*. Addison-Wesley, Reading, Massachusetts.

Wright, G. H. v., 1951, *An Essay in Modal Logic*. North-Holland, Amsterdam.

Wright, G. H. v., 1963, *Norms and Action – a Logical Enquiry*. Routledge and Kegan Paul, New York.

Yourdon, E., 1989, *Modern Structured Analysis*. Prentice-Hall, Englewood Cliffs, New Jersey.

Yourdon, E. and Constantine, L., 1979, *Structured Design*. Prentice-Hall, Englewood Cliffs, New Jersey.

Yu, C. H., 1994, Abduction? Deduction? Induction? Is there a logic of exploratory data analysis? *The Annual Meeting of American Educational Research Association, New Orleans*, Louisiana, http://seamonkey.ed.asu.edu/~behrens/asu/reports/Peirce/Logic_of_EDA.html (accessed 7 August 1998).

Index

affordance 61–62, 65
agent 46, 65
antecedent 66
authority 69
axioms   75, 134

behaviour
  patterns 61
  semiotic 67
  substantive 45, 67

collateral analysis 43
communication 82
  addressee 84, 97
  preparatory conditions 86
  speaker 84, 97
conceptual graphs 54–56
conceptual model 50
CONTEST 180
CRIS 201

database
  deductive 134
  extensional 119, 134
  intensional 119, 134
  object-oriented 135
  relational 134
  semantic temporal 127, 133, 154,177
deontic logic 89–94
deontic operator 93
determiner 64, 68

empirics 28

FRISCO 6
functional grammar 87

generic–specific 68

identity 68
information analysis 56, 58

information systems 2, 109
  formal 110
  informal 109
  methodologies 5
  technical 110
intention 124
invariant 62

knowledge, types 50, 52

LEGOL 71–73, 143
  operator 145
learning 15

MEASUR 7–8, 37
mode
  affective 75
  denotative 75

norm 98
  proto- 103
  specification 105
Norm Analysis 79–80
NORMA 64–71
Normbase 150–152

object-oriented design 159, 191
object-oriented implementation 161
ontological dependency 46, 65
ontology chart 69–79
organisational morphology 112
organisational onion 109

paradigm 21
  objective 21–24
  subjective 24–26
particular 61
physics 23
position
  epistemological 57
  ontological 57

217